Endorsements

When water-rich clouds join together, they produce copious rain. Likewise, apologetics scholars gather together in this volume to produce a powerful rain that will pour the wisdom of each of them on the church. This is a highly recommended book for all lovers of Scripture and for those who wish to have a definitive vision of the future.

Jorge Mendizabal
Spanish Ministries Director, South Texas District UPCI

We must earnestly contend for even the basic tenets of our Apostolic faith. We must know what we believe, why we believe it, and be able to explain it by rightly dividing the Word of truth. I appreciate the way Scripture is used to interpret Scripture in this compilation. Thank you, Brother Jorge and all other contributing authors, for a job well done.

Timothy L. Pickard
Pastor, First United Pentecostal Church of Toronto, Toronto, Ontario
Foreign Missions Director, Ontario District UPCI

As the apostle Peter prophesied, some are beginning to fall away from "the promise of his coming." This book gives solid biblical answers to those who deny the imminent future appearing of Jesus Christ to come and catch away His church.

Paul D. Dugas
Editor, *The Apostolic Contender*, Keizer, Oregon

Through the dark and murky clouds of error, half-truth, and gross misrepresentation, shines an unmistakable light to illuminate the pathway of end-time prophecy. The contributors to this book leave no stone unturned in their relentless quest to refute the fallacy of preterism. This book is written without compromise or equivocation and is a must read for every serious student of the Word of God.

Ron Macey
Presbyter, Houston Metro East, South Texas District UPCI

This is a book whose time has come. I highly recommend it for every pastor, preacher, and student of the Word. Preterism is an erroneous doctrine that undermines biblical last-days teaching. I have thoroughly studied preterism and have found nothing biblically sound in it.

Fred J. Foster
Pastor Emeritus, The Pentecostals of West Monroe, West Monroe, Louisiana

Apostolic Bible Institute commends Brother Jorge Medina and the other contributing writers for their scholarship in writing this book that reveals the error of preterism. It is a work that we will include in our classes on end-time prophecy.

Gerald F. Grant
President, Apostolic Bible Institute, St. Paul, Minnesota

Our movement has made allowance for unity in diversity. We must not, however, seek diversity at the expense of truth. We must at all times take a firm stand for biblical truth, as the authors of this book have done. They have thoroughly demonstrated that preterism contradicts the Holy Writ. While we can allow for a pre-trib, mid-trib, or post-trib Rapture, we cannot allow preterism to rob us of "that blessed hope, and the glorious appearing of the great God and our Saviour Jesus Christ."

Anthony Mangun
Pastor, The Pentecostals of Alexandria, Alexandria, Louisiana

I am happy to recommend this work that calls us back to a renewed emphasis on "that blessed hope," the glorious appearing of our great God and Savior, Jesus Christ. Since two men in white stood by the awestruck disciples as they watched Jesus ascending into heaven, believers have waited for Him to "come in like manner" as they saw Him go. I join with the writers of this book to confess, as the apostle Paul did, that we who are alive and remain when the Lord descends from heaven shall be caught up with the dead in Christ to meet the Lord in the air. There is, as Paul says, comfort in these words.

Daniel L. Segraves
President, Christian Life College, Stockton, California

As a pastor, I have seen the pride, problems, and perils that all too frequently accompany the teaching of preterism. This error has contributed to division, discord, and delusion in many of the churches of our fellowship. My hat is off to G. Jorge Medina and the men of God who have given us fresh insight into end-time prophecy. I gladly recommend this timely and scholarly work to you. Read it! Run with it! Keep looking for that blessed hope!

Chancy Gore
Senior Pastor, The Refuge of the Lake Cities, Wylie, Texas

With every generation there comes a new gust of theological error. Once again, however, truth has prevailed in the pages of this wonderful book as the authors thoroughly refute preterism. Truly this is a book whose time has come!

Bret A. Cooley
President, Texas Bible College, Lufkin, Texas

Without hesitation I wholeheartedly endorse this book on preterism by G. Jorge Medina and the other contributing authors. This book is necessary to correct misconceptions regarding end-time prophecy. It should be compulsory reading for UPCI Bible colleges and for candidates desiring to hold UPCI credentials.

Garth Hatheway
Vice Chair, Urshan Graduate School of Theology Board
Honorary presbyter, Atlantic District Board UPCI, New Brunswick, Canada
Member, UPCI Sunday School Curriculum Committee

Early Pentecostals were convinced that they were living on the cusp of the coming of the Lord, and this belief motivated them to live their lives fully committed to the gospel. This book takes a fresh look at the importance of the coming of the Lord in the life of the church. I trust it will renew our committment to the coming King.

Robin Johnston
Vice President, Gateway College of Evangelism
Director, The Center for the Study of Oneness Pentecostalism

Brother Jorge Medina and the other contributors have provided Apostolics with a long-needed book. For several years, we have needed biblical answers to the many questions that preterism has raised. This book gives us the biblical answers to refute this unbiblical doctrine. Thank you, Brother Medina, for the many hours you have spent compiling such excellent writings.

James L. Kilgore
Bishop, Life Tabernacle, Houston, Texas

This timely book gives a strong defense of the church's blessed hope. The authors have passionately written to prove that the coming of the Lord is still our future hope. This book is a must for students of eschatology.

Ricky D. Treece
Pastor, Apostolic Temple, Lake Charles, Louisiana

I commend the many gifted individuals who have contributed their talents, experience, passion, and biblical insight to make this book a reality. We need to receive their message! I wholeheartedly endorse this book and highly recommend it to every minister and student of Scripture.

Jonathan Urshan
Pastor, Bethel Pentecostal Church, St. Peters, Missouri

COMPILED BY G. JORGE MEDINA

DAVID K. BERNARD • WILLIAM CHALFANT • PHILLIP A. DUGAS • J. R. ENSEY
KEN GURLEY • JOHN T. LARABELL • DAVID S. NORRIS • STEVE PIXLER

WORD AFLAME PRESS

Upholding Our Future Hope

An Apostolic Response to Preterism

Compiled by G. Jorge Medina

Hazelwood, MO 63042-2299

Cover Design by Simeon Young, Jr.

Unless otherwise indicated, all quotations of Scripture are from The Holy Bible, King James Version.

Printed in the United States of America

Printed by

8855 Dunn Road, Hazelwood, MO 63042
www.pentecostalpublishing.com

Library of Congress Cataloging-in-Publication Data

Upholding our future hope : an apostolic response to preterism / compiled by G. Jorge Medina.
p. cm.
Includes bibliographical references.
ISBN-13: 978-1-56722-663-8 (pbk.)
ISBN-10: 1-56722-663-9 (pbk.)
1. Realized eschatology. I. Medina, G. Jorge.
BT824.5.U64 2005
236'.9—dc22
2005023686

Where no counsel is, the people fall:
but in the multitude of counsellers
there is safety.

—Proverbs 11:14

Contents

Preface

The topic of end-time prophecy, described in theological circles as eschatology, is increasing in popularity. Although the word *apocalypse* sounds ominous, it simply means "revelation." Nevertheless, in today's language it is usually taken to refer to the catastrophic end-time events that will precede the second coming of Christ to earth.

"When will these things be?" the disciples asked our Lord in Matthew 24. His response in the Olivet Discourse described the destruction of Jerusalem and beyond, including the glorious second coming of our Messiah. All Apostolic teachers until recently have taught that the second coming of Jesus will be a future climatic event that will end this present age. Within the last few years, however, some Pentecostal teachers have begun to promote an eschatological system known as *preterism*, which asserts that Jesus actually returned in A.D. 70. Holy Scripture disagrees, as this book will show.

The only way to make a preterist view of prophecy fit the Bible is to interpret references to specific persons, things, and events as actually referring to someone or something entirely different. Pentecostal preterists teach, among other things, that Jesus returned in A.D. 70 when the Roman army sacked Jerusalem, that Israel is Revelation's Babylon the Great, that the church has replaced Israel, that the Jews are God's "public enemy number one," that the Great Tribulation has already occurred, that Satan has been bound for the last two thousand years, that we are currently living in the promised Millennium, and that the geographical land of Israel and the city of Jerusalem have no more bearing on end-time prophecy today than, say, La Paz, Bolivia. It seems that preterism, then, has a bad case of mistaken identities, where no one is who they are supposed to be, and end-time events will not occur as the inspired writers of Scripture described them. Indeed, preterist interpretation of prophecy has brought to the surface the crucial need for teachers to employ valid hermeneutical principles when interpreting Scripture, namely the grammatical-historical method, for all too often preterists resort to allegorizing or spiritualizing prophecies in order to fit them into an A.D. 70 mold.

Truths dearly held by Apostolics for a century have come under fire; cardinal doctrines have come under scrutiny. Some preterists have branded those who choose to remain true to their Apostolic roots as old-fashioned and unwilling to receive new revelations, and some have even claimed that we are "deceived by the enemy." And so this book is a critically needed tool to assure Apostolics that our dearly held doctrines are not simply old-fashioned traditions, but are truths deeply rooted in Holy Scripture.

This book is intended to assist any honest student of the Word in understanding that the blessed hope of the apostle Paul (Titus 2:13) is still a future event and is thus our blessed hope as well. We must uphold this truth! We sincerely pray that many will be led to an utter and complete confidence in the promise of the Lord, who said, "In my Father's house are many mansions: if it were not so, I would have told you. I go to prepare a place for you. And if I go and prepare a place for you, I will come again, and receive you unto myself; that where I am, there ye may be also" (John 14:2-3).

We confidently await the final trumpet when we will be "caught up together . . . in the clouds, to meet the Lord in the air" (I Thessalonians 4:17), knowing that "when he shall appear, we shall be like him; for we shall see him as he is" (I John 3:2). Like the apostles, we are earnestly looking for our blessed hope.

I wish to thank the contributing scholars for taking time out of their busy schedules to share with us a little bit of the wealth of their knowledge and for standing fast in the defense of the faith once delivered to the saints. I am indebted to David K. Bernard for his assistance in the editorial process, along with Johnny Celey. Brother Bernard's zeal for the truth is a constant source of inspiration. My gratitude also goes to the publishing committee and staff at the Pentecostal Publishing House, who worked tirelessly in order to have this book printed in a timely manner. May our Lord continue to utilize their efforts for the glory of His kingdom.

G. Jorge Medina

1

What Is Preterism Anyway?

David K. Bernard

Preterism

Preterism is an interpretation of end-time prophecy. According to this view, most, if not all, passages of Scripture that conservative Christians generally regard as end-time prophecies, including the Book of Revelation, were fulfilled as of the Roman conquest of Jerusalem in A.D. 70. This event is identified as "the day of the Lord."

For instance, preterists typically believe that Revelation 1-19 was fulfilled by A.D. 70 and that most of Revelation 20-22 (the Millennium and the New Jerusalem) describes the current existence of the New Testament church.

Historically, preterism has been embraced primarily by some mainline Protestants, particularly those who are postmillennialists or amillennialists. In recent years, it has gained some acceptance in conservative evangelical circles, including Baptists, through the writings of R. C. Sproul, John Bray, and others.

These adherents typically link their view of end-time

prophecy with a denial of the present reality of the baptism of the Holy Spirit with the initial sign of speaking in tongues and of the supernatural gifts of the Spirit. For example, Joel 2:28-32, as quoted in Acts 2:17-21, speaks of the outpouring of the Spirit in the latter days followed by signs in heaven and earth and "the great and terrible day of the Lord." Since preterists believe that "the great and terrible day of the Lord" took place in A.D. 70 with the destruction of Jerusalem, they typically restrict the miraculous outpouring of the Spirit to the apostolic church before that time.

Partial Preterism

In recent years, a form of preterism has entered the ranks of Pentecostals. These teachers claim that most prophecies of the end times have been fulfilled, yet they still believe in the miraculous outpouring of the Holy Spirit and in a literal, future coming of Christ. Therefore, as some have acknowledged, their view can be called "partial preterism," as opposed to "full preterism," which asserts that all end-time prophecies have been fulfilled and denies a literal, future coming of Christ.

Here are some typical examples of the interpretation of Scripture by preterists (full or partial). In Matthew 24:30, Jesus predicted that in the future people would see "the Son of man coming in the clouds of heaven with power and great glory." According to some preterist teachers, the "clouds" refer to the clouds of dust stirred up by the Roman armies as they marched against Jerusalem, and thus the coming of the Lord refers to that event. In John 14:2-3, Jesus promised, "In my Father's house are many mansions: if it were not so, I would have told you. I go to prepare a place for you. And if I go and prepare a place for you, I will come again, and receive you unto myself; that where I am, there ye may be also." Some preterist teachers explain that the "mansions" are "rooms" that Jesus has prepared in the hearts of people. Thus, this passage has been fulfilled in the New Testament church. Moreover, the passages that refer to the second "coming" (*parousia*) of Christ actually refer to the spiritual "presence" of Christ. Thus the church has already experienced His coming.

Partial preterists imply that the Millennium is either past or present, but typically they have not been definitive, because the Articles of Faith of the United Pentecostal Church International (UPCI) require belief in a literal Millennium. However, they believe that the specified time of one thousand years is symbolic and that the UPCI should not have an official position on the Millennium. Moreover, it appears that, according to their interpretation, the eternal destiny of the church is to remain on the renovated earth.

Partial preterists acknowledge that at some point in time the church will see Jesus on the earth in His glorified humanity. Ultimately, there will be the resurrection of the dead, the last judgment, eternal reward for the righteous, and eternal judgment for the unrighteous. However, they do not find any prophetic indication of when this could take place; it could be a thousand years away.

As a necessary part of their belief system, partial preterists reject all aspects of dispensationalism and any role for the nation of Israel in God's future plan. They regard the church today as "spiritual Israel."

Some Pentecostal teachers of preterism have stated

that they received their beliefs personally from God through many hours and days of prayer, fasting, and Bible study. They also state that this message and their key role in disseminating this message have been confirmed by "prophets." Consequently, some have shifted the main focus of their ministry to studying and propagating these teachings.

Although preterists regard the prophecies concerning the Tribulation as already fulfilled, some partial preterist teachers do foresee a time of trouble in the near future because of an alleged attempt by Jews to dominate the world. In this connection, they regard Jerusalem as the Babylon of the Book of Revelation and the mother of false doctrine. As evidence of a worldwide Jewish conspiracy, they cite the *Protocols of the Elders of Zion*, an anti-Semitic forgery from Czarist Russia. The Russians used this document to justify pogroms against the Jews, and the Nazis likewise used it in their attempt to discredit the Jews. Scholars have conclusively demonstrated that it is false, however.

Some partial preterist teachers also cite the Noachide laws as evidence of a Jewish conspiracy to dominate the world. Jews derive these laws from the commandments that God gave to Noah after the flood. (See Genesis 9.) While they do not believe that Gentiles need to adhere to the Old Testament, since God did not establish that covenant with them, they do believe that Gentiles should keep God's covenant with Noah in order to be righteous in His sight.

Finally, many full preterist and partial preterist teachers regard prophetic schemes other than their own not merely as erroneous or incorrect but as "deception."

They see their mission as one of leading the Apostolic movement out of allegedly false doctrines inherited from trinitarian Christianity, such as the imminent Rapture, the future Tribulation, the New Jerusalem as a heavenly city and future abode of the saints, and so on.

Problems and Concerns

From a biblical perspective, there are serious flaws with both full preterism and partial preterism.

1. *The allegorical interpretation of Scripture.* Christians should use the grammatical-historical method of interpreting Scripture, sometimes called the literal method. This means to interpret the words and phrases of Scripture according to their grammatical, historical meaning in context, understanding the words and phrases in their ordinary and apparent meaning. It does not exclude the use of types, symbols, and figures of speech, but it recognizes them when the context indicates them. This method is the only way of finding an objective meaning in Scripture, so that it "is profitable for doctrine, for reproof, for correction, for instruction in righteousness" (II Timothy 3:16).

By contrast, the preterist view requires an allegorical interpretation of most passages dealing with the end times—ignoring the apparent, ordinary, literal meaning and instead choosing a hidden, secret meaning that corresponds with a preconceived doctrinal scheme. For example, under this view, Jesus does not return visibly in actual clouds, the Millennium is not an actual period of one thousand years, and the church does not have the promise of a literal abode in an eternal city.

By the allegorical method of interpretation, one could

easily destroy many other important doctrines of Scripture. For instance, by this method one could deny the teaching of literal water baptism, communion, speaking in tongues, divine healing, and so on. All of these things could be just as symbolic as the physical Second Coming, the Millennium, the mansions of heaven, and the New Jerusalem. Moreover, a logical application of the preterist view would result in the conclusion that the baptism of the Holy Spirit with tongues and the gifts of the Spirit are not for today.

2. *Discounting the message of the Book of Revelation.* The preterist view requires an extremely early date for the Book of Revelation, before A.D. 70. Moreover, it means that Revelation has very little relevance for Christians after that time. For the most part, it would have benefited only believers who lived in the few years between the time it was supposedly written and the time it was supposedly fulfilled. Thus it would be the only book of the New Testament that would have little or no application or blessing for the church today.

However, the general consensus of both ancient and modern writers is that the book was written around A.D. 96. Most scholars say the Book of Revelation was written in the latter part of the reign of the emperor Domitian (81-96). Writers in the second through fourth centuries uniformly testified that Domitian banished John to Patmos, and some said he did so in A.D. 95. From the description of the seven churches in Revelation 2-3, it is apparent that a considerable amount of time had passed from their founding. In particular, the church at Ephesus was no longer as fervent in love as when Paul wrote to them in the late 50s or early 60s. (See Ephesians 1:15;

3:17; Revelation 2:4.) Both from external and internal evidence, then, we see that the Book of Revelation was not written in the 60s but in the 90s.

3. *False teaching concerning the end times.* While there is considerable diversity among Apostolics regarding the doctrine of the last things, and to some extent this diversity is healthy, the Bible does affirm several key doctrines that the preterist view minimizes or denies. Examples are as follows, with supporting Scripture references:

- The Rapture (the imminent catching away of the saints into heaven to be with the Lord): I Corinthians 15:51-52; I Thessalonians 4:16-17.
- The Tribulation (a definite, future time period unlike any other in history): Matthew 24; II Thessalonians 2; Revelation 6-19.
- The Second Coming (the literal return of Jesus Christ to earth in visible form as the hope of the church): Acts 1:9-11; I Thessalonians 3:13; Titus 2:13; Zechariah 14; Revelation 19.
- The Millennium (the thousand-year reign of Christ on earth): Revelation 20:1-6; Zechariah 14:9.
- Expectancy of the soon coming of the Lord: Matthew 24:42-44; I Thessalonians 4:15-17; Hebrews 10:37; Revelation 22:20.

4. *Misunderstanding the role of spiritual gifts and experiences.* Some preterists rely upon the exercise of spiritual gifts and upon personal spiritual experiences to establish the credibility of their doctrine. However, this is a misunderstanding of the role of such gifts and experiences. The Bible is our sole authority for doctrine and

instruction. (See II Timothy 3:15-17; Acts 17:2, 11-12; Galatians 1:8; Revelation 22:18-19.) According to John 16:13, the manifested Spirit, or the Spirit within believers, does not grant independent authority to them but illuminates what God has already revealed and what Jesus taught on earth. Prophecy is given for edification, exhortation, and comfort and is subject to the judgment of the hearers (I Corinthians 14:3, 29).

5. *Anti-Semitism.* It is true that the church, not Israel, is the New Testament covenant people. Nevertheless, God still has a future plan for national Israel to lead them to salvation through Christ (Romans 11:25-29). Moreover, in the church, there can be no prejudice whatsoever. (See Galatians 3:28; James 2:9.) Therefore, we must vigorously reject all forms of anti-Semitism as contrary to the gospel and to Christian holiness.

6. *Undermining other churches, contrary to ministerial ethics.* Teaching that the Apostolic movement as a whole is in "deception" and false doctrine is dangerous and divisive. Whether intended or not, it has the effect of undermining the trust of members in their pastor, local church, and international organization. A number of reports have come of members leaving their churches after listening to tapes of this teaching or receiving this teaching in person. Jesus said we would know teachers by their fruit. (See Matthew 7:15-20.) It is not the will of God for teachers to promote doctrines that bring confusion, doubt, division, and personal spiritual failure.

7. *Undermining the message of practical holiness.* One of the strongest motivators for people to live a holy life is the expectation of the catching away of the saints and the physical return of Christ. (See Titus 2:11-14;

II Peter 3:1-14; I John 3:2-3.) Thus it is no coincidence that there seems to be a trend among some preterists to discard scriptural teachings concerning Christian lifestyle and dress.

Conclusion

Adherents of full preterism and partial preterism promote an allegorical interpretation of Scripture, discount the value of the Book of Revelation for believers today, and contradict the position of Scripture on a number of important points. When preterism has entered Pentecostal ranks, this view has typically led to a faulty understanding of spiritual experiences and gifts, the use of anti-Semitic material, questionable ministerial ethics, disruption of local churches, and compromise of practical teachings of holiness. Therefore, the doctrines of full preterism and partial preterism are incompatible with the Apostolic understanding of Scripture.

David K. Bernard is founder and pastor of New Life United Pentecostal Church of Austin, Texas, out of which have come ten additional works. He is also superintendent of the South Texas District UPCI and president of Urshan Graduate School of Theology. He holds a J.D. with honors from the University of Texas, an M.Th. from the University of South Africa, and a B.A. with high honors from Rice University.

2

A Hope Destroyed: Preterism's Origins and Implications

Ken Gurley

A Paradise Lost

Imagine the joy of receiving an all-expense-paid trip to paradise. To heighten the joy, family and friends are permitted to come as well. The day of departure finally arrives, and the trip is made to the airport, but there is no jet waiting at the gate. A ticket agent mournfully shares the news: the plane already came and went. Then, imagine that the ticket agent says the plane came two thousand years ago and no one got on board. The disappointment one might feel is roughly akin to that offered by the doctrine of preterism.

Preterists believe that Jesus came in the dust clouds of Roman chariots, not with a wedding, but a funeral on His mind. Christ, according to preterists, did not return with the sparkling New Jerusalem, but He came to destroy dusty, old Jerusalem. For those who cherish the many promises of Christ's soon return and the bliss awaiting the faithful, preterism represents a certain heart sickness—not of a hope deferred, but of a hope destroyed.

This chapter attempts a threefold purpose: first, to briefly discuss the importance of studying prophecy; second, to trace the change from the premillennial view of the early church to the postmillennial view, culminating with preterism; and third, to illustrate a few of the practical implications of holding to the doctrine of preterism.

Why Study Prophecy?

Much ink has been spilled over prophetic themes. Bookshelves are lined with books that purport to shed light on some hidden end-time truth. For the eight million or so prophecy buffs in the United States,[1] such material is fodder for endless and often idle speculation. For the remaining majority, the study of prophecy represents a minefield that is best viewed from a distance, if at all.

The sensationalism and misses behind the doomsday scenarios, Rapture scares, and Antichrist sightings contribute to the reluctance of many believers to study prophetic themes. Couple this with the daunting challenge of understanding and adopting a particular prophetic view, and the task seems insufferable. For example, within the premillennial view of prophecy, one finds those who hold to either the historicist view or to a wide variety of dispensational views regarding the Tribulation (pre-, mid-, post-, pre-wrath, progressive, and so forth). And this is just the tip of the prophetic iceberg. One easily sympathizes with the minister who when asked his view of the Tribulation replied that he was pan-tribulational. By this, he meant that it would all "pan out" in the end.

It is little wonder that many sincere believers find the prophetic shelves too long and too high. Adding to the challenge is the unique vocabulary employed in eschatology, the study of last things. Seemingly inscrutable and often frightening words, such as *parousia, apocalypse, Day of the Lord, Tribulation, Millennium,* and so forth, contribute to a sense of eschatological exclusiveness.

Compounding the problem is that the mere use or understanding of such terms does not necessarily render a degree of confidence in one's study of prophecy. When discussing the prophecies of the Book of Revelation, commentators commonly admit some degree of uncertainty.[2] Students of prophecy sympathize with the quip of American humorist Mark Twain: "The researches of many commentators have already thrown much darkness on this subject, and it is probable that, if they continue, we shall soon know nothing at all about it!"

A final explanation for the reticence or even apathy towards the study of prophecy lies in the attitude and behavior of some who study it. One may often observe a distinct smugness if not arrogance in some who make the study of prophecy a hobby or a hobby horse. The study of prophecy can easily become an obsession consuming a person's time, attention, and energy.

In spite of these obstructions, the study of prophecy cannot rightfully be ignored. Tipping the scales in favor of a serious study of eschatology are extremely weighty considerations, the first of which is that so much of Scripture is prophetic.[3] Since it is Scripture, it must have been given for man's study and instruction (II Timothy 3:16). Ministers who seek to declare the whole counsel of God cannot easily overlook the major prophetic themes (Acts 20:27). After all, of the six elementary teachings of the New Testament church, two are prophetic: resurrection from the dead and eternal judgment (Hebrews 6:1-2).

Thus, one-third of these basic Christian teachings points to the future.

Finally, the study of prophecy is needful since eschatology is not merely a category of one's systematic theology. Prophetic viewpoints impact lifestyles. A vision for the future is absolutely necessary. As Jürgen Moltmann once said, "From first to last, and not merely in the epilogue, Christianity is eschatology, is hope, forward looking and forward moving, and therefore also revolutionizing and transforming the present. . . . Hence eschatology cannot really be only a part of Christian doctrine. Rather the eschatological outlook is characteristic of all Christian proclamation, and of every Christian existence and of the whole Church."[4]

The primary practical concern for writing this chapter is found in this final point: the varied and significant effects that a prophetic view can have upon a person's lifestyle. The doctrine of preterism—the teaching that all or nearly all of the prophecies in the Olivet Discourse and in the Book of Revelation were fulfilled by the fall of Jerusalem in A.D. 70 or the subsequent fall of Rome in 410—like all other prophetic views has an impact on a person's conduct. God has placed eternity in man's heart (Ecclesiastes 3:11), and from one's deeply cherished beliefs flow thoughts, concepts, attitudes, words, beliefs, and lifestyles. The preterist viewpoint is not a doctrine to be considered in isolation from other doctrines and lifestyles.

Before turning to the implications of preterism, it is beneficial and perhaps necessary to look at the origins of this doctrine. From this, one can develop a heightened awareness of the implications of holding to such a view.

Origins of Preterism

As a general rule, proponents of preterism do not claim that the early church was postmillennial in its beliefs,[5] nor is there ample evidence in the extant writings of the ante-Nicene theologians to indicate that the early church believed that Christ had returned in A.D. 70 or that the Millennium was anything but in the future. Papias (ca. 130), bishop of Phrygian Hierapolis, viewed the Millennium as a future time of peace on the earth as described by the prophets.[6] Justin Martyr, Irenaeus, Tertullian,[7] and Lactantius adopted and augmented this premillennial view, although at least Justin and Irenaeus acknowledged that others held different views.[8]

The ante-Nicene theologians' literal and eschatological approach to understanding Revelation soon waned with the waxing of the Alexandrian theologians' allegorical hermeneutic. The Alexandrian theologians rejected the notion of a future, literal Millennium.[9] Of note in this regard is Origen (ca. 185-254), who not only popularized this method of interpretation but also predicted that Christianity would "gain the dominion over the world."[10] Tyconius (ca. 390) is credited as the first to allegorize the Millennium as an interval between the first and second advents of Christ. Both Jerome (ca. 340-420) and Augustine (ca. 354-430),[11] and to some extent Athanasius (ca. 296-372), adopted Tyconius's teaching, and it became the normative view through the Middle Ages.[12]

Contributing to the rise of this teaching and to its subsequent prominence was the Roman Empire accepting Christianity and later adopting it as the official state religion. Among some, the felt need for Christ to return and set up His kingdom diminished in the face of Christianity's apparent triumph over a physical, earthly kingdom.[13] This reinforced the spiritualizing of the Millennium into a present "golden age" of the gospel. As the empire faded, Augustine put forth his view that the first resurrection equaled regeneration and that the Millennium was the church in its role as the "city of God."[14] Such postmillennial thought held sway during the Middle Ages.

The Reformation did not initially challenge such thought. The Reformers adopted a historicist viewpoint of Revelation popularized by Joachim of Fiore (1130-1201), who originated one of the more detailed early forms of postmillennialism.[15] Although Fiore was loyal to Rome, others (e.g., John Knox and John Bale) would use his system to identify the Roman papacy as the first beast mentioned in Revelation. Such a view was compatible with the teaching of the Reformers, who equated the papacy with the Antichrist.

Spanish Jesuit scholar Luiz de Alcazar (1554-1613) came to Rome's defense with his preterist approach to Revelation. Although Dutch Protestant theologian Hugo Grotius (1583-1645) followed Alcazar's model and helped preterism gain acceptance outside Catholicism,[16] the Reformers did not widely accept the teachings of preterism.

Postmillennialism—albeit not of the preterist variety—remained imbedded in Protestantism from the seventeenth to the nineteenth centuries and spanned both the Old and New Worlds and many of the great theological divides as well. The most prominent names in Christendom, such as John Calvin (1509-1564), Isaac Watts (1674-1748), and Jonathan Edwards (1703-1758) adopted some form of postmillennialism.[17]

Two centuries after the Reformation, a marked ambivalence towards postmillennial thought developed. In the fourteen-volume collection of John Wesley's works, there is not a single mention of the words *premillennial* or *postmillennial.*[18] Wesley saw an "already" and a "not yet" fulfillment with the Millennium. He tried to reconcile the contrasting pictures of a flourishing church and the deception of the last days by arguing for "two distinct thousand years."[19] In line with the English sentiment that the coming of the Lord was drawing near, Wesley predicted that the "time, and times and a half a time" of Revelation 12:14 were the years from 1058-1836, thus calling for the Millennium to begin in the year of 1836—a non-event that he would not live to witness.[20]

About the same time as Wesley's failed prediction, however, several events revealed people's disenchantment with the traditional postmillennial viewpoint. William Miller, founder of the Seventh-Day Adventists, predicted unsuccessfully that the Lord would return in 1843. John Nelson Darby (1800-1882), a minister with the Plymouth Brethren, offered his Rapture theory and dispensational viewpoints. Another important event was the writings and teachings of J. Stuart Russell (1816-1895), a Congregational pastor. In his work *The Parousia* Russell advocated a viewpoint that Christ had returned at the destruction of Jerusalem, fulfilling the Jewish economy, the resurrection, and judgment.

The failure of the church to witness a "golden age" of evangelism, the entrenched worldliness in the church, the rise of the Arminian/Wesleyan view of sanctification, and the weariness of wars on both sides of the Atlantic were possible contributors to the rise of the Holiness Movement and the resurgence of premillennialism. The Christian and Missionary Alliance adopted a fourfold mantra of Christ as Savior, Sanctifier, Healer, and Coming King. From this movement eventually emerged modern Pentecostalism.

In the latter part of the twentieth century, postmillennialism saw its own resurgence in the form of theonomy (a.k.a. Christian reconstructionism, dominion theology, and kingdom now). The evangelical strain of this doctrine argues that society must once again come under the Mosaic judicial laws.[21] Proponents in the charismatic branch of this doctrine (e.g., Earl Paulk and John Meares) hold that the church, as a manifestation of the kingdom of God, will conquer each kingdom of the world. At a conference in 1988, the evangelical and charismatic proponents of theonomy met and claimed to have effected a merger between their various viewpoints.[22] At least two of the speakers at this meeting, Gary DeMar and the late David Chilton, went on to become ardent proponents of preterism.[23]

The past decade has witnessed the ascension of preterism. Popular radio personalities R. C. Sproul and Hank Hannegraff have fueled the doctrine through their teachings and respective writings: *The Last Days According to Jesus* and *The Last Disciple*. Of perhaps greater impetus was the "Rapture fatigue" brought on by such scares as Edgar Whisenant's *88 Reasons Why the Rapture Could Be in 1988*, which sold nearly five million copies. The crowning moment of "Rapture fatigue" came with the Y2K fiasco, where Christian soothsayers peddled their prophetic theories to a concerned public. A post 9/11 America might also be more attuned to a dominion message. Rather than a King to come, preterism offers a kingdom come.

In summarizing the origins of preterism, it cannot be shown that any in the apostolic age or in the immediate years following embraced preterism. Once an allegorical/spiritual hermeneutic was applied to prophecy, postmillennial thought developed, which was the common belief throughout the Middle Ages. The first two hundred years of Protestant history do not show a serious departure from postmillennialism. The Holiness Movement, which led to the rebirth of modern Pentecostalism, embraced premillennialism. The latter part of the twentieth century witnessed a rise in theonomy, followed by preterism. The doctrine of preterism, originally a Catholic response to Protestant attacks, has now spread throughout the Protestant ranks.

Astoundingly, the doctrine has entered into Apostolic Pentecostal ranks. A doctrine whose origins and hermeneutics seem so incompatible with the restorationist impulse and the fervently held doctrines of Apostolic Pentecostalism has made inroads in churches across North America. Proponents of this doctrine eagerly try to prove the error of those who hold a premillennial view and seem confident of their ability to do so. While fervency in studying Scripture may be commendable, one must wonder if proponents of preterism adequately understand its origins and the immense implications of its teachings.

Implications of Preterism

Doctrines, whether biblically sound or not, have ramifications (I Timothy 4:6). Preterism challenges many of the beliefs of Apostolic Pentecostalism and more specifically of the United Pentecostal Church International. Preterism can serve to undermine many of these beliefs.

Turning to the implications of preterism and to the more practical portion of this chapter, it is easy to see the problems preterism poses for Apostolic Pentecostals.

1. Preterism teaches that Christ came in judgment against Jerusalem. If A.D. 70 marks Christ's return, then it follows that much of the church's beliefs are now in vain.

Of course, preterists offer different views of this supposed return in A.D. 70. Inconsistent or partial preterists maintain that this was not the Second Coming while consistent or full preterists maintain the opposite. The former posits the return in A.D. 70 as a "judgment-return," which somehow differs in character from the Second Coming. Yet, in the partial preterist schema, it is often difficult to tell which coming is which. For example, in the Olivet Discourse in Matthew, Christ mentioned His coming seven times, four of those times using the Greek word *parousia* (Matthew 24:3, 27, 37, 39). A number of significant New Testament passages describing the Second Coming use the same word (I Corinthians 15:23; I Thessalonians 2:19; 3:13; 4:15; 5:23; II Thessalonians 2:1, 8; James 5:7-8; II Peter 1:16; 3:4, 12; I John 2:28). Yet, which of these passages—and others using different Greek terms for the Lord's coming—involve the "judgment-return" at Jerusalem versus a future Second Coming is difficult to tell. After all, an allegorical hermeneutic does not lend itself to an exact answer to many texts.

To illustrate, the apostle Paul mentions the coming of the Lord five times in I Corinthians. He instructs the believers to "come behind in no gift; waiting for the coming of our Lord Jesus Christ" (1:7). He commands them to "judge nothing before the time, until the Lord come" (4:5). The apostle connects the partaking of the Lord's Supper with showing "the Lord's death till he come" (11:26). Prophesying, speaking with tongues, and other gifts are present in the church until "that which is perfect is come, then that which is in part shall be done away" (13:10). Finally, he discusses the order of the resurrection, with Christ being the "firstfruits," followed by "they that are Christ's at his coming" (15:23). In one New Testament book, there are five items linked with the coming of the Lord: obtaining spiritual gifts, judging, the Lord's Supper, using spiritual gifts, and being resurrected from the dead. If Christ returned in A.D. 70, which of these five items, if any, "abideth" and which of these five items, if any, have been "done away"?

Consistent preterists maintain that the resurrection occurred with Rome's invasion of Jerusalem while all preterists maintain that the "first resurrection" (Revelation 20:5-6) is regeneration. In addition to battling charges of the Hymenaean heresy (II Timothy 2:17-18), such full preterists must face other unforeseen, perhaps humorous, consequences. For example, Jesus said that at the resurrection, people will neither marry nor be given in marriage, but will be as the angels in heaven (Matthew 22:30). Several preterist writers have recently come to the defense of marriage to explain why preterists do not have to be "as the angels."[24]

In addition to the obvious doctrine of the Second

Coming,[25] many of the doctrines of the United Pentecostal Church International are similarly anchored to the coming of the Lord: holiness,[26] translation of saints,[27] the Lord's Supper,[28] and the baptism of the Holy Ghost.[29] That so many of the church's beliefs involve the Second Coming is not surprising. The Christian's hope is motivated largely by the anticipated return of his King. Numerous are the verses that connect a person's godly lifestyle with the Second Coming: Mark 8:34-38; I Thessalonians 5:1-7; Titus 2:11-14; II Peter 3:10-12; Jude 14-16; Revelation 1:5-7. With its ill-defined "coming of the Lord," preterism compromises the scriptural understanding of other doctrines as well.

A curious comparison can be made regarding extreme forms of preterism and dispensationalism. One preterist noted that a "consistent preterist" believes that "all prophecy is fulfilled in the A.D. 70 destruction of the Temple, including the Second Advent, the resurrection of the dead, the great Judgment and so forth."[30] He described various characteristics of this view: exaggerating the "at hand" prophecies to force a fulfillment by A.D. 70; a complete removal of the physical resurrection; no future Second Coming; time is eternalized; the lack of any gospel message; and such things as the Lord's Supper are no longer necessary.

The extreme form of dispensationalism echoes similar themes: the Book of Acts is largely Jewish in character and no longer applies to today's believers; the gospel preached by Peter in the early part of the Book of Acts is Jewish and by Acts 15 has changed its character; water baptism and the Lord's Supper were given to Paul before he turned to the Gentiles and no longer apply.[31] Just as preterism pushes huge portions of Scripture and monumental doctrines aside—the Olivet Discourse, most if not all of the Book of Revelation, doctrines such as the Second Coming, the resurrection, and spiritual gifts—extreme forms of dispensationalism do the same. In this, extreme forms of preterism and dispensationalism agree in their exclusionary and "cessationist" tendencies.

Of special interest to Pentecostals is the treatment of spiritual gifts by any preterist view. Ed Stevens, in his recent work *What Happened in A.D. 70?*, arrives at a conclusion curiously similar to that of hyperdispensationalism. "The charismatic gifts which the Paraclete poured out upon the first century church for revelatory, confirmatory, and consummatory purposes [ceased] . . . once the plan [of redemption] was completely revealed and consummated [in A.D. 70]. . . . The last days of the Jewish nation ended then. A new age had begun. The charismata associated with the last days ceased."[32] Another consistent preterist also stated that "Christ's advent at the time of the destruction of Jerusalem to receive the kingdom . . . terminated an altogether exceptional state of things which had prevailed since the Day of Pentecost, and caused these abnormal miraculous gifts of the Holy Spirit to cease."[33]

One might argue that this represents only an extreme form of preterism, and this would be correct. Yet, as the doctrine of preterism continues to push forward, there appears to be a steady increase in consistent preterism. Consistent preterism accentuates its bias against the doctrines and practices of the early church, especially those that Apostolic Pentecostals hold precious.

Phil Johnson, executive director of the *Grace to You*

radio broadcast, regularly ranks Christian Web sites. Johnson recently identified one of the more common Web sites for preterism, The Preterist Archive, as "really bad theology." In his ranking, he made an interesting and telling statement:

> Hyper-preterists [consistent preterists] react to the end-of-the-world doom-and-gloomers by running to an opposite extreme, but their fanaticism is actually driven by a similar spirit. Here's a rule of thumb: when you encounter someone whose whole view of theology is shaped and driven by any eschatological theory (be it pre- post- or a-millennial), so that eschatology becomes their primary concern, you've found a candidate for the "really bad theology" category.[34]

2. Preterism teaches a present spiritual kingdom, but denies a future physical kingdom (Millennium). Since the apostles taught both of these, preterism in effect calls into question the reliability of the Lord's chosen witnesses and of the New Testament canon.

One Pentecostal preterist maintains that the present Apostolic church has not "sought out" two areas, namely the Lord's coming in the "clouds" and the kingdom of God. He quotes several verses[35] illustrating the spiritual aspect of Christ's kingdom and uses these to justify his view that Jesus and His apostles did not believe in a coming physical kingdom. He concludes:

> It is easy to see that Jesus and his Apostles believed the kingdom of God to be the Spirit of God

> indwelling in the hearts of believers after they are born again. The Apostles wrote as if the kingdom of God was something they had already received rather than something they were waiting to receive in the future.[36]

Preterism resides in the postmillennial camp, meaning that it teaches that the church is the kingdom. However, one cannot find that the apostles prophesied of the "golden age" of the gospel, rather they saw the cause of Christ moving forward amid rejection, persecution, and martyrdom.[37] Jesus clearly taught that His kingdom was "not of this world" (John 18:36). However, He instructed the disciples to pray, "Thy kingdom come" (Matthew 6:10). The coming kingdom is frequently associated with Christ's second coming (Matthew 25:34; Luke 19:11-15). After His ascension, Jesus taught the apostles the things "pertaining to the kingdom of God" (Acts 1:3). Shortly thereafter, the apostles asked Jesus if at that time would He "restore again the kingdom unto Israel" (Acts 1:6). Jesus told them that it was not for them to know the "times or the seasons" that the kingdom would come—language that Paul relates to the coming Day of the Lord (I Thessalonians 5:1-2). Paul not only spoke of the present reality of the spiritual kingdom;[38] he consistently spoke of a future kingdom.[39]

Two passages in Paul's writings are of special interest in this regard. In I Corinthians 15:23-24, Paul describes the order of the resurrection: "Christ the firstfruits; afterward they that are Christ's at his coming. Then cometh the end, when he shall have delivered up the kingdom to God." Obviously, the apostle did not see the kingdom as being a past or merely a present event, but one with future implications. The second passage that is particularly noteworthy is in the final chapter of the final letter written by Paul. In II Timothy 4:1, Paul begins by giving Timothy a solemn charge before "the Lord Jesus Christ, who shall judge the quick and the dead at his appearing and his kingdom." He closes this chapter with a prayer that the Lord will preserve him "unto his heavenly kingdom" (II Timothy 4:18). That a future kingdom is in view can hardly be denied.

In Simon Peter's discourse on the heavenly virtues, the chief apostle promises that those who do them will "never fall" and will also be granted a "rich welcome" into the eternal kingdom (II Peter 1:10-11). John declared himself as being "in the kingdom" (Revelation 1:9), but also recorded heaven's words deep into the Tribulation: "Now is come . . . the kingdom of our God" (Revelation 12:10).

When John wrote Revelation, it is thought that only he remained of the original apostles. Each died expecting a coming kingdom. This hope did not die with the closing of the apostolic age. Rather, those who came after the apostles continued to teach what preterists believe to be error. Justin Martyr (100-165) was born in Samaria close to the newly destroyed city of Jerusalem. Justin interpreted the apostolic teaching in light of the Old Testament prophecies of a future, coming kingdom. In his *Dialogue with Trypho*, Justin responded to a question about whether there would be a resurrection and a literal thousand years, saying, "But I and others, who are right-minded Christians on all points, are assured that there will be a resurrection of the dead, and a thousand years in Jerusalem, which will then be built, adorned, and enlarged, [as] the prophets Ezekiel and Isaiah and others declare."[40] Other significant writers of this era, such as Papias,[41] Irenaeus,[42] and Tertullian,[43] confirmed the chiliastic (from the Greek *chilia* meaning one thousand) view of the kingdom.

From secular historian Edward Gibbon to Daniel Whitby, father of modern postmillennialism, and a host of scholars in between, the common sentiment is that for at least the first two centuries after Christ, the belief in a literal, coming kingdom was nearly universal in the church.[44]

The New Testament church was chiliastic, that is, it believed in a physical return of Jesus Christ to set up His earthly kingdom that would last for a thousand years.[45] Preterism teaches that such expectations were in error and recasts the apostles' hopes to a mere destruction of Jerusalem—something no apostle was ever known to have desired. Preterism further holds that the kingdom is not a future physical reality, but a present spiritual one. Although one can find references to a present spiritual kingdom in the New Testament, it does not exclude the New Testament writers' belief in a future kingdom as well.

The United Pentecostal Church International believes in a literal Millennium preceded by the Second Coming and followed by the judgment.[46] This is fairly typical of classical Pentecostal organizations and represents the eschatological doctrines brought from the Holiness Movement. Preterists interpret the Scripture references cited by the UPCI to substantiate such a coming kingdom to mean that this was either fulfilled in A.D. 70 or spiritually through the church.[47]

The preterist interpretation notwithstanding, it is incredulous to assert that the apostles and believers somehow missed Christ's coming and His kingdom in His purported return in A.D. 70.[48] Since preterism appeared in church history after the apostolic age, it comes as little surprise that from Scripture or known extant writings, there is no evidence that the early church understood the prophecies relating to the Lord's return or His kingdom in a preterist manner. Not all preterists would agree with these statements, but several admit to this. For example, one preterist recognizes this lack of support for the preterist view in the early church:

> How could it be that some of the apostles and their traveling companions lived through the events of A.D. 70 without recognizing the significance of it and saying something about it? This is the single most significant factor shaping the history of eschatological study that I am aware of. All of church history and its consequent interpretation of Bible Prophecy is deeply affected by this silence.[49]

He goes on to suggest that the reason for the silence in the early church on this matter is that believers were raptured in A.D. 66.[50] He says that his viewpoint coincided with some of the earliest modern preterists.[51]

Another preterist suggested that the absence of preterist understanding was not that the believers were raptured, but that the passage of A.D. 70 caused the prophecies to become "unintelligible for the most part."[52] Finally, another preterist admits that preterism is a recent development and concludes:

> Modern Christian eschatology is based upon an early church error: assuming the second coming was delayed, but misunderstanding its spiritual fulfillment in A.D. 70. We need not remain in this wilderness of misplaced hope. Rather, through sound biblical scholarship, we can recover the transforming hope that the early church embraced. Herein lies our hope for the third Christian millennium.[53]

These preterist authors offer three choices for the omission of any preterist viewpoint in the early church: The apostles and their followers were raptured, confused, or mistaken. Keeping with this last theme of being mistaken, preterism largely insists that Christ had to return within a generation of the apostles, or God's Word would be in error.[54]

One Pentecostal preterist avows something with which all sincere believers might agree: "To take the position that statements made in the New Testament were in error in order to make a futurist viewpoint correct is to side with the agnostics and criticizers of Christianity and to take away all foundation for determining what is truth."[55] While valid, the opposite is equally so: One must not wrest the Scriptures in an attempt to prove preterism. This also undermines the foundation for truth.

3. Preterism denies the soon return of the Lord, thus arguably denying believers the motivation for much of the evangelism witnessed in the New Testament.

Preterism thoroughly mutes the imminence of Christ's coming and its urgent appeal. The church, according to preterists, is in the midst of a Millennium/kingdom without a sense of urgency. One preterist spoke of this day as a "vast, undefined period of time. . . . It may require a million years."[56] Another preterist notes, "The New Testament suggests long 'seasons' pass before Christ returns. . . . Postmillennialism does not hold to the imminence of Christ's return."[57]

One amillennialist made a cogent observation about postmillennial thought, of which preterism is a part:

> [Postmillennialism] alters the focus of the believer's hope for the future. . . . Whereas the New Testament depicts the church in the present age as a church continually participating in the sufferings of Christ and eagerly awaiting the return of Christ at the end of the age, the postmillennial view encourages an outlook for the future that is focused on an anticipated period of largely undisturbed blessedness in the millennial kingdom. . . . The golden age postmillennialist has his sights fixed upon the coming golden age rather than the return of Christ at end of the age.[58]

A Christian reconstructionist-turned-preterist lends credence to the above observation:

> Every day brings us closer to the realization of the knowledge of God covering the entire world. . . . God promises that He will bless His people for one thousand generations. By the analogy of Scripture, then, this means that a figure of forty thousand years is a bare minimum. This world has tens of thousands,

> perhaps hundreds of thousands of years of increasing godliness ahead of it, before the Second Coming of Christ.[59]

The only sense of urgency one derives in reviewing preterist materials is a seeming iconoclastic bent to debunk yet another strongly held belief. This particular form of zeal differs from that possessed by the early church as she anticipated the return of Jesus Christ. "To those who eagerly await for Him," the writer of Hebrews said, "He will appear a second time, apart from sin, for salvation" (Hebrews 9:28, NKJV). In many other places in Scripture, believers are encouraged to "watch" for His soon return. "To live without watchfulness," observed William Barclay, "invites disaster."[60]

Preterists view much, if not all, of the Olivet Discourse as past history. Jesus said that the "gospel of the kingdom" would be preached through the whole world "and then shall the end come" (Matthew 24:14). Later in the same Gospel, Jesus commands His disciples to go into "all the world" and promises that He will be with them until the "end of the world" (Matthew 28:19-20; compare with Mark 16:20). Preterists are fond of saying that the world was reached with the gospel during the apostles' lifetime and that A.D. 70 marked the end. It follows—according to the preterist logic—that the great commission has been fulfilled, and thus Christ is no longer "with us" (Matthew 28:20). One preterist has followed this same logic and contends that in fact the great commission was fulfilled by A.D. 70.[61]

One Pentecostal preterist believes that by the destruction of Jerusalem the spreading of the gospel "had already been completed. This left no hindrances in the way of Jesus coming in their day to execute his judgment. Because of this, the disciples worked all the more to preach the Gospel. . . . This burden was heavy because they wanted every soul . . . to have a chance to be born again before His coming."[62] If the world was indeed evangelized by A.D. 70, then is it reasonable to assume that from this point forward the body of Christ has operated without its Head, since Christ is no longer "with us"? Another curious point in the quote is that he acknowledges that a belief in Christ's soon return motivates evangelism.

In his *Evangelism in the Early Church*, Michael Green, senior research fellow at Oxford's Wycliffe Hall, makes a telling comment: "There can be no doubt that the expectation of the imminent return of Christ gave a most powerful impetus to evangelism in the earliest days of the Church." The preaching and spreading of the gospel "was set in the context of an urgent eschatological hope as they awaited the return of God's Son from heaven." Not only did the imminent return of Christ motivate the apostles, the focus of their preaching "frequently came to its climax in a proclamation of the imminent return of Christ and a challenge to repentance and faith in light of the culmination of all things."[63]

The New Testament describes the Lord's return as imminent, meaning that it could happen at any moment. Believers are instructed to watch for His coming. In Paul's writings, the apostle spoke of "waiting for the coming of our Lord Jesus Christ" (I Corinthians 1:7); he gave the hopeful watchword of waiting Christians, "maranatha" (I Corinthians 16:22); he encouraged believers to remember that they had a citizenship in heaven and that they should "look for the Saviour" (Philippians 3:20); he reminded the same church that "the Lord is at hand" (Philippians 4:5). Additionally, other apostles joined in this eschatological chorus: James 5:7-9; I Peter 1:13; Jude 21.

In the Book of Revelation, the risen Christ gave a fourfold assurance of His anticipated return (3:11; 22:7, 12, 20). The New Testament closes with the assurance of the Lord's return. In other places in Revelation, John focuses his reader's attention on the coming of the Lord (1:7; 2:26; 3:3; 19:11-16). Clearly, the belief and preaching of the Lord's return is not a distraction from the church's business on planet earth; rather it is part and parcel of the church's deeply held hopes and beliefs.

A Pentecostal preterist poses an interesting question: "I have always tried to remain true to the Apostle's first century doctrines on salvation, godly living, and every other doctrine that they deemed important enough to write on, so why shouldn't I support a belief that these same Apostles held about prophecy as well?"[64] That is the question. Why insist upon a prophetic viewpoint that opposes what the apostles preached? Why insist upon a prophetic viewpoint that also differs widely from what marked the rebirth of Apostolic Pentecostalism in the previous century?

The resurgence of modern Pentecostalism cannot be separated from its eschatological impulse. The fathers of modern Pentecostalism, Charles Parham and William Seymour, illustrate this. Parham believed that speaking in tongues was a sign of the last days and was indicative of the Spirit's empowerment to evangelize.[65] Prior to Seymour's Pentecostal experience, he joined a "reformation" Church of God in Cincinnati, Ohio, more popularly known as the "Evening Light Saints." He became steeped in the various elements of the Holiness theology, including premillennialism and the promise of a worldwide revival before the Rapture. The subsequent missionary emphasis of Azusa Street can be traced to modern Pentecostalism's eschatological impulse.

With the background of the apostolic age and the rampant growth of modern Pentecostalism, it is somewhat dissonant to turn to one Pentecostal preterist's writings, where he states, "Rather than whether there is a premillennial coming or not does not enter into the picture as much as other issues which will determine where we stand and what we believe."[66] This is incorrect. The other issues that he lists as being of premier importance pale in comparison to one's anticipation of Christ's second coming. The premillennial coming of the Lord occupied center stage in the hopes of the New Testament church, the post-apostolic age, and in the resurgence and great revival of modern Pentecostalism. To cavalierly push it aside as being inconsequential is misinformed at best and reckless at worst.

The United Pentecostal Church International holds to a premillennial viewpoint while permitting great latitude of prophetic beliefs within that framework. This tolerance has been demonstrated through the years. However, the antagonism displayed by certain proponents of preterism makes this no easy union.[67]

Summary and Final Thoughts

The origins of preterism are beyond the apostolic age. Preterism is a postmillennial doctrine derived initially from a Jesuit priest in defense of the Roman papacy. The focus of preterism is not on a coming King or a kingdom, but on a kingdom here and now. In this sense, it is similar to the evangelical reconstructionists and the charismatic dominionists. The doctrine of preterism can be used to argue for the cessation of spiritual gifts, and it can also bring confusion to other teachings, such as holiness, resurrection, communion, and so forth. Preterism erodes the restorationist impulse of Apostolic Pentecostalism and deprives the modern church of the evangelistic zeal shared by the early Christians.

One is reminded of the words of a Christian sociologist who said, "Any theology that does not live with a sense of the immediate return of Christ is a theology that takes the edge off the urgency of faith. But any theology that does not cause us to live as though the world will be here for thousands of years is a theology that leads us into social irresponsibility."[68] The Second Coming has proven to be an effective instrument in keeping "the edge" on the urgency of faith while also causing Christians to be conscious of their actions.

Jesus, in the Olivet Discourse, warned His hearers to be ready for His return. In one of His parables, Jesus told of an "evil servant" who believed that his lord would delay his return (Matthew 24:48-51). Because the servant believed his master was not coming soon, his behavior and his treatment of others suffered. Jesus will return for those who "love his appearing" (II Timothy 4:8). The King will soon return for those who await Him. This may be a hope deferred, but it is not a hope destroyed.

Ken Gurley is pastor of the First Church of Pearland and secretary of the South Texas District UPCI. He is the author of the Worth the Wait *material, the* Preaching for a New Millennium *series, and numerous other books, articles, and pamphlets. He lives in Pearland, Texas, with his wife and three children.*

Notes

[1]As estimated by Paul Boyer, *When Time Shall Be No More: Prophecy Beliefs in Modern American Culture* (Cambridge, Mass.: Harvard University Press, 1992), 2-3.

[2]Assorted quotes of such uncertainty: "No portion of the Holy Scripture has been the subject of so much controversy and of so many varying interpretations" (Milton S. Terry, *Biblical Hermeneutics* [Grand Rapids: Zondervan, n.d.], 466). "To comment on this great prophecy is a harder task than to comment on a Gospel, and he who undertakes it exposes himself to the charge of presumption. I have been led to venture upon on what I know to be dangerous ground" (Henry B. Swete, *Commentary on Revelation* [Grand Rapids: Kregel, rep. 1977], 1). "No other book, whether in sacred or profane literature, has received in whole or in part so many different interpretations. Doubtless no other book has so perplexed biblical students throughout the Christian centuries down to our own times" (John T. Beckwith, *The Apocalypse of John: Studies in Introduction* [Grand Rapids: Baker, 1919], 1). "Some of the problems of this book are enormously difficult and I certainly have not the capacity to solve them . . . by common consent of the most difficult of all the books of the Bible" (Leon Morris, *The Revelation of Jesus Christ* [Chicago: Moody, 1966], 7).

[3]Dr. George Sweeting estimated that "more than a fourth of the Bible is predictive prophecy." He further stated that there are 1,845 references to Christ's second coming in the Old Testament. In the 260 chapters of the New Testament, there are 318 references to the Second Coming, equivalent to 1:30 verses of the entire New Testament. (As quoted in Moody Bible Institute's "Today in the Word" radio broadcast, December, 1989, 40).

[4]Jürgen Moltmann, *The Theology of Hope* (San Francisco: Harper and Row, 1980), 16.

[5]Prolific writer and preterist Kenneth L. Gentry, Jr., notes that no millennial view is found in any of the early creeds and that a "gradual development of millennial schemes" is to be expected. Gentry cites classic dispensationalist John F. Walvoord's statement that "the development of most important doc-

trines took centuries" as bolstering the understanding that important doctrines evolve over time. He also noted Millard J. Erickson's surprising statement that "all three millennial positions have been held virtually throughout church history." *Three Views on the Millennium and Beyond* (Grand Rapids: Zondervan, 1999), 15.

[6]F. F. Bruce, "Revelation" in the *International Bible Commentary* (Nashville: Abingdon, 1962), 1594.

[7]Tertullian, in his *Against Marcion* 3.24, noted, "For we do profess that even on earth a kingdom is promised us: but this is before we come to heaven, and in a different polity . . . we shall be changed in a moment into angelic substance . . . and be translated into that heavenly kingdom" (Oxford: Clarendon Press, 1972), 1:247-9.

[8]In a footnoted reference in Michael Green's *Evangelism in the Early Church*, the author stated, "Belief in an earthly Millennium seems to have been nothing short of Christian 'orthodoxy' from Justin to Irenaeus, though both are aware of some Christians who spiritualize it." See Justin's *Dialogue with Trypho*, 80f; Irenaeus's *Against Heresies*, 5.35 (Grand Rapids: Eerdmans, 2003), 415. Also, in Steve Gregg's *Revelation: Four Views*, Robert Clouse notes that the extant writings of the early church writers "bear witness" to their "premillennial convictions" (Nashville: Thomas Nelson, 1997), 29.

[9]The Alexandrian approach of allegorizing Scripture was noted by the following individuals: Eusebius of Caeserea (260-340, Bloesch), Clement of Alexandria (150-215, Swete), Methodius (ca. 311, Swete), Tyconius (ca. 390, Swete).

[10]Philip Schaff, *History of the Christian Church*, 5th edition (Grand Rapids: Eerdmans, 1919), 2:591, cf. 122. Origen anticipated that "every form of worship will be destroyed except the religion of Christ which alone will prevail. And indeed it will one day triumph, as its principles take possession of the minds of men more and more every day" (Origin, *Against Celsus*, 8:68). Origen would posthumously be condemned at the Fifth Ecumenical Council in Constantinople (553) for his denial of the physical nature of the resurrection, his teachings on the preexistence of the soul, and universal salvation.

[11]Gentry argues that Augustine and Athanasius held to a "nascent [budding, hopeful] postmillennialism." He cites both Millard J. Erickson and David Chilton in support of this (*Three Views on the Millennium and Beyond*, 16). In Augustine's commentary on Mark 13:26, he asks, "Will not the Lord come again in later times, when all the peoples of the earth shall lament? He came first in preaching, and filled the whole wide world. Let us not resist his first coming, that we may not tremble at his second" ("On the Psalms" 96.14, in *Mark*, Ancient Christian Commentary on Scripture [Downers Grove, Ill.: InterVarsity Press, 1998], 188).

[12]Bruce, *Revelation*, 1594.

[13]As premillennialist Craig Blaising notes, "Many believed that the new Christian imperial order was the fulfillment of the Millennium. And this order functioned as a type of eternal spiritual reality" (*Three Views*, 172). Blaising also cites D. M. Nicol, "Byzantine Political Thought," in *The Cambridge History of Medieval Political Thought, c. 350-c. 1450* (Cambridge: Cambridge University Press, 1988), 52-53.

[14]Augustine, *City of God*, 20.

[15]John Walvoord, *The Revelation of Jesus Christ* (Chicago: Moody, 1966), 18.

[16]Swete, *Revelation*, ccxiv.

[17]Donald G. Bloesch, *Essentials of Evangelical Theology: Volume 2* (San Francisco: Harper and Row, 1979), 193. In Calvin's rebuke of premillennialism, he spoke of "the error of the chiliasts" and said that "their fiction is too childish either to need or to be worth a refutation. And the Apocalypse, from which they undoubtedly drew a pretext for their error, does not support them" (*Institutes of the Christian Religion*, Volume 21 in the Library of Christian Classics, editor John T. McNeill [Philadelphia: Westminster, 1960], 995).

[18]See Vic Reasoner's *Introduction to Wesleyan Eschatology* (Evansville, Ind.: Fundamental Wesleyan Publishers, 1999) for a discussion of this. Reasoner argues that, although Wesley never utilized these words, his sermons, doctrines, and his brother's songs indicate that he was postmillennial.

[19]In his *Explanatory Notes upon the New Testament*, 2 volumes (Baker Reprint, 1983 from an undated work published by the Wesleyan-Methodist Book Room, London), Wesley comments on Revelation 20:4-7 with these words: "By observing these two distinct thousand years, many difficulties are avoided. There is room enough for the fulfilling of all the prophecies, and those which before seemed to clash are reconciled; particularly those which speak, on the one hand, of a most flourishing state of the church as yet to come; and, on the other, of the fatal security of men in the last days of the world."

[20]See the listing in Tom McIver's *The End of the World: An Annotated Bibliography* (Jefferson, N.C.: McFarlane & Co., 1999), preface.

[21]For more information, see Meredith G. Kline, "Comments on an Old/New Error," *Westminster Theological Journal* 41:1 (1978): 172-89 and *Theonomy: A Reformed Critique*, ed. William S. Barker and W. Robert Godfrey (Grand Rapids: Zondervan, 1990). Kenneth L. Gentry, Jr., *God's Law in the Modern World: The Continuing Relevance of Old Testament Law* (Tyler, Tex.: Institute for Christian Economics, 1997). Greg L. Bahnsen, *By This Standard: The Authority of God's Law Today* (Tyler, Tex.: Institute for Christian Economics, 1997).

[22]William M. Alnor, "News Watch," *Christian Research Journal* (Fall, 1988), 5.

[23]In his chapter, "Some Practical Dangers of Preterism" (*The Endtimes Controversy* [Eugene, Ore.: Harvest House, 2003], 426), Thomas Ice observes, "Once a person accepts the basic tenets of preterism, it is hard to stop and resist the appeal to preterize all Bible prophecy." He traces the route of David Chilton and Walt Hibbard through Christian reconstructionism deeper into the various stages of preterism. Please note that Larry Smith consistently gives this caveat to his partial preterist beliefs: "This viewpoint is probably closest to the position that I currently endorse on Bible prophecy. However, I strive to remain open so that I can always walk in the light as God reveals more understanding about the Scriptures" (Norris, *Reponse*, 9).

[24]Ward Fenley, "Why are People Still Given in Marriage, an Analysis of Luke 20," and J. P. Holding, "Rezza Wreckin': On a Hyper-Preterist Take on resurrection," (www.eschatology.com/whymarriage.html); and (http://www.tektonics.org/esch/rezwreck.html).

[25]Excerpted from "Second Coming of Jesus" Article of Faith: "That Jesus is coming again the second time in person, just as He went away, is clearly set forth by the Lord Jesus Himself, and was preached and taught in the early Christian church by the apostles; hence, the children of God today are earnestly, hopefully, looking forward to the glorious event (Matthew 24; Acts 1:11, 3:19-21; I Corinthians 11:26; Philippians 3:20-21; I Thessalonians 4:14-17; Titus 2:13-14)."

[26]Excerpted from "Holiness" Article of Faith: "We admonish all of our people to refrain from any of these practices in the interest of spiritual progress and the soon coming of the Lord for His church."

[27]Excerpted from "Translation of Saints" Article of Faith: "We believe that the time is drawing near when our Lord shall appear; then the dead in Christ shall arise, and we who are alive and remain shall be caught up with them to meet our Lord in the air (I Thessalonians 4:13-17; I Corinthians 15:51-54; Philippians 3:20-21.)"

[28]Excerpted from "Sacrament or Communion" Article of Faith: "On the night of our Lord's betrayal, He ate the Passover supper with His apostles, after which He instituted the sacrament. 'And he took bread, and gave thanks, and brake it, and gave unto them, saying, This is my body which is given for you: this do in remembrance of me. Likewise also the cup after supper, saying, This cup is the new testament in my blood, which is shed for you' (Luke 22:19-20). Paul instructed the church how to observe it (I Corinthians 11:23-34)." Thus, if the Lord has returned, there is no longer a new covenant in His blood.

[29]Excerpted from "The Baptism of the Holy Ghost" Article of Faith: "It is scriptural to expect all who receive the gift, filling, or baptism of the Holy Spirit to receive the same physical, initial sign of speaking with other tongues. The speaking with other tongues, as recorded in Acts 2:4,10:46, and 19:6, and

the gift of tongues, as explained in I Corinthians, chapters 12 and 14, are the same in essence, but different in use and purpose." Thus, if the Lord has returned, the seeking and use of spiritual gifts have ceased.

[30]Kenneth Gentry, "A Brief Theological Analysis of Hyper-Preterism," (article posted on www.preteristarchive.com).

[31]Curiously enough, an extreme form of dispensationalism is argued by a group called "Rightly Divided." In its founder's recent book, *One Book Rightly Divided: The Key to Understanding the Bible* (McCowen Mills, 2000), Douglas Stauffer poses several questions: "What is the real meaning of Acts 2:38? Is baptism a requirement for salvation?" "Since the New Testament does not begin in Matthew chapter one, where does it begin?" "Which of the seven types of baptism was Paul implementing when he re-baptized the converts of John the Baptist?"

[32]Stevens, 23, 29. The late David Chilton who steadily moved from reconstructionism into consistent preterism stated in the preface to Ed Steven's book, "Stevens presses Christ's declaration in Luke 21:22 to its limit: 'Jesus said that all Old Testament prophecy would be fulfilled by the time Jerusalem was destroyed.' The more I pondered the awesome implications of Jesus' words, the more I realized their truly revolutionary significance for eschatology. Without exception, every event foretold by the Biblical prophets was fulfilled within that generation, as Jesus had said (Matt. 16:27-28; 24:34)."

[33]Max R. King, *The Cross and the Parousia of Christ* (Warren, Ohio: Parkman Road Church of Christ, 1987), 370.

[34]Phillip Johnson's rankings of Christian websites can be found at www.spurgeon.org/~phil/bookmark/bad.htm.

[35]Matthew 3:1-2; 4:17; 10:7; 12:28; Luke 17:20-21; John 3:5; John 18:36; Romans 14:17.

[36]Larry Smith, *The Coming of the Lord, the Last Days, and the End of the World As Taught by Jesus and His Apostles* (El Campo, Tex.: Rightly Dividing the Word, 2000), 48.

[37]Amillennialist Robert B. Strimple, when commenting upon Kenneth Gentry's postmillennial/preterist view, says, "In all the major eschatological texts of the New Testament—no mention is made of a golden age prior to Christ's second coming. None of the Old Testament messianic psalms or prophetic passages is ever applied to such a golden age by the New Testament writers" (*Three Views*, 70).

[38]See references in Romans 14:17, I Corinthians 4:20, and Colossians 1:13.

[39]See references in I Corinthians 6:9, Galatians 5:21, Ephesians 5:5, and II Thessalonians 1:5.

[40]Chapter LXXX.

[41]Papias (ca. 60-130), bishop of Hierapolis, was a student of the apostle John. He wrote extensively, but few of his writings remain. Eusebius, bishop of Caesarea, said of Papias, "Among other things he says that a thousand years will elapse after the resurrection of the dead and there will be a corporal establishment of Christ's kingdom on this earth" ("The Apostolic Fathers" in *The Fathers of the Church,* edited by Ludwig Schopp, et al, translated by Francis X. Glimm, Joseph M. F. Marique, and Gerald G. Walsh [Washington, D.C.: The Catholic University of America Press, 1962] I, 378).

[42]Irenaeus (120-202), student of John and pupil of Polycarp, wrote extensively in *Against Heresies* of the future aspect of the kingdom and other matters. He spoke of a future Antichrist—not of a past Antichrist in Nero as taught by preterism—who would set himself up in a temple for three years and six months. Jesus would then come in glory ushering in the kingdom (Book V, XXX). He described a coming resurrection of the just "which takes place after the coming of the Antichrist" followed by the kingdom (Book V, XXXV). In another writing, *The Treatise on Christ and Antichrist*, Irenaeus described the coming of the Lord followed by the future reigning together with Christ (5). Irenaeus also interpreted the "time, and times, and half a time" to be a literal 1,260 days, and he also called this "the half of the week," presumably linking this with the midpoint of Daniel's seventieth week (60, 61, 64). Such was the chiliastic interpretation of the forthcoming kingdom.

[43]Tertullian in his writings against Marcion said, "But we do confess that a kingdom is promised to us upon the earth, although before heaven, only in another state of existence; inasmuch as it will be after the resurrection for a thousand years in the divinely-built city of Jerusalem, 'let down from heaven,' which the apostle also calls 'our mother from above'; and while declaring that our citizenship is in heaven, he predicates of it that it is really a city in heaven. This both Ezekiel had knowledge of and the Apostle John beheld. And the word of the new prophecy which is a part of our belief attests how it foretold that there would be for a sign a picture of this very city exhibited" (Chapter XXV, "Christ's Millennial and Heavenly Glory in Company with His Saints"). Tertullian went on to say that recent reports had spied just such a city hovering at that time over the city of Jerusalem. The obvious conclusion is that a future kingdom was in view. Other writers in the first three centuries of the Christian era who believed in a future coming kingdom are Hippolytus, Methodius, Lactantius, Barnabas, Clement, Cyprian, and Commodianus (Elwell, Editor, *Evangelical Dictionary of Theology*, Baker, 714).

[44]See the chapter by Joseph A. Seiss for numerous quotes to this effect, "The Millennium in the Early Church," in *The Last Times* (A. Seiss, D. D., [Philadelphia, 1866], 141. See also Henry Alford, *Alford's Greek Testament: An Exegetical and Critical Commentary*, vol IV, part I (Grand Rapids:

Guardian Press, 1875, 1986), 245.

[45]The Greek word *chilia* is used six times in Revelation 20 in relation to the Millennium. (See Revelation 20:2-7.)

[46]The UPCI article of faith regarding the Millennium reads, "We believe that the distress upon the earth is the 'beginning of sorrows' and will become more intense until there 'shall be a time of trouble, such as never was since there was a nation even to that same time' (Matthew 24:3-8; Daniel 12:1), and that period of 'tribulation' will be followed by the dawn of a better day on earth and that for a thousand years there shall be 'peace on earth and good will toward men.' (See Revelation 20:1-5; Isaiah 65:17-25; Matthew 5:5; Daniel 7:27; Micah 4:1-2; Hebrews 2:14; Romans 11:25-27.)"

[47]The *crux interpretum* for the Millennium is Revelation 20. Preterists deny that this refers to a coming kingdom of 1,000 years. Fairly typical is Kenneth Gentry's explanation: "The thousand years in Revelation 20 seem to function as a symbolic value, not strictly limited to a literal thousand year period" (*Three Views*, 51). One of the preterist prophecy sites, www.eschatology.com, purports that Isaiah's kingdom picture of the wolf lying down with the lamb is actually the time in which "Messiah would come to save His people from the animals that devoured them, which were the ravenous wolfen [sic] Pharisees" ("The Wolf and The Lamb").

[48]Edward E. Stevens, "Silence Demands a Rapture," privately printed paper by the International Preterist Association, 2. It can be obtained from the Web site www.preteristarchive.com. A summarized form of Larry Smith's book *Last Days* is also posted on the same Web site. Stevens maintains, "If apostle John was still around (which this Rapture theory denies), surely he would have said something about what he had just seen at A.D. 70. It is impossible (in my thinking) for John to have still been on earth after A.D. 70 and not say something about the Parousia having occurred."

[49]Stevens, 2.

[50]Stevens, 10. "I see the Rapture as occurring in A.D. 66, at the time the Jewish war with Rome was shaping up. This was the time when Christ appeared, raised the rest of the dead out of Hades, raptured the 'living and remaining ones' and began his three and a half year PRESENCE (Parousia) from A.D. 66-70."

[51]Stevens, 12. "I am not the first one to invent this Rapture idea. Four scholars a century ago (J.S. Russell, Milton S. Terry, Richard Weymouth, and Ernest Hampden-Cook) suggested the A.D. 70 Rapture idea, and wrote several pages in defense of it in their books. They suggested that there may have been a Rapture of the true Christians, so that the mere professing (but not true) 'Christians' were left behind to carry on. I am merely reminding all of us about their theory, and asking us to keep it in the back of our mind as the best way (maybe the only way) of resolving the 'documentation problem.'"

[52]R. H. Charles, *Studies in the Apocalypse* (Eugene, Ore.: Wipf and Stock Publishers, 1913, 1996), 8.

[53]Samuel M. Frost, *Misplaced Hope: The Origins of First and Second Century Eschatology* (Colorado Springs: Bimillennial Press, 2002), 210.

[54]See the paper written by David Norris, "Larry Smith, Preterism and the Apostolic Movement" for an excellent discussion on this issue (2003 UGST Symposium), 12-13, 29.

[55]Smith, *Last Days*, 3.

[56]David Chilton, *The Days of Vengeance* (Fort Worth: Dominion Press, 1987), 506-507.

[57]Gentry, *Three Views*, 48.

[58]Corenlis P. Venema, "Evaluating Post-millennialism (II)," *The Outlook*, January 1998), 22.

[59]David Chilton, *Paradise Restored* (Fort Worth: Dominion, 1985), 221-22.

[60]William Barclay, *The Gospel of Matthew Volume II, The New Daily Study Bible* (Louisville: Westminster John Knox Press, rev. 2001), 370.

[61]Don K. Preston, *Into All the World: Then Comes the End!* (no publishing information, 1996).

[62]Smith, *Last Days*, 52-53.

[63]Michael Green, 369.

[64]Smith, *Last Days*, 23.

[65]See comments by Daniel G. Reid, ed., *Dictionary of Christianity in America* (Downers Grove, Ill.: InterVarsity Press, 1990), "Pentecostalism," by R. G. Robins.

[66]Larry Smith, "Response to David Norris" UGST 2003 Symposium, 9

[67]In Smith's writings, he makes various statements about dispensational theology, a common feature of Apostolic Pentecostalism. One must note that few who hold to dispensational theology will agree with Smith's characterization of it. Smith describes the prevalent view amid the UPCI as being a "man-made" teaching (*Last Days*, 3, "70th Week of Daniel" 2002, 4); "false teaching" ("70th Week," 3); "hand me down Jewish theology that has been put in the church to make the Jews God's chosen people instead of the church" (Response to Norris, 7); "a wicked system" (*The Last Days*, 45); "deception" (*The Last Days*, 45-46); part of a "modern day satanic plot" (*The Last Days*, 45); ". . . done by Satan to make the Church believe that there is still seven years remaining of law-keeping" ("70th Week," 22); "annuls the work of the cross" ("70th Week," 22); is "anti-Christian" and is motivated by the spirit of the Antichrist (*The Last Days*, 72-73), is based on the trinity (Response to Norris, 7); a defeatist theory (*The Last Days*, 45); in reference to a Joe McCarthy quote, represents a conspiracy of "unholy Jews" and "freemasons" (*The Last*

Days, condensed online version www.preteristarchive.com, 19); in an audio message, "Take Clarence Larkin's dispensational truths and build a fire with it" ("Identifying the Four Beasts and Two Witnesses," Spirit and Truth Conference 2003).

[68]"Interview: Tony Campolo," *The Door* (September/October 1993), 14.

3

Could Preterism Be Apostolic?

David S. Norris

The twentieth century has been called the century of Pentecostalism because it experienced the modern rebirth of Pentecostal doctrine and practice. A hunger to have both the experience and the doctrine of the apostolic church gave birth to this revival. Oneness Pentecostals, in particular, determined that, if there was a difference between what churches had traditionally taught for hundreds of years and what was taught by the apostles, they would reject church tradition and teach what the apostles taught. For this reason many modern scholars suggest that these Apostolics were even more "Pentecostal" than the Pentecostals up until that time.[1]

To be Apostolic is to conform one's beliefs and practices to those of the apostolic church, regardless if later Christians came to believe and practice something else. Modern Apostolics reject, for example, infant baptism, the trinity, and baptism in the titles, though they ultimately became the normative belief and practice of most Christians, because the apostolic church neither believed nor practiced them. To determine if preterism could be Apostolic is to first determine if preterism was taught by the apostolic church. If it was, we must embrace it; if it was not, we must reject it. In this chapter, it will be shown that the apostolic church did not, in fact, teach preterism.

The reason why preterism cannot be Apostolic, then, is quite simple: Since the apostolic church did not believe and teach preterism, modern Apostolics must not. There simply were no preterists among the apostles or other leaders in the first centuries of the church. Tellingly, the early church continued to look for the coming of the Lord after A.D. 70. Indeed, no one in the first sixteen hundred years of the church ever thought that the coming of the Roman armies in A.D. 70 to destroy Jerusalem was the coming of the Lord. Without exception, all of the church leaders of the earliest centuries believed in the future second coming of Christ, in the future Antichrist, in the future Tribulation, and in the future Millennium—none of which is believed by preterists. Until recently, all modern Apostolics accepted these doctrines, following the example of the apostolic church.

Another significant belief universally embraced by the apostolic church, but rejected by all preterists, is that Jesus is coming soon and that the church should be ready as a bride adorned for her husband.[2] This belief was instrumental in the very founding and formation of the modern Apostolic church. In fact, the first recorded modern interpretations of messages in tongues were that Jesus was coming soon.[3] Again, until recently all modern Apostolics have embraced this view. It must be emphasized that preterists among Apostolics were not commonly known until recent years and that the restoration of the apostolic church is based on an understanding that is directly against anything that preterists teach.

Preterists make several claims about how long preterism has been believed. Some of the claims are flatly false; some are partially true. One claim that is absolutely false is that the apostles believed in preterism. Preterism, however, was actually invented in the 1600s by a Catholic Jesuit named Luis de Alcazar (1554-1613). The claim that is partially true is that a particular aspect of preterism has been believed for hundreds of years, namely, that the Millennium is not a literal future reign of Christ on earth, but rather is symbolic of the present experience of the church under the lordship of Christ—but this is not a preterist doctrine; it is a Catholic doctrine. Let us briefly consider how the Roman Catholic Church came to believe this.

In the first centuries of the church, the testimony was unanimous: The church believed in the premillennial coming of Jesus Christ.[4] There was an imminent expectation of Jesus Christ's return. After the destruction of Jerusalem, but before the close of the first century, Clement wrote, "Let us then wait for the kingdom of God from hour to hour in love and righteousness, seeing that we know not the day of the appearing of God."[5] At the beginning of the second century, Ignatius wrote, "These are the last times."[6] In the middle of the second century, Justin Martyr wrote, "But I and whoever are on all points right-minded Christians know that there will be a resurrection of the dead and a thousand years in Jerusalem, which will then be built, adorned, and enlarged as the prophets Ezekiel and Isaiah and the others declare . . . and John, one of the Apostles."[7] Such a view is also found in Papias,[8] Barnabas,[9] Irenaeus,[10] and Tertullian.[11]

During the third and fourth centuries, some began to challenge the premillennial expectation of the coming of Jesus, particularly the Alexandrian theologians, who were known for their allegorical interpretation of Scripture.[12] With the marriage of the Catholic church with Rome, the millennial reign of Christ was reinterpreted as the church itself, largely for political reasons.[13] The Catholic father of theology, Augustine, in his interpretation, equated the Catholic church with the kingdom of God. Since the Catholic church equaled the kingdom of God, they felt they had a right to interpret Scripture allegorically, suggesting that it had a particular meaning because they said that it did. When preterists say that they interpret Scripture the same way it has been interpreted for hundreds of years, they are correct: They agree with the Catholic interpretation.

It would be wrong, though, to say that the Catholic church is preterist. While they did allegorize Revelation, they never believed it referred to A.D. 70 and the coming of the Roman armies. It was not until the Reformation that such a view was even considered. When Protestant theologians equated the Beast of Revelation with the Catholic church, the Catholic Jesuit Luis de Alcazar developed preterism to rebut their charges.

Few adopted Alcazar's views, and soon various groups developed other forms of preterism. Some Protestants who had a low view of the biblical text held to a preterist view for academic reasons. Some among Reformed groups also began to look at preterism as an eschatological option. Other views of prophecy were also held.

The real question that must be asked, though, is how

Pentecostals came to view prophecy the way they did. What were the steps that allowed them to reclaim an apostolic understanding of prophecy? At the beginning of the Reformation, most of the emphasis was on reclaiming the Bible and in disallowing the Catholic church's claim that they alone could grant salvation. One is hard pressed to find many people who were seriously looking at the Roman Catholic Church's view of prophecy. Soon after the Reformation began, however, there were some among the Moravians, Anabaptists, and Huguenots who did begin to teach the premillennial return of Jesus Christ. Some in these groups also began receiving the Holy Spirit and speaking in tongues.[14]

Revivals in England and America in the 1800s were accompanied by sporadic speaking in tongues as well as a prophetic expectation of the soon return of Christ.[15] By the middle of the nineteenth century, many believing Christians began focusing on the biblical understanding of the soon return of Christ, a future Tribulation, and a future millennial reign of Christ.[16] There was a specific emphasis on these beliefs in those movements that were the forerunners of the Apostolic revival. Scholars tell us that one of the most important elements in twentieth-century Pentecostalism was the anticipation of the soon return of the Lord.[17]

Preterists sometimes claim that preterism is a new revelation that has been given to Apostolics. Based on reasons already given, this should be categorically denied: First, the apostles did not believe in preterism; second, the early church after the apostles did not believe in preterism; third, no one believed in preterism until the seventeenth century when the Catholic church first offered it as an interpretation. The preterist view of Revelation that equates the future kingdom of God with the present church began with the Catholic church. It would seem, then, that the preterists' new revelation actually implies that the Catholics were correct all along.

There is another part of the argument that ought to be suspicious to Apostolics as well. Preterists often claim that Satan has deceived most modern Apostolics. The theory is that Satan was "loosed" in the 1800s to deceive the nations and that this is how he has been effective in deceiving Apostolics.[18] Since this is such an incredible claim, it is important to address this in some detail.

First, the Bible does not indicate that Satan was bound when Jesus died and rose again. There are more than a few problems with such a view. First of all, it contradicts Scripture. If Satan had been bound, how could Peter tell Ananias that Satan was working in him (Acts 5:3)? Why would Paul say that Satan could affect families in the church (I Corinthians 7:5) and that Satan would blind people to be lost (II Corinthians 4:3-4) and that he was even transformed into an angel of light (II Corinthians 11:14)? As John F. Walvoord offers, "Satan is seen to tempt, to deceive, to blind, to buffet, to hinder, to work signs and lying wonders, to influence unbelievers, to seek to devour individuals. Is this a picture of Satan bound? Is this in harmony with the amillennial interpretation of Revelation 20:1-3? The obvious answer is that Satan is not bound."[19]

The problem with the theory that Satan has been bound is not simply a biblical one but a historical one as well. If Satan has been bound, how could the church have fallen away from the original apostolic teaching, and how could there have been wars, atrocities, and egregious sin for the last two thousand years? Isaiah's prophecies that a wolf will lie down with a lamb (Isaiah 11:6) and that the nations will beat their swords into plowshares (Isaiah 2:4) obviously have not been fulfilled. Even if an interpreter were to suggest that these prophecies from Isaiah about the future Millennium were in some way metaphorical, the suggestion that Satan has been kept from working during the last two thousand years is clearly indefensible.

The claim that Satan was loosed in the 1800s with the specific intent to deceive Apostolics regarding prophecy is suspicious for another important reason. If Satan had been so empowered to deceive Apostolics, why was he unable to keep them from receiving the Holy Spirit in the first place—or at least to keep them from understanding its meaning and significance? Why did he not prevent them from understanding the oneness of the Godhead? If he was going to attack Apostolics in their doctrine, why did he allow them to baptize once again in Jesus' name? It is amazing to think that Satan was unable to deceive Apostolics in any of these foundational truths, but then was somehow able to deceive them regarding prophecy.

Were twentieth-century Apostolic pioneers such as G. T. Haywood, Andrew Urshan, and Frank Ewart in fact deceived by Satan? Did the entire first generation of modern Apostolics swallow a lie? Were the people who formed the United Pentecostal Church International tricked by Satan? Is this current generation of Apostolics bound by Satan's continued deception? There are preterist teachers who are suggesting this, but the truth is that they are proposing a doctrine that is rooted in Roman Catholicism instead of the ancient apostolic church and that has never been accepted by modern Apostolics.

In short, since preterism contradicts the teaching of the ancient apostolic church and disregards the teaching of the modern Apostolic church, it follows, then, that preterism could not be Apostolic. Preterism is guilty on both counts.

David S. Norris received an M.A. in theological studies from Eastern Baptist Theological Seminary and a Ph.D. in religion from Temple University in Philadelphia. He is an ordained minister of the UPCI and is professor of biblical theology at Urshan Graduate School of Theology. He has written several books, scholarly papers, and articles.

Notes

[1]Douglas Jacobsen, *Thinking in the Spirit: Theologies of the Early Pentecostal Movement* (Bloomington and Indianapolis: University of Indiana, 2003), 259.

[2]George Taylor, *The Spirit and the Bride: A Scriptural Presentation of the Operations, Manifestations, Gifts and Fruit of the Holy Spirit in Relation to his Bride with Special Reference to the Latter Day Revival* (Dunn, N.C.: the author, 1907); see also D. William Faupel, *The Everlasting Gospel: The Significance of Eschatology in the Development of Pentecostal Thought* (Sheffield: Sheffield Academic Press, 1996), 26.

[3]Vincent Synan, *The Century of the Holy Spirit*, notes that, even in the nineteenth century, people received the Holy Ghost, sometimes manifesting spiritual gifts without understanding all that was going on theologically. For instance, the Presbyterian minister Edward Irving quested for a return to biblical Pentecost. He sought it, preached it, and waited to see the fruit of his search. When he heard that a group was speaking in tongues, he went to investigate. In one meeting, Irving found two brothers, George and James MacDonald, speaking in tongues. "On April 20, 1830, in the first recorded tongues message and interpretation in modern times, James gave an utterance in tongues and George interpreted it. 'Behold He cometh—Jesus cometh—a weeping Jesus!'"

[4]See Hans Bietenhard, "The Millennial Hope of the Early Church," *Scottish Journal of Theology* 6 (1953):12-30. The references for the church fathers below largely draw from Bietenhard.

[5]*Second Letter to the Corinthians*, chap. 12.

[6]*The Letter to the Ephesians*, 11.1; Frend, 128.

[7]*Dialogue with Trypho*, 80, in *The Ante-Nicene Fathers*, ed. Alexander Roberts and James Donaldson, rev. A. C. Coxe (1884; reprint, Grand Rapids: Eerdmans, 1967), 1:239.

[8]Irenaeus gives the view of Papias as found in *Against Heresies*, 5.33.3-4, *Ante-Nicene Fathers*, I, 562-63.

[9]The *Epistle of Barnabas*, 15.3-9, in the *Ante-Nicene Fathers*, trans. Kirsopp Lake, Loeb Classical Library (Cambridge: Harvard University Press, 1912), I:395-97.

[10]Irenaeus, *Against Heresies*, 5.28-36, in the *Ante-Nicene Fathers*, I:556-67.

[11]Tertullian, in *Against Marcion* 3.24, in *Tertullian*, trans. Ernest Evans, (Oxford: Clarendon, 1972), 1:247, and *On the Resurrection of the Flesh*, 19, 25, in *The Ante-Nicene Fathers*, 3:558-59, 563.

[12]Walter C. Kaiser, "Response 3: An Evangelical Response," *Dispensationalism, Israel and the Church: The Search for Definition*, ed. Craig A. Blaising and Darell L. Bock (Grand Rapids: Zondervan, 1992), 362-63.

[13]"The major break with this theology came in the fourth century A.D. during the reign of Emperor Constantine in the work *Ecclesiastical History* by Eusebius Pamphili. Eusebius did not believe that there was a distinct future for the Jews; rather, the church was God's new Israel. Any proposal about a millennium was thought by Eusebius to be heretical." Walter C. Kaiser, "Response 3: An Evangelical Response." *Dispensationalism, Israel and the Church: The Search for Definition*, ed. Craig A. Blaising and Darell L. Bock (Grand Rapids: Zondervan, 1992), 361-62.

[14]Morton T. Kelsey, *Tongue Speaking* (Garden City, N.Y.: Doubleday & Company Inc., 1964), 52.

[15]George M. Marsden, *Fundamentalism and American Culture* (New York: Oxford University Press, 1980), 51.

[16]Ibid.

[17]In his study, Dayton first shows the commonality of all these themes in the literature of the early twentieth century. Then, he demonstrates that these were actually themes carried over from late nineteenth century Perfectionism. The added element, of course, was speaking in other tongues. See Donald Dayton, *The Theological Roots of Pentecostalism* (Metuchan, N.J.: The Scarecrow Press, 1987), 21-23.

[18]A prominent Pentecostal preterist has said, "What I believe is this: I believe Satan was loosed approximately two hundred years ago. Since that time he has gained power, power, power. 1830 and the restoration period that we had . . . there was three major doctrines that came that were not restorations, they were taking us backwards. One was Jehovah[sic] Witness doctrine . . . another was Mormonism, and the other was Dispensational theology, they all three were created by Masonry." Larry T. Smith, *Controversies Against the Time Text of the Book of Revelation*, Spirit & Truth Conference, 2002, (www.rightlydividingtheword.com/st2002.htm. Web site accessed on 07-12-2005.)

[19]John F. Walvoord and Roy B. Zuck, *The Bible Knowledge Commentary*, 93.

4

Preterism, the Allegorical Method, and the Old Testament

David S. Norris

The Bible is meant to be understood. While it is true that prophetic books are sometimes more difficult to understand than other parts of the Bible and are often subject to conflicting interpretations, we should neither ignore prophecy nor simply allow any fanciful reading to go unchallenged. Prophecy can be understood; but we must use sound principles of interpretation, namely the grammatical-historical method, when approaching prophetic passages of the Bible. Preterists sometimes use the Scripture extensively to support their case. The problem, however, is in their method of interpreting the Scripture. Merely citing Scripture does not establish correct doctrine; the right interpretation of Scripture does. In the next two chapters we will demonstrate the tendency among preterists to interpret prophetic passages of Scripture allegorically.

This is a serious problem. Allegorical interpretation ignores the specific context of Scripture and asserts a meaning for a text that is not based on any solid criterion from the context. In the end, the interpreter himself is the final authority for what a text means. A verse will be said to have a particular meaning simply because the interpreter *says it has that meaning*. To make his case, the interpreter sometimes emphasizes one aspect of a verse and ignores the rest; other times, he gives a machine gun burst of texts that supposedly support a doctrine, but that, when examined closely, do not support the stated position at all. In the end, followers of allegorical interpreters trust the interpreter for reasons not confined to the text: They may deem the interpreter to be more spiritual than others, or the interpreter himself may claim to have a "new revelation" or to have "discovered heresy" and is attempting to root it out. The task of this chapter is to reveal the kind of allegorical method preterists employ and to explain principles that will allow for a normative reading of prophetic Scripture.

Consider, for example, how a preterist interpretation turns Matthew 24 on its head in an effort to demonstrate that the text does not mean that Jesus will come again in the future, but rather that He came in A.D. 70. In Matthew 24:30, Jesus states that "they shall see the Son of man coming in the clouds of heaven with power and great glory." In verse 31, He continues, "And he shall send his angels with a great sound of a trumpet, and they shall gather together his elect from the four winds, from one end of heaven to the other." In verse 34, He goes on to say, "This generation shall not pass, till all these things be fulfilled." Now let us consider how preterists interpret this passage allegorically.[1] Preterists say that "this generation" must be the generation that Jesus lived in,[2] and therefore the text cannot mean that Jesus will *really* come again. The clouds are not real clouds, but are symbolic of the Roman armies attacking Jerusalem. The trumpet is not really a trumpet, but the preaching of the gospel. The angels are not really angels, but are preachers. The gathering of the elect is not the literal second coming of Jesus, and instead of referring to a single event, this "gathering of the elect" has been going on for thousands of years.

How do preterists come to such a mystical interpretation that is so distant from a normal, literal reading of this passage? There is only one answer: A preterist must believe that someone has the authority to interpret this passage in a way that goes beyond the normal, literal reading of the text. This teacher must be given the right to determine meaning. If a preterist accepts the authority of such a teacher, it hardly matters what the teacher says when interpreting the text; it will be the correct interpretation—despite the scriptural context, the historical setting, or the overall message of the biblical text. The interpretive authority rests upon the teacher and not on the text.

Let us consider some important verses from both the Old and New Testaments that preterists marshal to support their position. In the remainder of this chapter, we will focus on texts from the Old Testament and will follow these texts in chronological order. We begin with Leviticus 26 where Moses warns the Jewish people that judgment awaits them if they disobey the Word of God. Preterists insist that Leviticus 26 is about the final judgment against the Jews—a final judgment that they say is described in the Book of Revelation. There are several reasons why such an interpretation cannot stand. First, although Leviticus 26 does promise judgment on the nation of Israel if they disobey, it is clearly not the final judgment, for the Lord promises the restoration of the Jewish people in this very chapter (Leviticus 26:44-45). Although we will not deal with it in detail in this chapter, there is another crucial reason why Leviticus cannot confirm that Revelation is a prophecy of the Jew's final judgment at the destruction of Jerusalem in A.D. 70: Revelation was not written until ca. 95. (For more information on this issue, see the chapter on "Dating the Book of Revelation" later in this book.)

What is the proof, then, that Leviticus 26 points to the Book of Revelation? Preterists teach that there are four sevenfold judgments in Leviticus 26 that mirror four sevenfold judgments in Revelation. And since the judgment in Leviticus 26 describes the judgment on Israel, it must follow that the judgment in Revelation must also describe the destruction of Israel, as it was fulfilled by the Romans in A.D. 70.[3]

The basic problem is that preterists misread both Leviticus and Revelation. There is no promise of four sevenfold judgments in Leviticus. What is foretold, however, is a single sevenfold judgment if Israel disobeys.[4] Despite the clear reading of various translations and commentaries that describe this as a thematic repetition of one sevenfold-judgment, preterists read into the text what they want to find.[5] Both the Hebrew original and the English translation are clear: A prophecy of judgment is repeated successively in poetic parallelism, but it is not meant to introduce new sets of judgments. There are not four sevenfold judgments in Leviticus, just Hebrew poetic parallelism. Further, there are not four sevenfold judgments in Revelation either.[6] Revelation teaches three sevenfold judgments. In short, only an allegorical interpretation will allow a preterist to identify parallelism between Leviticus 26 and Revelation.

Another preterist argument is derived by combining Deuteronomy 28 and Deuteronomy 32 and attempting to link these chapters with Revelation 15 and 16. One preterist teaches that the "Song of Moses" in Deuteronomy 32 is somehow connected to the curses of Deuteronomy 28 and further that both these are connected with Revelation 15 and 16. He says Revelation 15 and 16 describe the destruction of Jerusalem, "a judgment that God said He would bring against those who forsook His covenant."[7] Consider the logic of the argument.

> This judgment [destruction of Jerusalem] is the fulfillment of the **curse of the Law** that is **recorded in Deuteronomy 28:15-68** [*CLAIM 1*] and also in the **Song of Moses** [*CLAIM 2*], which is mentioned in Revelation 15:3, and is **recorded in Deuteronomy 32:1-44.** Moses' song speaks of the judgments that God said He would bring against Israel if they disobeyed the Law. These judgments were prophesied to take place during one particular generation [*CLAIM 3*] that we now know to be the final Jewish generation [*CLAIM 4*] that rejected the New Covenant message and tried to keep the Law for salvation [bold and underlining in original].[8]

He assumes he has proved his point—when in fact he has merely strung together several unfounded assertions—and goes on to say:

> The Song of Moses was also heard being sung in the book of Revelation along with the Song of the Lamb. The Lamb's song proclaims the redemption that comes through Jesus' New Covenant message. These two songs being sung together are just one more proof that the book of Revelation does show that the destruction of Jerusalem was a judgment that God said He would bring against those who forsook His Covenant.[9]

The problem with this interpretation is that, instead of seeking to understand the original context of the Deuteronomy passage, this author imposes his own ideas upon the text. The same thing could be said for his assertion on how this is linked with "the final generation" or with the Book of Revelation. Deuteronomy 28 says nothing about the final generation—like Leviticus, these sets of chapters not only prophesy judgment on Israel but also restoration. In Deuteronomy 30, after predicting judgment, the Lord offers hope and promises a way back (Deuteronomy 30:1-14)—hardly a prediction of God's final rejection of the Jewish people. Nor is Deuteronomy 32 (the so-called Song of Moses) about final judgment. This is an imposition on the text.

Further, there is no reason to link Deuteronomy 32 to the Song of Moses in Revelation 15. More likely, the Song of Moses in Revelation 15 is derived from the Song of Redemption in Exodus 15. There is no indication that the Song of Moses in Revelation is connected to judgment at all. A simple reading of Revelation 15 demonstrates that the text is not at all about the Jews being cursed, but about the Jews being saved—Jews who have found Jesus.

The people singing in Revelation 15:3 are in fact Jewish saints who will be martyred by the Beast. The song they sing has nothing to do with the judgment of God on them. It celebrates their Jewishness as well as their faith in Christ. Revelation 15:3 reads, "And they sing the song of Moses the servant of God, and the song of the Lamb, saying, Great and marvellous are thy works, Lord God Almighty; just and true are thy ways, thou King of saints." Thus, preterists can marshal neither Leviticus nor Deuteronomy to support their reading of Revelation. They must resort to interpreting Deuteronomy allegorically in order to read it into Revelation. This attempt to link unrelated verses from the Old Testament with the alleged destruction of Jerusalem in Revelation 15 and 16 is tortured at best.

Preterists gather other Old Testament texts together as well to support their interpretive scheme. For instance, they list a whole set of alleged parallels to demonstrate that the Book of Ezekiel parallels the Book of Revelation. They do this to support their argument that Revelation was written before A.D. 70 and to suggest that the cosmic judgment in Revelation is about nothing more or less than the destruction of Jerusalem in A.D. 70.[10] There is only one way a preterist could come to this interpretation: the allegorical method. Further, while Ezekiel has much to say about the destruction of Jerusalem, the focal point of the book is the prophesied destruction of Jerusalem that happened in 586 B.C. not A.D. 70!

Preterists insist Ezekiel is the key to understanding Revelation because there are so many parallel phrases and metaphors in Ezekiel and Revelation. One Pentecostal preterist writer alleges, "Most people, however, put these judgments in the wrong time period because they fail to realize that the books of Revelation and Ezekiel are basically the same books written with the same biblical imagery, and that they are, in most cases, prophesying of the same time period, and dealing with the same events."[11]

While there are admittedly many allusions to Ezekiel in the Book of Revelation, Revelation contains the largest number of allusions, not merely from Ezekiel, but from the broad array of metaphors found in all the Old Testament prophets. Still, preterists attempt to buoy their case by three faulty assumptions: (1) The prophecies of Jerusalem's destruction in Ezekiel are really about A.D. 70 and not 586 B.C. (2) The cosmic judgments in Revelation are really not cosmic judgments at all, but are merely describing the Romans attacking Jerusalem in A.D. 70 (also assumed to be prefigured in Ezekiel). (3) Ezekiel's chronology of the destruction of Jerusalem roughly matches the chronology of these same judgments found in Revelation. The linchpin of this set of assumptions seems to be that the chapters in Ezekiel have the same chronological sequence as the chapters in Revelation. However, any such implication dissipates under scrutiny. This same preterist makes a sequential comparison of chapters in Ezekiel and Revelation, implying that such close symmetry is meant to demonstrate that these books parallel very closely in theme and content.[12] But the symmetry is more constructed than real. While Revelation 8 apparently parallels Ezekiel 10, and Revelation 10:1-7 apparently parallels Ezekiel 12, the exceptions to such a common chronological order quickly mount up. This preterist says that Revelation 10:8, instead of paralleling

Ezekiel 13 or 14, actually parallels Ezekiel 2. He then says that Revelation 11:1-2 parallels Ezekiel 40-43 and that Revelation 11:8 parallels Ezekiel 16. Rather than symmetry, the order in Ezekiel plays hopscotch. Further comparisons bring further confusion. In the end, the only thing that can be clearly said is that metaphors in Ezekiel are applied in Revelation; this is hardly an argument for preterism.

One Old Testament theme that preterists rely on in establishing their position is the way certain symbols are allegedly used to consistently prophesy specific types of judgments. For instance, one important theme for preterists is the way clouds are presented in Scripture. One preterist claims that "'coming in the clouds' is Old Testament imagery that usually refers to God's coming in judgment on a nation."[13] Several verses are offered in succession where clouds apparently represent armies.[14] This claim about clouds is unusual, and it plays strongly in preterist interpretation. The notion is largely to deconstruct the literal understanding of Scripture that Jesus is literally returning in clouds and to replace this with the notion that this is a kind of metaphor for the judgment of the Roman armies upon Jerusalem.

But it is just this kind of interpretation that amounts to something of a shell game. Several texts are put forth as proof, as if they are the lion's share of testimony as to how clouds are used in the biblical text. The weight of the biblical text, however, is against any such claim. A simple check of the 162 references to "cloud" and its cognates in the Bible demonstrates that most of the references to clouds are, in fact, literal; some references actually relate to the glory of the Lord. Even the best evidence of clouds being associated with armies is uneven. In Isaiah 19:1, there is one cloud, and it is a means of transport, not an army. In Jeremiah 4, it is the quickness of how clouds develop that is used metaphorically. In Ezekiel 30:3, a cloudy day is used to portend doom. And in Nahum 1, though the text says of God that clouds "are the dust of his feet," this text does not do the kind of work that preterists suggest that it does—nor do the other verses.

Despite the fact that preterists have said otherwise, there is a consistent theme of hope for the church connected to Christ's literal return in the clouds. In Acts 1, two angels stand by the believers who had watched from the Mount of Olives as Jesus "was taken up; and a cloud received him out of their sight." The angels state simply, "Ye men of Galilee, why stand ye gazing up into heaven? this same Jesus, which is taken up from you into heaven, shall so come in like manner as ye have seen him go into heaven." We cannot take the Book of Acts any other way than literally. Jesus literally ascended in clouds. The "two men in white apparel" promised that Jesus would return in the same literal way that He was taken up. We can depend upon it. Jesus will literally return in the same way that He ascended—in clouds. A number of texts that we will refer to in the next chapter corroborate this promise. But we must not miss one important point: If the ascension of Jesus was literal—and it was—then we can count on the return of Jesus to be literal as well.

We have argued in this chapter that preterism is only possible through the allegorical interpretation of prophetic texts. As we explored important Old Testament themes and passages of Scripture utilized by preterists to make their claims, we showed that only a mystical interpretation would allow texts in Leviticus and Deuteronomy to be linked with Revelation in the way that preterists link them. Further, we showed that the claims about Ezekiel paralleling Revelation were overstated. Finally, we showed how a preterist allegorizing of "clouds" so that Jesus' coming necessarily refers to Roman armies destroying Jerusalem ignored the specific context of both Old and New Testament texts. In the next chapter, we will seek to demonstrate how this allegorical method undermines a clear reading of prophecy in the New Testament.

Notes

[1]Preterists variously interpret this verse. Full preterists discount all future prophecy and say that Jesus really did come and that all end-time events predicted in the New Testament have taken place. Some even suggest that Jesus literally came in A.D. 70, despite any historical record to that effect. The partial preterist position represented by the interpretation I am arguing against is that of Larry T. Smith, based upon an interview I had with him on March 1, 2003, in El Campo, Texas.

[2]Preterists do not address how this is contrary to the interpretation of the earliest church. Universally, the earliest church writers, all writing after A.D. 70, looked forward to the soon return of Christ, the future Tribulation, and the millennial age. Absent is any mention at all of the destruction of Jerusalem as any kind of coming of Christ.

[3]See Larry T. Smith, *The Coming of the Lord, The Last Days, and The End of the World* (El Campo, Tex.: Rightly Dividing the Word, 2000), 21-22.

[4]See Leviticus 26:18, 21, 24, 28. Verse 18 reads, "And if ye will not yet for all this hearken unto me, then I will punish you seven times more [Hebrew *yasaph*] for your sins." (Some translators render this "seven times over.") Verse 21 reads, "And if ye walk contrary unto me, and will not hearken unto me; I will bring seven times more plagues [continue to plague you sevenfold—these are not additional plagues] upon you according to your sins." Verse 24

reads, "Then will I also walk contrary unto you, and will punish you yet [Hebrew *gam*] seven times for your sins." (Most translators do not represent the Hebrew *gam*, and these are not additional plagues). Verse 28 reads, "Then I also will walk contrary to you in fury; and I, even I, will chastise you seven times for your sins." (There is no suggestion, either in Hebrew or in English, that these are additional plagues.)

[5]Larry Smith writes on p. 20 of his *The Coming of the Lord*, "Its occurrence is based on Leviticus 26, which says that God will bring FOUR SEVEN-FOLD JUDGMENTS upon those who break His covenant [bold, underline, and caps are all original with Smith]. He said that except they repent, He would judge them until they were destroyed. This judgment is exactly the same judgment that you find recorded in Revelation. So the foundation of the book of Revelation is found in Leviticus 26."

[6]Revelation clearly teaches three sevenfold judgments: Seals, Revelation 6-8:1; trumpets, Revelation 8-10; vials, Revelation 15-16. Whereas the seals, trumpets, and vials are identified as judgments, or plagues, nothing of the sort is said about the "seven thunders." They appear in the context of the seventh trumpet, just as other thunders occur in the context of other events in Revelation. (See Revelation 4:5; 8:5; 16:18.)

[7]Smith, *The Coming of the Lord*, 22.

[8]Ibid., 17.

[9]Ibid.

[10]Ibid., 31-32, claiming to follow David Chilton's *The Days of Vengeance.*

[11]Ibid., 31.

[12]Ibid., 32.

[13]Smith, *The Coming of the Lord*, 14. Smith appears to be following Kenneth Gentry on this. For an example of Gentry's argumentation, see his *He Shall Have Dominion: A Postmillennial Eschatology* (Tyler, Tex.: Institute for Christian Economics, 1992), 216.

[14]Isaiah 19:1; Jeremiah 4:13-14; Ezekiel 30:3; Nahum 1:2-6.

5

Allegorical Interpretation, Time Texts, and the New Testament

David S. Norris

A preterist reading of the New Testament does not merely vary from a normative Apostolic understanding in some minor fashion. Rather, such a reading reinterprets the theme and tenor of the entire New Testament. Thus, instead of looking forward with hope to Jesus returning, preterists teach that the coming of Jesus was really a past judgment upon the Jewish people. Instead of the old covenant clearly ending at Calvary and the new covenant beginning on the Day of Pentecost, preterists artificially extend a "Jewish age" until A.D. 70 and make the focus of the New Testament church to be on the imminent judgment upon the Jewish people. Instead of the literal coming of Christ, what the church got was Roman armies destroying Jerusalem. Accepting a preterist reading turns the scholarly understanding of the New Testament on its head and necessarily redefines what it means to be Apostolic.

In this chapter, we will work to reveal the allegorical assumptions behind a preterist interpretation of prophetic texts in the New Testament. Ironically, preterists claim to be defending a consistent and literal understanding of Scripture. They argue that specific verses must be taken seriously that prophesy the coming of the Lord within a generation of Jesus. It is these "time texts" that are the focus of this chapter. We will demonstrate that there are biblical reasons why no one in the early centuries of church history believed in preterism.[1] Indeed, we will show that strictures placed on identifying specific time texts in the New Testament are inconsistent and selective.

Before beginning to address specific New Testament texts, let us review why prophets often prophesied in the present tense or portrayed an event as occurring soon, even though such prophecies might not be fulfilled for hundreds, or in some cases, thousands of years. Prophecy did not originate with the prophet, of course. The prophets were merely the mouthpiece of God, who unfolds His eternal plan in this way. Romans 4:17 says God "calleth those things which be not as though they were." Because of this, it is not surprising to read that the church was ordained before the foundation of the world or that prophetic foreshadowing of Christ goes all the way back to the Book of Genesis. Revelation 13:8 says that Jesus was "the Lamb slain from the foundation of the world." Though Jesus was not literally slain before Calvary, in the mind of God, the event was certain. It is no accident that over seven hundred years before Calvary, Isaiah wrote of Christ in Isaiah 53:5: "But he was wounded for our transgressions, he was bruised for our iniquities: the chastisement of our peace was upon him; and with his stripes we are healed." Just as the initial coming of Christ was certain and could be spoken of in terms of "now," so too, the return of Christ was the universal promise to the church and was spoken of with continued anticipation as an event that should be eagerly anticipated with hope.

Now we may address the issue at hand. Preterists suggest that prophecies that promise the soon return of the Lord must be fulfilled within a specific time period, a time period that they designate. Of course, Jesus did not come. And here is the rub. While there are some preterists who insist that Jesus did come (despite there being no record of this), most preterists are content to allegorize His coming in the Roman armies attacking Jerusalem. There are at least some verses of Scripture that on the face of it could be construed to support this. That said, a preterist system can only work if one reads selectively and ignores texts that present problems.

Let us consider a preterist use of I Corinthians as an example of how their allegorical method works. Preterists argue that I Corinthians necessarily teaches the soon coming of the Lord (a coming of the Lord prior to A.D. 70). For preterists, references in I Corinthians that say that the "time is short" or that the "ends of the world" are come upon the Corinthian church must necessarily indicate that Paul was teaching that the coming of the Lord was fulfilled in the destruction of Jerusalem.[2] While we would interpret these texts in I Corinthians differently than preterists,[3] what is of interest now is the selective use of evidence in this allegorical system. A preterist largely ignores verses in I Corinthians that contradict his position. For instance, consider the clear statements of Paul to the Corinthians in chapter 1. In I Corinthians 1:7,

Paul prays for the Corinthians that they "come behind in no gift; waiting for the coming of our Lord Jesus Christ." Thus, the gifts of the Spirit were anticipated until the coming of the Lord (which preterists say was in A.D. 70). If a consistent preterist reading is allowed, the gifts of the Spirit must necessarily have ceased after the destruction of Jerusalem. But, of course, this is not the case.[4]

The Greek in I Corinthians 1:7 is clear. The church is to earnestly wait and hope for the coming of the Lord.[5] This is consistent with New Testament teaching as a whole. Indeed, Paul wrote to Titus that they were "looking[6] for that blessed hope, and the glorious appearing of the great God and our Saviour Jesus Christ" (Titus 2:13). Paul is definitely not speaking of the coming of Roman armies as that blessed event, nor is he speaking of some generic kind of hope for a final resurrection. Rather, he is speaking of the real and anticipated hope of the church: the literal appearing of Christ at His return.

There are other texts in I Corinthians that are problematic for preterists as well. Paul writes in I Corinthians 11:26, "For as often as ye eat this bread, and drink this cup, ye do shew the Lord's death till he come." Again, a consistent preterist understanding of I Corinthians would insist that communion should no longer be taken because we no longer look forward to the coming of the Lord. But preterists are inconsistent. The allegorical method allows them to impute whatever meaning they desire to a text. In these specific texts, preterists may suggest that this particular coming of the Lord may not be A.D. 70, but perhaps a kind of "final coming" of the Lord, a sort of general resurrection at the end of time. But this will hardly do, as most interpreters consistently understand that both I Corinthians 1:7 and I Corinthians 11:26 refer to the promised literal return of Jesus Christ.[7] Thus, it is only if one grants the preterist interpreter the right to interpret difficult texts allegorically that a preterist reading of I Corinthians can be sustained. Further, the method preterists utilize in I Corinthians is the same method they employ throughout the rest of the New Testament. Consequently, when the text does not support a preterist reading, it is ignored or reinterpreted. Preterists say that perhaps the coming of the Lord in that instance is not speaking of A.D. 70, but is likely the "final end."[8]

There will be yet a future turning of the age; on this the Scripture is clear. But on this point as well, preterists reinterpret the clear biblical meaning of this future promise. A preterist interpretive scheme is based on the notion that the "end of the world" must necessarily have occurred in A.D. 70. Preterists suggest rightfully that when the New Testament talks about the "end of the world" it does not necessarily refer to the end of the physical world. They suggest wrongfully, however, that this "end of the world" occurred in A.D. 70 when the "Jewish age" was completed after the destruction of Jerusalem. Determining that A.D. 70 is the closure of this Jewish age is only possible with a hefty bit of allegorical gymnastics. The New Testament is clear about how the Old Testament (the so-called Jewish age) ends. Jesus said, "The law and the prophets were until John: since that time the kingdom of God is preached, and every man presseth into it" (Luke 16:16). The writer of Hebrews declares, "But this man, after he had offered one sacrifice for sins for ever, sat down on the right hand of God" (Hebrews 10:12). Paul writes, "For Christ is the end of the law for righteousness to every one that believeth" (Romans 10:4). Paul writes to the Colossians that Jesus "[blotted] out the handwriting of ordinances that was against us, which was contrary to us, and took it out of the way, nailing it to his cross" (Colossians 2:14). The old covenant ended at the cross of Calvary, and the church age began on the Day of Pentecost. Preterists wrongfully say that Apostolics ascribe the kingdom to the future. When people receive the Holy Ghost, they are in the kingdom of God. That said, this does not prevent God from fulfilling literal promises about the kingdom in the future.[9]

Actually, there is not in any sense a Jewish age that ended with the destruction of Jerusalem. Despite claims to the contrary, neither the offering of sacrifice nor the keeping of the law ceased at the destruction of the Temple.[10] Nor did the church reap sudden benefits when the Temple was destroyed. Regardless of what preterists insist, there is not a shred of historical evidence that suggests evangelism by the church was greatly increased by the destruction of Jerusalem.[11] Indeed, there were not any Christians in the first centuries of the church who ever looked back and regarded the destruction of Jerusalem as a coming of the Lord.[12] In actuality, there is nothing that happened in A.D. 70 in terms of any eschatological turning of the age—nothing at all! The turning from the law happened on the cross of Calvary, and the Day of Pentecost inaugurated the new covenant. The coming of the Lord is certainly not in the past; it is yet to come.

Preterists seek to marshal evidence that the "end of the world" was the end of the Jewish age in A.D. 70 by pointing to the questions the disciples asked Jesus in Matthew 24, Mark 13, and Luke 21.[13] Because the disciples asked about both the destruction of Jerusalem and the "end of the world," preterists assume that both events necessarily occurred at the same time. Recently, a preterist who was debating me made the claim that the "end of the world" in Matthew 24 was fulfilled at "the end of the Jewish age," an event he believed took place in A.D. 70.[14] In response, I pointed out that this could hardly be the case. The same Greek phrase used in Matthew 24 to describe the future "end of the world" (*sunteleias tou aionos*) is used other places as well in the New Testament in ways that clearly would not support his premise. For instance, in Matthew 28:20 Jesus explains that He will always be present with believers: "And, lo, I am with you alway, even unto the end of the world [*sunteleias tou aionos*]. Amen." The same Greek phrase—*sunteleias tou aionos*—is found in both Matthew 24 and Matthew 28. Thus, if a preterist understanding of "the end of the word" were actually correct, then Matthew 28:20 would be superfluous. Jesus would have promised to be with the church only until A.D. 70! When I explained this, the preterist debating me had no response.

Evidence put forth to demonstrate that the coming of Jesus was allegorically fulfilled in the coming of the Roman armies is based upon verses that preterists label "time texts." For preterists, when Jesus promised to come "soon" and when the text says that the coming of the Lord is "at hand," such words necessarily mean that Jesus' coming would occur within a brief period of time. Consequently, for preterists, Revelation 1:1-7 is an absolute demonstration that Jesus must come within just a few years of the writing of Revelation.[15] Consider what one preterist has written:

> Revelation 1:1 **The Revelation of Jesus Christ**, which God gave unto him, to shew unto his servants **things which must shortly come to pass**; and he sent and signified *it* by his angel unto his servant John: He didn't say this was going to happen 2,000 to 3,000 years in the future. He said this was "shortly" coming to pass. Revelation 1:3 Blessed *is* he that readeth, and they that hear the words of this prophecy, and keep those things which are written therein: **for the time *is* at hand**. He said the time is "at hand." Compare the phrase "at hand" with its usage in the rest of the New Testament, and you will discover that this is a reference to it being close by, not far off, something that was soon to take place [underline and bold type are his].[16]

Let us consider what John meant in his introduction to the Book of Revelation. When Revelation 1:1 speaks of things that must "shortly" come to pass, the Greek that underlies the word "shortly" is *en tachei.* This use of *en tachei* does not necessarily indicate temporal shortness or shortness in chronological sequence. Considering the larger prophetic context of Scripture, *en tachei* here emphasizes the certainty that the event will happen, not how soon it will happen.[17] This does not promise that Jesus would come (allegorically or otherwise) in the next few years. Rather, it promises the certainty of His coming. Further, Revelation 1:3 says that "the time is at hand." This phrase translates the Greek "*ho gar kairos engus.*" The Greek word *engus* (translated "at hand") is an adverb. Again, the word does not so much predict how soon the events will be fulfilled, but rather its prophetic certainty.[18]

These same kinds of prophetic promises, using similar language, appear in the Old Testament. Scores of prophecies, though described as if they would be fulfilled soon, were actually not fulfilled for hundreds of years—or in some cases have yet to be fulfilled. For example, when the Old Testament was translated into Greek (the Septuagint, LXX), the translators used these same words that are found in the Book of Revelation. Zephaniah 1:14 says, "The great day of the LORD is near [*engus*], it is near [*engus*], and hasteth [*tacheia*] greatly, even the voice of the day of the LORD: the mighty man shall cry there bitterly." The Day of the Lord is prophesied again and again in the Old Testament, and it was still anticipated in II Peter as future for the church.[19] Clearly the use of these words does not necessitate a time of fulfillment that must be within a few years.

The next few verses in Revelation prove that the Lord's return has yet to be accomplished. Revelation 1:7 further explains, "Behold, he cometh with clouds; and every eye shall see him, and they also which pierced him: and all kindreds of the earth shall wail because of him. Even so, Amen." While preterists allegorize these clouds to be fulfilled in the coming of Roman armies, we have already demonstrated the fallacy of such an argument.[20] The Greek is clear: John says of Jesus that "every eye shall see him." This cannot be allegorically fulfilled by the Roman armies. It says that every eye shall see *Him*. The word *every* could not be plainer; it must mean "every eye," "all eyes," or the "the eye of every person." The *New Jerusalem Bible* rightfully translates this, "Everyone will see him!" The *New Living Translation* translates this exactly the same. Historically, this was not fulfilled when the Roman armies destroyed the Temple, but it will be fulfilled when Jesus Christ returns.

Preterists argue vehemently for the necessity of these time texts in the New Testament. They insist that either Jesus and His apostles were telling the truth and these texts were fulfilled in the first century, or else (those who oppose preterist teaching must be saying) Jesus and His apostles were liars![21] But by only allowing these two options, preterists are guilty of a logical fallacy.[22] In fact, there is clearly the possibility of another interpretation.

Consider a simplistic preterist interpretation of Hebrews 10:37. Citing the verse, "For yet a little while, and he that shall come will come, and will not tarry," a preterist interpreter writes, "He said it is not much longer and He is coming. Was He wrong? I don't think so."[23] The ironic thing about such an assessment of these words is that the writer of Hebrews was not the first to write this startling prophecy. In fact, Hebrews is quoting the prophet Habakkuk, who originally gave the prophecy in the seventh century B.C.[24] How is it possible for this to be a time text that demands immediate fulfillment when the words were first uttered hundreds of years earlier and had yet to be fulfilled? In view of this, the necessity of time texts being fulfilled in ten or thirty or even forty years is simply erroneous.

When confronting a preterist about this apparent inconsistency in interpreting so-called time texts, one response is that there is a kind of mystical formula that demonstrates which texts must be taken as demanding immediate fulfillment. In this scheme, texts "within a vision" do not have to be fulfilled in a specific time, but texts "outside a vision" must necessarily be fulfilled very soon.[25] But who is to say which texts have to follow a preterist's scheme or are located "within a vision"? As we have suggested earlier, in the end, such authority is granted to the one making such an allegorical choice. This is certainly not surprising. In allegorical interpretation, authority must necessarily be granted to some individual, for authority is not found in the text itself.

One thing that preterists consistently agree on is that New Testament texts that speak in the present tense about the coming of the Lord must necessarily happen in the lifetime of those present in the audience. Thus, a number of Gospel texts and promises in the Epistles are not merely promises for the imminent coming of the Lord to the church at large; for the preterist they are undeniable proof that Jesus was coming in the first century. The problem, of course, is that this scheme is not foolproof either. I sat down with a preterist and went through I Thessalonians in depth in order to determine which of those texts were deemed by preterists to be about the coming of the Lord and which might possibly just refer to a kind of "final judgment."[26] It was both an interesting and confusing conversation trying to discern whether, for this preterist, a particular reference was speaking of Jesus coming in A.D. 70 (Jesus coming allegorically in the Roman armies) or whether the text was referring to some distant resurrection of the saints. In the end, I failed to be convinced that there was any objective criterion at all. Sometimes the interpreter said a particular text meant A.D. 70, sometimes a general resurrection; sometimes the interpreter did not know for sure. That said, one fruitful part of the conversation occurred when we began to discuss I Thessalonians

4:15-17, for the interpreter was certain this text was speaking of the final resurrection.

Consider the words of Paul in I Thessalonians 4:15-17:

> For this we say unto you by the word of the Lord, that we which are alive and remain unto the coming of the Lord shall not prevent them which are asleep. For the Lord himself shall descend from heaven with a shout, with the voice of the archangel, and with the trump of God: and the dead in Christ shall rise first: Then we which are alive and remain shall be caught up together with them in the clouds, to meet the Lord in the air: and so shall we ever be with the Lord.

These verses do not sound like some distant eschatological resurrection. Rather, they seem to fulfill the preterist rule that verses in the present tense should be fulfilled in the first century. Indeed, these verses are alive with expectation; Paul clearly uses the present tense verb to talk about the event. The manner of speaking is anticipating a present hope, and the language is the language of looking, watching, and waiting. The present participle translated by the words "we which are alive" is *zontes*. It is clearly addressing Paul's present hearers. This then qualifies as a time text. If preterists were at all consistent, this could not be an event scheduled for thousands of years later but must be immediate. Again, using a preterist scheme, if this were not the case, then Paul was a liar! Paul said, "We which are alive and remain unto the coming of the Lord . . ." The word *remain* comes from *perileipomenoi*. This participle, too, is in the present tense: "We, the remaining ones . . . " If the scheme for creating preterist time texts is correct and if one is only allowed one of two choices, then either there was a general resurrection in the lifetime of some of Paul's hearers or Paul is a deceiver! But, of course, Paul was not lying. The reason Paul could use language like this is that he was writing to the church at large of a hope that should be present in every generation until Jesus returns. This way of speaking denotes the certainty of the event, and it gives a message to the covenant people of God to always be watching, waiting, and anticipating the redemption of His creation.

Finally, let us briefly address Matthew 24 and the Olivet Discourse at large, the chapter that becomes the principal focus of preterist interest. Jesus said, "This generation shall not pass, till all these things be fulfilled" (verse 34). Although there is no historical evidence that the first-century church considered this a time text specifically applying to their generation, preterists insist this must be the case. Despite the universal anticipation by the early church theologians for a future coming of the Lord after A.D. 70, and despite the fact that not one of them ever referenced A.D. 70 as any sort of coming of the Lord at all, preterists insist that they alone are taking the Scripture literally. Yet, the glaring inconsistency of such a claim is obvious. In order to insist that this verse is a necessary time text (something not believed by the early church), every other portion of this section in Matthew 24 must be allegorized. Clouds are not clouds, but symbolism. Jesus' coming is not really His coming. Angels are not really angels, but preachers; and in the end, the "gathering of the elect"—interpreted as preaching the gospel—did not take place within a single generation but is still going on today (obviously not fulfilled in that first generation of the church).

While all interpreters agree that some part of the Olivet Discourse was fulfilled in the first century, in order for preterists to be correct, all of the Olivet Discourse must only apply to events leading up to the destruction of Jerusalem in A.D. 70. This requires considerable historical and biblical gymnastics to make such a system believable to anyone. Preterists, of course, are aided by allegorical interpretation, which allows the greatest amount of flexibility to ignore context.

Preterist teachers expend considerable effort to link historical events leading up to the fall of Jerusalem as described by Josephus to the biblical prophecies given by Jesus.[27] Unfortunately, despite their best effort, the absolute linking of Matthew 24 with the historical record is just too great a stretch. The first century can hardly be said to fulfill the statement of Jesus, "And except those days should be shortened, there should no flesh be saved: but for the elect's sake those days shall be shortened" (Matthew 24:22). Nor can the statement made by Jesus possibly refer to the destruction of Jerusalem when He pronounced that this time of judgment was a "great tribulation, such as was not since the beginning of the world to this time, no, nor ever shall be" (Matthew 24:21). Were there not multiplied thousands of elect outside of the concern of Rome's invading armies? Absolutely. Were the battles of the First Jewish War from A.D. 66-70 the *greatest* tribulation that has ever occurred in the world or ever would occur? The obvious answer is an unequivocal no. More Jews were killed in the Second Jewish War in A.D. 132-135 than in the war of A.D. 66-70. Consider all of the persecution of the Jewish people through the last two millennia. In the last century alone, Hitler killed millions of Jews. When I asked a leading preterist about the millions killed in the Holocaust, he categorically denied that the Holocaust took place in the way that has been reported historically![28]

It is difficult to speak of what all preterists may believe or even to summarize how they universally argue, for preterists are not a monolithic group. What we have tried to demonstrate is the kind of method that preterists employ as a group and to show how subjective it is. Particularly, as we have focused on the so-called time texts, it becomes apparent that the allegorical method allows preterists to selectively pick and choose which texts are usable and how they can be interpreted to make their scheme work.

In conclusion, the truth of the future coming of Jesus should not be abandoned or reinterpreted. We cannot say with certainty in what generation Jesus will come again. Jesus stated clearly that no one knows the day or hour of His return (Matthew 24:36); yet the New Testament admonishes the church to be ever watching and ever waiting His return. (See Matthew 25:13; II Timothy 4:8; Hebrews 9:28.) At the Last Supper, Jesus told the disciples that He would literally go away, and He did. In this same context, Jesus also told His disciples that, if He did literally go away, He would literally return—the Greek is unambiguous: "I am coming again" (*palin erchomai*), clearly indicating His literal return.[29] This was not fulfilled when Roman armies invaded Jerusalem and destroyed the Temple. It will be fulfilled, however, when Jesus literally returns and takes believers to Himself.[30] Now, more than ever, it is important to remain faithful to this truth as it was understood both by the early church and as a foundational premise for the very identity of the Apostolic Pentecostal movement.

Notes

[1]See my chapter "Could Preterism Be Apostolic?" earlier in this book.

[2]See Larry T. Smith, *The Coming of the Lord, The Last Days, and The End of the World* (El Campo, Tex.: Rightly Dividing the Word, 2000), 51; cf. 70-71.

[3]As we discuss below, both the Old Testament and New Testament treat salvation history as imminent. Both the Old Testament and New Testament can speak collectively to the way in which God will act in the present tense, whether the particular prophecy is fulfilled immediately or sometime in the future. Further, temporal judgment is often seen against the backdrop of the eternal judgment of God. On this, see Gordon Fee and Douglas Stuart, *How to Read the Bible for All Its Worth* (Grand Rapids: Zondervan, 1993), 182.

[4]Some preterists might suggest that gifts of Spirit ceased; this is certainly not consonant with an Apostolic reading of the New Testament.

[5]The Greek word translated "waiting" is *apekdekomenous*. It means to "await eagerly or expectantly," "look forward eagerly," and it is always used of Christian hope in the New Testament. On this, see Walter Bauer, William F. Arndt, and F. Wilbur Gingrich, *A Greek-English Lexicon of the New Testament and Other Early Christian Literature*, 2nd ed., rev. F. Wilbur Gingrich and Frederick W. Danker (Chicago: University of Chicago Press, 1979), 890.

[6]The word "looking" (*prosdechomenoi*) has reference to anticipating, waiting with expectation. In A. T. Robertson's *Word Studies*, he demonstrates the sense of this verb by pointing out the similar usage when describing how Simeon (Luke 2:25) and others (Luke 2:38) were looking for the Messiah.

[7]Gordon Fee suggests that the Corinthians had an "overrealized eschatological understanding connected to their experience of tongues." Gordon D. Fee, *The First Epistle to the Corinthians* (Grand Rapids: Eerdmans, 1987), 42, n. 36.

[8]Even the notion of whether there is a final end or not is sometimes questioned. See Larry Smith's "Two Cups, One Choice," part I (El Campo, Tex.: Rightly Dividing the Word). He offers, "The Bible said, 'world without end.' It just might be that. The Bible said, 'His kingdom would not end.' The Bible said

His kingdom was an everlasting kingdom. . . . This thing may go on forever."

[9]It has been my observation that a "straw man" employed by preterist advocates is to suggest that Apostolics teach that we are not in the kingdom of God or that Apostolics teach a necessary return to law keeping in the future. That we are in the kingdom is certain. That there are future prophecies of the kingdom that will be fulfilled is also certain. Preterists deny a future Millennium. They suggest that we are currently living in it. But Apostolics have not sacrificed anything in the present to allow that God has a plan for the future.

[10]While studying for my dissertation, I discovered that the Jews contrived a way for sacrifices to be made on the Temple Mount even after the destruction of Jerusalem in A.D. 70. Indeed, it was not until the Second Jewish War in 132-135 that the Jews were thwarted in all such attempts. Certainly the Jews keep the Torah to this day.

[11]Such a claim made by preterists (see Larry Smith, "Two Cups but One Choice," part I) has no historical basis whatsoever.

[12]On the initial development of preterism in the seventeenth century, see Thomas Ice, "The History of Preterism," in *The End Times Controversy: The Second Coming under Attack*, Tim LaHaye and Thomas Ice, gen. eds. (Eugene, Ore.: Harvest House Publishers, 2003), 37-66.

[13]Matthew 24:3; Mark 13:4; Luke 21:7; it is important to read the composite narrative to explore all that Jesus taught on the Mount of Olives. Note that the Lukan question deals more with the details of the Temple in A.D. 70. The Matthean account goes beyond A.D. 70 and deals in greater detail with events surrounding the coming of the Lord.

[14]"Prophecy Debate on Preterism Between David Norris and Larry Smith," Houston, Texas, January 31, 2005; Defenders of the Faith Conference on Apostolic Doctrine and Apologetics, sponsored by Los Pentecostales de Royalwood (faithdefenders@hotmail.com).

[15]Smith, *The Coming of the Lord*, 56.

[16]Ibid., 41.

[17]See p. 103 of Thomas Ice, "Preterist Time Texts," in *The End Times Controversy*, 83-122. See also p. 118 of F. Blass and A. Debrunner, *A Grammar of New Testament Greek*, trans. and revised by Robert Funk (Chicago: University of Chicago, 1961).

[18]On this see Thomas Ice, "The War Over Words," in *The End Times Controversy*, 283-305.

[19]Joel 2:1-3 states that the Day of the Lord is near (LXX *engus*); see Ezekiel 30:3. It states that the Day of the Lord is near (LXX *engus*); II Peter 3:10-12 warns the church to continue to look for the imminent Day of the Lord!

[20]See my chapter on the Old Testament; cf. Jorge Medina's chapter "Coming in the Clouds."

[21]Larry Smith certainly deals in this kind of argumentation on p. 5f. of his *The Coming of the Lord*, under the heading, "Was Jesus a Deceiver?" and in the next section, "Can the Writers of the Bible Be Trusted?"

[22]Fallacy of the excluded middle; that is, limiting the possibilities to a false antithesis. On this, see D. A. Carson, *Exegetical Fallacies.*

[23]Smith, *The Coming of the Lord*, 51.

[24]Habakkuk 2:3 "For the vision is yet for an appointed time, but at the end it shall speak, and not lie: though it tarry, wait for it; because it will surely come, it will not tarry."

[25]Interview with Larry Smith, March 1, 2003, El Campo, Texas.

[26]Ibid.

[27]Larry Smith, "Two Cups but One Choice": Part 1; See also Larry Smith on p. 54 of his *The Coming of the Lord.* Smith cites Josephus's record of the destruction of Jerusalem after offering from Matthew 24:21, "For then shall be great tribulation, such as was not since the beginning of the world to this time, no, nor ever shall be."

[28]Interview with Larry Smith, March 1, 2003.

[29]Just as Jesus had a literal death, followed by a literal ascension, so the return must too be literal. Just prior to the opening of the chapter, Peter asks, "Lord, whither goest thou? Jesus answered him, Whither I go, thou canst not follow me now; but thou shalt follow me afterwards." Peter understands that Jesus is speaking of His death and indicates his own willingness to join His Master. He then says, "Lord, why cannot I follow thee now? I will lay down my life for thy sake." Only then does Jesus tell them that He is literally going away, literally preparing rooms for them in His Father's house, and is literally going to take them to the Father's house. Nowhere in the Bible is this ever used as imagery for receiving the Holy Ghost. On this, see Robert Gromacki, "The Imminent Return of Jesus Christ," *Grace Theological Journal* 6 (fall 1965): 18.

[30]The Greek for receive is *paralempsomai* and indicates that Jesus will literally take them Himself.

6

Coming in the Clouds

G. Jorge Medina

"And the high priest arose, and said unto him, Answerest thou nothing? what is it which these witness against thee? But Jesus held his peace. And the high priest answered and said unto him, I adjure thee by the living God, that thou tell us whether thou be the Christ, the Son of God. Jesus saith unto him, Thou hast said: nevertheless I say unto you, Hereafter shall ye see the Son of man sitting on the right hand of power, and coming in the clouds of heaven" (Matthew 26:62-64).

When Jesus was brought before the Sanhedrin, they had only one goal in mind: Convict Him of blasphemy, a charge serious enough to merit death. Before we analyze the situation that fateful day at the high priest's palace, it is important that we understand what preterists claim regarding Matthew 26:62-64. One preterist says, "Here the Lord informs the high priest and the other members of the Jewish Sanhedrin that they will 'see' His coming. Obviously, they are not still alive today! Jesus must be referring to an event in their first-century life spans."[1] He continues:

> Here Christ informs the Sanhedrin that they will see His coming. As I argue above, this is not a physical, visible coming, but a judgment-coming upon Jerusalem. They "see" it in the sense that we "see" how a math problem works: with the "eye of understanding" rather than the organ of vision. . . .[2] In fact, Scripture often mentions "seeing" in a nonliteral sense. . . . Paul teaches that "since the creation of the world His *invisible attributes*, His eternal power and divine nature, have been *clearly seen*, being understood through what has been made, so that they are without excuse" (Romans 1:20, emphasis mine). The writer of Hebrews says that "by faith" Moses was "seeing Him who is unseen" (Hebrews 11:27).[3]

We see that preterists think Jesus told the high priest, "I will come back in judgment soon, and I will destroy you and this whole nation." For preterists, the high priest would "see" the judgment of God coming against them. Although it is incredible to think that anyone would "see" Jesus in the face of the Roman soldiers coming against Jerusalem, this is, in fact, a cardinal belief of preterism. Let us analyze this passage to show that the preterist interpretation is wrong. We must examine the whole of the New Testament record in order to arrive at the right interpretation.

First-Century Judaism

Second Temple Judaism had two religious symbols that no one would ever speak against: (1) the Torah, the law God gave directly to Moses, and (2) the Temple, the only place where Jews could offer sacrifices for sins, and whose Holy of Holies was the abode of the very presence of God. The Jewish leadership first attempted to convict Jesus of blaspheming against the law of Moses.[4] Next, they tried to convict Him of blaspheming against the Temple, but to no avail: "For many bare false witness against him, but their witness agreed not together. And there arose certain, and bare false witness against him, saying, We heard him say, I will destroy this temple that is made with hands, and within three days I will build another made without hands. But neither so did their witness agree together" (Mark 14:56-59). Finally, when they thought all hope was lost, the high priest in desperation put Jesus under oath: "And the high priest arose, and said unto him, Answerest thou nothing? what is it which these witness against thee? But Jesus held his peace. And the high priest answered and said unto him, I adjure thee by the living God, that thou tell us whether thou be the Christ, the Son of God" (Matthew 26:62-63). The Lord could have been released due to lack of evidence for a conviction, but He decided to speak: "Thou hast said: nevertheless I say unto you, Hereafter shall ye see the Son of man sitting on the right hand of power, and coming in the clouds of heaven" (Matthew 26:64). Not only does He confirm His Messiahship ("you said it"), but He also hands them the evidence they have been seeking against Him. With those words Jesus sealed His fate.

Until

Jesus could not have meant that the high priest himself would see Him coming in judgment against

Jerusalem as preterists teach. Why? Because He placed a requirement on His coming. Let us see it in a favorite passage of preterists and study it in context: "O Jerusalem, Jerusalem, thou that killest the prophets, and stonest them which are sent unto thee, how often would I have gathered thy children together, even as a hen gathereth her chickens under her wings, and ye would not! Behold, your house is left unto you desolate" (Matthew 23:37-38). Jesus was lamenting over the fate of those who rejected Him, and He announced the destruction of the Temple (their "house"). He then proclaimed a truth that preterists would like to hide away so no one would notice: "For I say unto you, Ye shall not see me henceforth, *till* ye shall say, Blessed is he that cometh in the name of the Lord" (Matthew 23:39, emphasis mine).

When did Jesus say the inhabitants of Jerusalem would see Him again? Not until His second coming when they will accept Him as the promised Messiah. The prophet Zechariah also foretold this:

> And I will pour upon the house of David, and upon the inhabitants of Jerusalem, the spirit of grace and of supplications: and they shall look upon me whom they have pierced, and they shall mourn for him, as one mourneth for his only son, and shall be in bitterness for him, as one that is in bitterness for his firstborn. . . . And one shall say unto him, What are these wounds in thine hands? Then he shall answer, Those with which I was wounded in the house of my friends. . . . And it shall come to pass, that in all the land, saith the LORD, two parts therein shall be cut off and die; but the third shall be left

> therein. And I will bring the third part through the fire [of the Great Tribulation], and will refine them as silver is refined, and will try them as gold is tried: they shall call on my name, and I will hear them: I will say, It is my people: and they shall say, The LORD is my God. . . . And his feet shall stand in that day upon the mount of Olives, which is before Jerusalem on the east, and the mount of Olives shall cleave in the midst thereof toward the east and toward the west, and there shall be a very great valley; and half of the mountain shall remove toward the north, and half of it toward the south. . . . And the LORD my God shall come, and all the saints with thee (Zechariah 12:10; 13:6, 8-9; 14:4-5).

It would be very difficult to have it any clearer. Scripture is its own best interpreter. It is indeed unthinkable for a Oneness Pentecostal to try to deny this truth. Spiritualizing these verses, along with the passages in Matthew 24 and Matthew 26 about His second coming, takes away from the glorious revelation of the mighty God in Christ. This will become clearer as we progress in our study.

Jesus was indeed saying, "Let Me give you a time text: When Jerusalem is destroyed, you will not see Me; when armies surround Jerusalem, you will not see Me; when the Temple is burned, you will not see Me. If fact, you will not see Me again until you receive Me as your King and Lord."[5]

A Rescue Mission

Notice also that Yahweh (YHWH) will come to fight for the Jewish nation, not against it, as preterism teaches: "In that day shall the LORD defend the inhabitants of Jerusalem; and he that is feeble among them at that day shall be as David; and the house of David shall be as God, as the angel of the LORD before them. And it shall come to pass in that day, that I will seek to destroy all the nations that come against Jerusalem" (Zechariah 12:8-9). Compare this with what Jesus says in Luke 21:27-28: "And then shall they see the Son of man coming in a cloud with power and great glory. And when these things begin to come to pass, then look up, and lift up your heads; for your redemption draweth nigh." This is not speaking about A.D. 70, but of the second coming of Christ. (Compare also Acts 1:9-11.) Since this has not yet happened, preterism's interpretation is patently false.

The High Priest Did Not Accept Messiah

Since the high priest did not accept Christ at the time of the destruction of Jerusalem, and since we believe Jesus was not deceitful or mistaken, then the inescapable conclusion is that Jesus did not come in A.D. 70. Now if the Jews would not see Jesus again until they accepted and welcomed Him, why did Jesus tell the high priest, "Hereafter shall ye see the Son of man" (Matthew 26:64)? Let us compare that verse with Matthew 23 again: "For I say unto you, Ye shall not see me henceforth, till ye shall say, Blessed is he that cometh in the name of the Lord" (Matthew 23:39). During the siege and destruction of Jerusalem, Israel did not accept Him. In fact, most of the inhabitants of Jerusalem perished in A.D. 70. How will they ever "see" the Lord? The conclusion is that Jesus was speaking to the nation of Israel as a whole, regardless of time or space.

Let us look at another passage that sheds more light on this: "Wherefore God also hath highly exalted him, and given him a name which is above every name: That at the name of Jesus every knee should bow, of things in heaven, and things in earth, and things under the earth; And that every tongue should confess that Jesus Christ is Lord, to the glory of God the Father" (Philippians 2:9-11). Someone may be inclined to say, "Lord, it is very difficult for a bunch of old, disintegrating bones to bow their knees to you or to confess you as Christ and Lord." Again, this is not limited by time or space; every knee will bow and every tongue will confess Him as Lord, even those who reject Him. This kind of "corporate" language is frequent in the New Testament. Note Paul's usage: "For this we say unto you by the word of the Lord, that we which are alive and remain unto the coming of the Lord shall not prevent them which are asleep. For the Lord himself shall descend from heaven with a shout, with the voice of the archangel, and with the trump of God: and the dead in Christ shall rise first: Then we which are alive and remain shall be caught up together with them in the clouds, to meet the Lord in the air: and so shall we ever be with the Lord" (I Thessalonians 4:15-17).

Interestingly, partial preterists do not interpret I Thessalonians in relation to A.D. 70; rather they admit that these verses proclaim the final coming of the Lord (the *second* Second Coming?), which has not happened yet. But when Paul wrote these words, he said, "We will be alive when He comes, and we will be caught up to Him." Question: Is Paul alive today? The answer is obviously no. Was Paul caught up to meet the Lord at His coming? The answer again is no. He employed a "corporate we," speaking about the church as a whole, including himself as a part of the body of Christ that would experience that event.

One preterist admits that the pronouncement of Jesus in Matthew 26 is a "corporate you." Notice what he writes:

> We must again recall Christ's interchange with the Sanhedrin at His ecclesiastical trial before His crucifixion: "The high priest said to Him, 'I adjure You by the living God, that You tell us whether You are the Christ, the Son of God.' Jesus said to him, 'You have said it yourself; nevertheless I tell you, hereafter you shall see the son of man sitting at the right hand of power, and coming on the clouds of heaven'" (Matthew 26:63-64). Here Christ informs the Sanhedrin that they will see His coming.[6]

He quotes the verse that says, "Jesus said to him [the high priest]" and then argues that the whole Sanhedrin ("they") would see His coming.[7] He understands that Jesus was not only addressing one person, but a group of people. He believes that group to be the Sanhedrin; other verses indicate it was the whole nation. (Compare with Matthew 23:37-39.)[8]

Jesus Did Not Threaten the Priest

Preterism makes Jesus out to be a spiteful individual, threatening His captors (and all of Israel) with total destruction and everlasting rejection, but this does not square with Scripture: "Who did no sin, neither was guile found in his mouth: Who, when he was reviled, reviled not again; when he suffered, *he threatened not*; but committed himself to him that judgeth righteously" (I Peter 2:22-23, emphasis mine). "Then said Jesus, Father, forgive them; for they know not what they do" (Luke 23:34).

When Jesus told the high priest, "Hereafter shall ye see the Son of man sitting on the right hand of power, and coming in the clouds of heaven," He was not being vindictive and threatening him with judgment, but was pronouncing Love's offer of grace to a condemned generation. Jesus is addressing the whole nation, once again proclaiming hope. Jesus is in fact saying, "You will suffer because you rejected Me, but in your time of greatest need, when you turn your hearts towards Me, you will see Me with power and glory, coming in the clouds of heaven to save My people from total annihilation." (Compare with Zechariah 13-14.)

Expressions used by Jesus such as "right hand of power," "the Son of man," and "coming in the clouds," need to be taken into account.

Right Hand of Power

The right hand of power is not a physical location where Jesus is sitting, but speaks of His authority and power, attributes He has because of His divinity. He has the power and authority of God, as the *International Standard Bible Encyclopedia* explains, "Christ at the 'right hand of God' is the highly suggestive picture of His universal dominion asserted by Himself (Matthew 28:18). . . . It is vain to speculate upon the relation of Christ's nature in this exalted state. We cannot distinguish between the human and Divine."[9]

The Son of Man

Jesus, knowing the Sanhedrin's failure to find proof to obtain a death conviction, gave them one. He calls to mind the vision of the Son of Man and the Ancient of Days in the Book of Daniel: "I saw in the night visions, and, behold, one like the Son of man came with the clouds of heaven, and came to the Ancient of days, and they brought him near before him. And there was given him dominion, and glory, and a kingdom, that all people, nations, and languages, should serve him: his dominion is an everlasting dominion, which shall not pass away, and his kingdom that which shall not be destroyed" (Daniel 7:13-14). Was the coming of the Son of Man really an army marching against the Ancient of Days? Of course not. Thus, "coming in the clouds" does not have to be a "judgment coming." Since Jesus referred to Daniel's vision when speaking to the high priest, His coming in the clouds cannot be an army either, but rather a glorious appearing. (See Titus 2:13.)

Why Was Jesus Accused of Blasphemy?

"There are two general forms of blasphemy: (1) Attributing some evil to God, or denying Him some good that we should attribute to Him (Lev 24:11; Rom 2:24). (2) Giving the attributes of God to a creature—which form of blasphemy the Jews charged Jesus with (Matt 26:65; Luke 5:21; John 10:36)."[10] Notice that *Unger's Bible Dictionary* recognizes that Jesus, in Matthew 26:65, was charged with blasphemy when He claimed He would come in the clouds. Jesus was in fact saying, "Remember the magnificent glory of the Ancient of Days? Remember the Son of Man that comes in the clouds?

That is exactly how I am coming again. You will not be able to distinguish me from God."[11]

Jesus knew what the answer from the high priest and the Sanhedrin would be: "Then the high priest rent his clothes, saying, He hath spoken blasphemy; what further need have we of witnesses? behold, now ye have heard his blasphemy. What think ye? They answered and said, He is guilty of death" (Matthew 26:65-66). To Jewish eyes, Jesus had indeed blasphemed: He was making Himself out to be God, as He had done before. (See John 8:56-59.) Therefore they accused Him before Pilate, saying, "We have a law, and by our law he ought to die, because he made himself the Son of God" (John 19:7).[12]

Coming in the Clouds

The coming of the Lord must be visible and literal because the New Testament context demands it. Proper hermeneutics teach us that the meaning of any passage is governed by its context. So when we interpret a verse, we must look to other verses in the context that can shed light on its meaning. The context of a verse is not limited to just those verses nearby, but increases outwardly to ultimately include the entire Bible. For example, when interpreting a verse in the New Testament, we should consider the context in the following order:

- the passage in question
- other verses in the same chapter
- other chapters within that book
- other books by the same writer
- other books in the New Testament
- passages in the Old Testament

Preterists forsake all New Testament verses relating to a "coming in the clouds"[13] and go straight to the Old Testament, looking for support for their point of view. They miss the New Testament forest for a few Old Testament trees.

Jesus declared His divinity when He spoke about the right hand of power and when He spoke about the Son of Man, and He powerfully declared His absolute divinity when He said He would come in the clouds of heaven. The misguided identification preterism makes between "cloud" passages in the New Testament with certain passages in the Old Testament strips this verse of its depth of revelation because they want to limit its significance to "judgment": "In the Old Testament, clouds are frequently employed as symbols of divine wrath and judgment. Often God is seen surrounded with foreboding clouds. . . . God is poetically portrayed in certain judgment scenes as coming in the clouds to wreak historical vengeance upon His enemies."[14] This author goes on to say, "This actually refers to Jesus' ascension. In the destruction of the temple, the rejected Christ is vindicated as the ascended Lord and shown to possess great power and glory."[15]

Clouds in the Old Testament

Scripture does use the image of Yahweh riding a cloud: "The burden of Egypt. Behold, the LORD rideth upon a swift cloud, and shall come into Egypt: and the idols of Egypt shall be moved at his presence, and the heart of Egypt shall melt in the midst of it" (Isaiah 19:1). Clouds could mean God's swift action or arrival. (See Deuteronomy 33:26; II Samuel 22:10-12; Psalm 18:9-11; 104:3.) But clouds do not have that exclusive meaning.

For instance, they could also mean groups of people (Isaiah 60:8; Hebrews 12:1), an invading army (Isaiah 14:31), impending judgment (Isaiah 18:4), or even a Babylonian army (Jeremiah 4:13). Note that the last three verses do not mention Yahweh riding around or coming in those clouds. When applied to Yahweh, the meaning of clouds is a lot richer than just a coming in judgment: They portray God's dwelling. (See Exodus 40:35; Numbers 9:17; I Kings 8:12; II Chronicles 6:1; Psalm 97:2.) They also portray His glory. (See I Kings 8:10; II Chronicles 5:13; Ezekiel 10:3-4.)[16]

Old Testament passages show God coming in clouds, but with no army following, and therefore no judgment coming. For example:

Exodus 19:9: "And the LORD said unto Moses, Lo, I come unto thee in a thick cloud, that the people may hear when I speak with thee, and believe thee for ever. And Moses told the words of the people unto the LORD."

Exodus 24:16: "And the glory of the LORD abode upon mount Sinai, and the cloud covered it six days: and the seventh day he called unto Moses out of the midst of the cloud." (See also Leviticus 16:2.)

I Kings 8:10-11: "And it came to pass, when the priests were come out of the holy place, that the cloud filled the house of the LORD, so that the priests could not stand to minister because of the cloud: for the glory of the LORD had filled the house of the LORD." (See also Ezekiel 10:4.)

In fact, sometimes clouds refer to the grace and mercy of God, not to judgment and destruction: "It came even to pass, as the trumpeters and singers were as one, to make one sound to be heard in praising and thanking the LORD; and when they lifted up their voice with the trumpets and cymbals and instruments of musick, and praised the LORD, saying, For he is good; for his mercy endureth for ever: that then the house was filled with a cloud, even the house of the LORD" (II Chronicles 5:13). No armies were seen, no destruction followed.

The *Dictionary of Biblical Imagery* says:

> Exodus 16:10 associates the cloud in the wilderness with the "glory of the LORD." The cloud and the fire represent God's presence with them during their sojourn. . . . As the people look at the mountain, they hear and see "thunder and lightning, with a thick cloud over the mountain" (Ex 19:16 NIV, cf. also 24:16, 18; 34:5). Once again God's appearance is marked by a cloud . . . [and] the temple later . . . too is filled with the cloud of God's glory (1 Kings 8:10-11; 2 Chron 5:13-14). . . . [When] he abandons his temple, Ezekiel sees this as the departure of the cloud from the Holy of Holies (Ezek 10:3-4). . . . While biblical writers associate clouds primarily with the appearance of God, they occasionally exploit other aspects of clouds to render vivid their ideas.[17]

Clouds in the New Testament

So the primary aspect of clouds in the Old Testament is as a symbol of the presence of Yahweh. This meaning does not change in the New Testament. Clouds do not exclusively refer to God's jugment. "The NT use of the cloud theme, however, returns to the theophanic, or more specifically Christophanic, function. At the transfiguration God spoke out of a cloud to identify Jesus as 'my Son, whom I have chosen' (Lk 9:35). Jesus, like God in the OT, rides on a cloud (Acts 1:9)."[18] It is evident that rather than exclusively accentuating God's judgment, the cloud in the Old Testament was, more often than not, a symbol of His presence and glory. The New Testament continues that tradition, which elucidates why the high priest accused Jesus of blasphemy; in his eyes Jesus was "giving the attributes of God to a creature": Himself!

They Could Not See Yahweh

Preterists may argue that in the Old Testament no one really saw God; therefore no one needs to see Jesus literally when He comes in the clouds. Old Testament comings of Yahweh were necessarily different from New Testament passages. Yahweh is a Spirit (John 4:24), who had no flesh and bones (Luke 24:39). No one *could* see Him: "No man hath seen God at any time; the only begotten Son, which is in the bosom of the Father, he hath declared him" (John 1:18). "And the Word was made flesh, and dwelt among us, (and we beheld his glory, the glory as of the only begotten of the Father,) full of grace and truth" (John 1:14).

In the New Testament, the invisible God became visible in His Son: "Jesus saith unto him, Have I been so long time with you, and yet hast thou not known me, Philip? he that hath seen me hath seen the Father; and how sayest thou then, Shew us the Father?" (John 14:9). Of course no one saw Yahweh as He came in the clouds in the Old Testament, He was invisible (see I Timothy 1:17; 6:16; Hebrews 11:27), but in the New Testament, that very same God came in a body (see Hebrews 10:5; I Timothy 3:16), and He can be seen. Seeing Jesus is the only way to see God. Paul says, "In whom the god of this world hath blinded the minds of them which believe not, lest the light of the glorious gospel of Christ, who is the image of God, should shine unto them. . . . For God, who commanded the light to shine out of darkness, hath shined in our hearts, to give the light of the knowledge of the glory of God in the face of Jesus Christ" (II Corinthians 4:4, 6). The author of Hebrews says, "Who being the brightness of his glory, and the express image of his person, and upholding all things by the word of his power, when he had by himself purged our sins, sat down on the right hand of the Majesty on high" (Hebrews 1:3).

Every Eye Shall See Him

The apostles expected a literal, visible coming in the clouds:

Luke 21:27: "And then shall they see the Son of man coming in a cloud with power and great glory."

Acts 1:9-11: "And when he had spoken these things, while they beheld, he was taken up; and a cloud received him out of their sight. And while they looked stedfastly toward heaven as he went up, behold, two men stood by them in white apparel; which also said, Ye men of Galilee, why stand ye gazing up into heaven? this same Jesus, which is taken up from you into heaven, shall so come in like manner as ye have seen him go into heaven."[19]

Note that Luke wrote both of the above passages. Whatever meaning we assign to one of them, it is logical to think that the other must have a similar meaning as well. Since preterists accept the Acts 1 statement as pointing to the Second Coming, they should accept that the statement in Luke points to the same event.

Revelation 1:7: "Behold, he cometh with clouds; and every eye shall see him, and they also which pierced him: and all kindreds of the earth shall wail because of him. Even so, Amen."

I Thessalonians 4:16-17: "For the Lord himself shall descend from heaven with a shout, with the voice of the archangel, and with the trump of God: and the dead in Christ shall rise first: Then we which are alive and remain shall be caught up together with them in the clouds, to meet the Lord in the air: and so shall we ever be with the Lord."

I John 3:1-2: "Behold, what manner of love the Father hath bestowed upon us, that we should be called the sons of God: therefore the world knoweth us not, because it knew him not. Beloved, now are we the sons of God, and it doth not yet appear what we shall be: but we know that, when he shall appear, we shall be like him; for we shall see him as he is."

The witness of the Scriptures is powerful. The world did not know the Father when He appeared about two thousand years ago, but we will know Him when He returns, for we shall see Him as He is! (See John 1:9-18.)

One futurist has concluded: "Certainly the burden of proof to take such expressions in another way, as preterists contend, would be on those who think that it is a symbol for something else. As with any literature, the proof would have to be textual, not just an argument that it could, maybe, or might mean something else."[20]

Jesus Shows Off

Following the flawed interpretation of Matthew 26:62-64, preterists want to force an A.D. 70 fulfillment on the following verse: "Verily I say unto you, There be some standing here, which shall not taste of death, till they see the Son of man coming in his kingdom" (Matthew 16:28). However, they forget, as some have said, that a text without a context is a pretext for a proof text. Let us analyze the setting of this verse: "For what is a man profited, if he shall gain the whole world, and lose his own soul? or what shall a man give in exchange for his soul?" (Matthew 16:26). Observe that the subject matter is the last judgment. Jesus is speaking of the eternal value of a soul; then in verse 27, He proclaims, "For the Son of man shall come in the glory of His Father with his angels; and then he shall reward every man according to his works." Then He announces that some shall not "taste death" but that they will taste something else. What is it? They will see "the Son of man coming in his kingdom" in the glory of His Father. Furthermore, Jesus did not say they would only see the kingdom of the Son of Man, as preterism asserts, but the Son of Man coming Himself.

"Some" Shall See Him

Based on the word "some," one preterist contends that most of the apostles "would be dead" before this event occurred: "But the transfiguration cannot be its fulfillment, since Jesus indicated that some who were standing with Him would still be alive when He came but most would be dead."[21] This author does this in order to buy his doctrine about forty years until the destruction of

Jerusalem. Of course, this is not the case, especially since Jesus never said that "most would be dead."

Regarding the word "some," a futurist says that the disputed phrase "refers not to length of life, but to privilege; some shall have the privilege of beholding Him in His glory even before they die."[22] Another futurist goes on to point out, "Besides this, all excepting John were deceased before the city was overthrown."[23] Jesus' prophecy would then have to be changed to: "Verily I say unto you, There be one standing here, which shall not taste of death, till he see the Son of man coming in his kingdom." Of course that is not what Jesus said.

Context Is King

Matthew 16 ends at this verse, but we must remember that the original Scriptures were not divided into chapters and verses. The very next verse is a continuation of the narrative. How do we know? It begins with the conjunction "and," which means He was not done talking about it:

> And after six days Jesus taketh Peter, James, and John his brother, and bringeth them up into an high mountain apart, and was transfigured before them: and his face did shine as the sun, and his raiment was white as the light. And, behold, there appeared unto them Moses and Elias talking with him. Then answered Peter, and said unto Jesus, Lord, it is good for us to be here: if thou wilt, let us make here three tabernacles; one for thee, and one for Moses, and one for Elias. While he yet spake, behold, a bright cloud overshadowed them: and behold a voice out of the

> cloud, which said, This is my beloved Son, in whom I am well pleased; hear ye him. And when the disciples heard it, they fell on their face, and were sore afraid (Matthew 17:1-6).

The other narratives of the same event also describe the value of a soul and the coming judgment. (See Mark 9:1-7; Luke 9:27-35.) They all have the promise of Jesus that some would not taste death until they saw Him in His kingdom, and then the fulfillment in the same exact order. Both Matthew and Mark say it happened after six days. Luke says it was about eight days later, counting, no doubt, the beginning and ending days together with the six days.

The Glory of His Kingdom

We read in the Scriptures of the glory of the Father, the Son of Man, His coming in His kingdom, etc. We recognize the same kind of theophanic language in Matthew 26:64. Notice some of the events:

- Jesus' face is transfigured and shines like the sun.
- His garments become white and glistening.
- Moses and Elijah appear "in glory."
- A glory cloud overshadows them (remember God at Sinai).
- A heavenly voice gives witness of the Son of God (See also Matthew 17:2; Luke 9:31.)

Luke gives the following details: "But Peter and they that were with him were heavy with sleep: and when they were awake, they saw his glory, and the two men that stood with him" (Luke 9:32). The appearance of Moses and Elijah is also very significant, as *The Bible Knowledge Commentary* points out:

> Why were Moses and Elijah, of all Old Testament people, present on this occasion? Perhaps these two men and the disciples suggest all the categories of people who will be in Jesus' coming kingdom. The disciples represent individuals who will be present in physical bodies. Moses represents saved individuals who have died or will die. Elijah represents saved individuals who will not experience death, but will be caught up to heaven alive (1 Thes. 4:17). These three groups will be present when Christ institutes His kingdom on earth. Furthermore the Lord will be in His glory as He was at the transfiguration, and the kingdom will take place on earth, as this obviously did. The disciples were thus enjoying a foretaste of the kingdom the Lord promised (Matt. 16:28). . . . Peter seemed to sense the significance of the event for he suggested that he erect three shelters, for Jesus, Moses, and . . . Elijah. He saw in this event the fulfillment of the Jewish Feast of Tabernacles which looked two ways: backward to the wanderings in the wilderness for 40 years, and forward to Israel's full enjoyment of God's blessings when He would gather His people to the land. Peter was correct in his understanding of what was taking place (he saw the kingdom) but he was wrong in his timing.[24]

That is exactly what Jesus said they would see. It is incredible that preterism tries to turn these passages of Scripture into the judgment on Jerusalem in A.D. 70.

Peter's Testimony

In fact, all we need to do is read the testimony of Peter: "For we have not followed cunningly devised fables, when we made known unto you the power and coming of our Lord Jesus Christ, but were eyewitnesses of his majesty. For he received from God the Father honour and glory, when there came such a voice to him from the excellent glory, This is my beloved Son, in whom I am well pleased. And this voice which came from heaven we heard, when we were with him in the holy mount" (II Peter 1:16-18). Notice all the similar words in this passage and in the description of the Transfiguration, including the power and coming of the Lord. II Peter was written around A.D. 64, yet Peter says that he and the apostles had been eyewitnesses of his majesty. How could Peter announce a future Second Coming based on something he says he had been an eyewitness to in the past—if Jerusalem was still standing? No one can be an eyewitness to an event that has not happened yet! It makes no sense apart from the experience on the mount, which Peter is describing here.

Certainly Jesus kept His word. They tasted His glory before they tasted death. Even the foretaste of His coming in glory during the Transfiguration was a literal event, with a literal, personal, corporeal Jesus, visible to all who were there. And so shall His second coming be since that was precisely what Jesus was trying to show his disciples: "And then shall appear the sign of the Son of man in heaven: and then shall all the tribes of the earth mourn, and they shall see the Son of man coming in the clouds of heaven with power and great glory" (Matthew 24:30).

G. Jorge Medina was born in La Paz, Bolivia. He attended Texas Bible College and is a licensed minister with the UPCI. He is founder and director of the Defenders of the Faith Conference on Apostolic Doctrine & Apologetics. In addition to translating several works into Spanish, he has written five books on the cults and world religions and teaches apologetics at Centro Teológico Ministerial, a Spanish Bible school in Houston, Texas.

Notes

[1]Thomas Ice and Kenneth L. Gentry, Jr., *The Great Tribulation: Past or Future?* (Grand Rapids: Kregel Publications, 1999), 53.

[2]This mystical coming sounds a lot like the Seventh-Day Adventist doctrine of Christ's "investigative judgment" or the Jehovah's Witness doctrine that Jesus came invisibly in 1914 to set up His kingdom. These two doctrines, along with preterism, have a "private interpretation" that is apparent only to those that receive the "new revelation." (See II Peter 1:20.)

[3]Gentry, *Tribulation*, 60-61. (Emphasis is Gentry's.)

[4]"The Sanhedrin members are obviously looking for a blasphemy conviction. The reason that standing against the Torah or the Temple was considered blasphemy was because those were the greatest 'incarnational' symbols of Second Temple Judaism. Yahweh dwelled in these symbols. He actually made His abode in the Holy of Holies and was identified with the Torah, His Word. His presence was manifest in both, as it would be in the Son when the fullness of time came (Galatians 4:4; Hebrews 1:1-3). 'In the beginning was the Word, and the Word was with God, and the Word was God' (John 1:1) could have been said by the Rabbis of the period about Yahweh and His Torah. John is not here writing something too foreign to Jewish theology, that is, until he identifies the Word with Yeshua" (G. Jorge Medina, *Jesus: Seen Through Jewish Eyes*, unpublished paper, 6).

[5]It seems there is an unspecified period of time between the rejection of Messiah and His acceptance by Israel as a people: *until*. This sounds like a time gap.

[6]Gentry, *Tribulation*, 60. (Emphasis is Gentry's.)

[7]Gentry repeats his "corporate you" interpretation on page 53 of *Tribulation*.

[8]It should also be remembered that when Jesus speaks of judgment and desolation to Jerusalem, preterists, paradoxically, interpret those words as applying not only to that generation but to all Jews everywhere from that time on (so much for the limitation of "this generation"). They view those judgments as corporate, applying to Jews throughout history forever; hence their need for "replacement theology."

[9]James Orr, general editor, *International Standard Bible Encyclopedia*, "Christ, The Exaltation of." Digital Edition, QuickVerse 6.0.

[10]*New Unger's Bible Dictionary*, "Blasphemy." Digital Edition. PC Study Bible 3.0.

[11]The interpretation of this passage is given by the angel in Daniel 7:18, 22, 27. Compare with Revelation 1:13-14; I John 3:1-2; Matthew 24:30.

[12]See John 10:33; Mark 14:60-65; Matthew 9:2-6; Luke 5:21; John 10:36-38. We should never forget the eternal difference between Jesus' death as a criminal with that of any other in history: Jesus did not die because of something He did. He died because of who He was.

[13]Or they divide them up between "Second Coming" and "A.D. 70 judgment" passages without any rationale for doing so. For more information, see the chapter "The Impending Peril of Full Preterism."

[14]Kenneth L. Gentry, Jr., *He Shall Have Dominion: A Postmillennial Eschatology* (Tyler, Tex.: Institute for Christian Economics, 1992), 273.

[15]Gentry, *Tribulation*, 61.

[16]Warren W. Wiersbe, *Index of Biblical Images* (Grand Rapids: Baker Book House, 2000), 26-27.

[17]Leland Ryken, James C. Wilhoit, Tremper Longam III , *Dictionary of Biblical Imagery*, "Cloud" (Downers Grove, Ill.: InterVarsity Press, 1998), 157.

[18]Ibid.

[19]Partial preterist Kenneth Gentry admits this is a reference to the Second Coming: "Here we have a clear and compelling reference to the Second Advent" (Gentry, *Dominion*, 275). If that is true, and for consistency, other passages in the New Testament that speak of a coming of Jesus and mention clouds should be taken as referring to the same event, unless the context dictates differently. In this case, we know that, since Jesus was received up into glory (Acts 1:9-11; I Timothy 3:16), He will also come back with power and great glory (Luke 21:27).

[20]Ice, *Tribulation*, 105.

[21]Gary DeMar, *Last Days Madness: Obsession of the Modern Church* (Powder Springs, Ga.: American Vision, 1999), 34.

[22]As cited by George N. H. Peters, *The Theocratic Kingdom*, vol. 2 (Grand Rapids: Kregel Publications, [1884], 1978), 563. Quoted in *The End-*

times Controversy, Tim LaHaye and Thomas Ice, eds. (Eugene, Ore.: Harvest House Publishers, 2003), 88.

[23]Peters, *Kingdom*, 563. Quoted by Thomas Ice in *Controversy*, 85.

[24]John F. Walvoord and Roy B. Zuck, *The Bible Knowledge Commentary: New Testament*, ed. 2, Matthew, digital edition, QuickVerse 6.0.

7

The Seventy Weeks of Daniel

Phillip A. Dugas

The prophecy of the seventy weeks in the Book of Daniel is crucial in understanding the end times. Taken by itself it may not seem so, but when we consider the larger context of Scripture, in particular the first coming of Jesus Christ and the enlightenment provided by other New Testament truths, we see that this passage gives the framework for what is going to take place at the end of this present age.

Preterists say this prophecy was totally fulfilled in the time of Christ and in the years immediately following His death and resurrection. This is untenable. In this chapter, we will explain that this prophecy has not been completely fulfilled and therefore has meaning for the future.

For this prophecy to have meaning for the future, it is necessary for a gap to occur between the sixty-ninth and seventieth weeks. In other words, the first sixty-nine weeks of the prophecy have been fulfilled, but there remains one week, a period of seven years, that is yet to be fulfilled. We believe there is a gap and will endeavor to show why.

The Prophecy: Daniel 9:24-27

"Seventy weeks are determined upon thy people and upon thy holy city, to finish the transgression, and to make an end of sins, and to make reconciliation for iniquity, and to bring in everlasting righteousness, and to seal up the vision and prophecy, and to anoint the most Holy. Know therefore and understand, that from the going forth of the commandment to restore and to build Jerusalem unto the Messiah the Prince shall be seven weeks, and threescore and two weeks: the street shall be built again, and the wall, even in troublous times. And after threescore and two weeks shall Messiah be cut off, but not for himself: and the people of the prince that shall come shall destroy the city and the sanctuary; and the end thereof shall be with a flood, and unto the end of the war desolations are determined. And he shall confirm the covenant with many for one week: and in the midst of the week he shall cause the sacrifice and the oblation to cease, and for the overspreading of abominations he shall make it desolate, even until the consummation, and that determined shall be poured upon the desolate."

This prophecy was given to Daniel during exile in Babylon around 539 B.C. Daniel was in his eighties. He understood by the writings of the prophet Jeremiah that God was going to let Jerusalem lie desolate for seventy years (Jeremiah 25:11). He knew that the time was about up so he set himself to seek God on behalf of himself and the people of Israel. While Daniel was praying and fasting, the angel Gabriel came to him with the prophecy that had to do with the future of the people of Israel and the city of Jerusalem.

Gabriel told Daniel, "Seventy weeks are determined upon thy people and upon thy holy city" (9:24). Most agree that the seventy weeks are weeks of years, and so the total time of God's dealing with Israel as relating to this prophecy is 490 years. (See the next chapter "Refuting Preterism's View of the Seventy Weeks" for more detail on this point.) In this 490-year period, six promises are to be fulfilled for Israel:

- to finish the transgression
- to make an end of sins
- to make reconciliation for iniquity
- to bring in everlasting righteousness
- to seal up the vision and prophecy
- to anoint the most Holy

The New Testament church is not in view in the prophecy. This prophecy has only to do with Israel and the city of Jerusalem. The question is, Have the promises of this prophecy been fulfilled for Israel? Have they stopped transgressing against God? Has their sinning ended? Have they been reconciled to God? Are they walking in everlasting righteousness? Have the vision and prophecy been sealed up? Has the most Holy been anointed? Since the answer to these questions is obviously no, then the prophecy has not yet been fulfilled. Since Israel as a nation and the city of Jerusalem are a force on the world scene today, it is evident that God is still with them and will in His time bring to fulfillment the promises of this prophecy. There is a gap in the prophecy to allow this to happen.

Verses 25-26

"Know therefore and understand, that from the going forth of the commandment to restore and to build Jerusalem unto the Messiah the Prince shall be seven weeks, and threescore and two weeks: the street shall be built again, and the wall, even in troublous times. And after threescore and two weeks shall Messiah be cut off, but not for himself: and the people of the prince that shall come shall destroy the city and the sanctuary; and the end thereof shall be with a flood, and unto the end of the war desolations are determined."

According to the prophecy, Messiah is cut off (crucified) after sixty-nine weeks or 483 years. The New Testament reveals what took place during the ministry of Messiah, the Lord Jesus Christ. He offered himself to Israel as their king in fulfillment of Zechariah 9:9: "Rejoice greatly, O daughter of Zion; shout, O daughter of Jerusalem: behold, thy King cometh unto thee: he is just, and having salvation; lowly, and riding upon an ass, and upon a colt the foal of an ass."

In response to Jesus' ministry as their Messiah, the elders consistently rejected Him and tried to turn the people against Him. They eventually succeeded in having Him crucified. As a result of their rejection of Jesus, He pronounced judgment upon the city of Jerusalem and the people (not exactly what the promises in Daniel 9:24 call for):

> O Jerusalem, Jerusalem, thou that killest the prophets, and stonest them which are sent unto thee. . . . Behold, your house is left unto you desolate (Matthew 23:37-38).

> And when he was come near, he beheld the city, and wept over it, saying, If thou hadst known, even thou, at least in this thy day, the things which belong unto thy peace! but now they are hid from thine eyes. For the days shall come upon thee, that thine enemies shall cast a trench about thee, and compass thee round, and keep thee in on every side, and shall lay thee even with the ground, and thy children within thee; and they shall not leave in thee one stone upon another; because thou knewest not the time of thy visitation (Luke 19:41-44).

What belonged "unto thy peace" (verse 42)? It had to include the promises of Daniel 9:24. "But now they are hid from thine eyes." The promises of the prophecy will not be completely fulfilled until the Lord returns to earth. The implication is that Israel will one day be blessed. It will happen when He returns the second time.

They did not know the time of their visitation by the Lord, but He will visit them again, and they will receive Him. The Book of Romans gives understanding on this truth:

> What then? Israel hath not obtained that which he seeketh for; but the election hath obtained it, and the

> rest were blinded (according as it is written, God hath given them the spirit of slumber, eyes that they should not see, and ears that they should not hear;) unto this day. . . . I say then, Have they stumbled that they should fall? God forbid: but rather through their fall salvation is come unto the Gentiles, for to provoke them to jealousy. Now if the fall of them be the riches of the world, and the diminishing of them the riches of the Gentiles; how much more their fulness? (Romans 11:7-8, 11-12).

The Jews who fully believed on the Lord Jesus Christ on the Day of Pentecost and all those after who believed became members of the church. And the door was opened for Gentiles who believed to become members of the church, so that Jew and Gentile make up one body (Ephesians 2:11-22; I Corinthians 12:13). This does not do away with God's plan for Israel as a nation blessed with the promises of God in the coming kingdom age (Romans 11:25-29).

Because of their rejection of Messiah at His first coming, the nation of Israel has been set aside, but not forever. The last question the disciples asked Jesus before He ascended was, "Wilt thou at this time restore again the kingdom to Israel?" He said, "It is not for you to know the times or the seasons which the Father has put in His own power" (Acts 1:6-7). What He did not say was, "Sorry, there isn't going to be any kingdom for Israel." In fact He had told them that when He came to sit upon the throne of His glory (Matthew 25:31), which is the throne of the kingdom age, they would sit upon twelve thrones judging the twelve tribes of Israel (Matthew 19:28).

The disciples came to realize that God was visiting the Gentiles to take out of them a people for His name and that He would return again to set up the tabernacle of David (Israel) that had fallen down (Acts 15:14-16). God, by divine foreknowledge, cognizant that Israel would reject the Messiah, ordained the church age, thus opening the door of salvation to believing Gentiles and believing Jews, who make up one body in Christ. They will be raptured and will return with Christ in their glorified bodies when He returns to set up His earthly kingdom (Revelation 20:1-6). The church age is the major reason for the gap in the prophecy.

Romans 11:25 says, "For I would not, brethren, that ye should be ignorant of this mystery, lest ye should be wise in your own conceits; that blindness in part is happened to Israel, until the fulness [full measure] of the Gentiles be come in." Blindness comes from the Greek *porosis*, primarily meaning "a covering with a callus," "a hardening," "hardness." It is metaphorical of a dulled spiritual perception.

Preterists think that verse 25 teaches that God is through with Israel and that the promises to Israel in the Old Testament are being fulfilled in the church and that there will be no future kingdom on this earth in which Jesus Christ rules over Israel and the world. This is incorrect, for Scripture reveals that the blindness to Israel is partial so that any Jew who sincerely seeks after the Lord can be saved, but someday it will be removed from all of Israel, but not before the church is completed. Romans 11:26-33 says:

> And so all Israel shall be saved: as it is written, There shall come out of Sion the Deliverer, and shall

> turn away ungodliness from Jacob: for this is my covenant unto them, when I shall take away their sins. As concerning the gospel, they are enemies for your sakes: but as touching the election, they are beloved for the fathers' sakes. For the gifts and calling of God are without repentance. For as ye in times past have not believed God, yet have now obtained mercy through their unbelief: even so have these also now not believed, that through your mercy they also may obtain mercy. For God hath concluded them all in unbelief, that he might have mercy upon all. O the depth of the riches both of the wisdom and knowledge of God! how unsearchable are his judgments, and his ways past finding out!

God will keep His promises to the "house of Israel," just as He is keeping and will continue to keep the New Testament promises to His church.

The rejection and crucifixion of Jesus as Messiah and promised King of Israel was disastrous for the people of Israel and the holy city. It ultimately led to the destruction of the city and the scattering of the people among the nations of the world. The rejection of Messiah the Prince ends the sixty-ninth week. But there is still one week left.

Verse 26

"And after threescore and two weeks shall Messiah be cut off, but not for himself: and the people of the prince that shall come shall destroy the city and the sanctuary; and the end thereof shall be with a flood, and unto the end of the war desolations are determined."

This statement constitutes a gap in the prophecy. History reveals that in A.D. 70 the Romans came and did exactly what this prophecy said and what Jesus had said before He was crucified. The major importance of this statement is that it reveals there will be another prince that will present himself to Israel. He will come from the Roman system at some time in the future.

Preterists, however, say that "the people of the prince" referred to in verse 26 are the Roman armies that would come in A.D. 70 to destroy Jerusalem and are actually the people of Messiah the Prince, the Lord Jesus Christ, rather than the people of a coming prince. They then assert that the "he" of verse 27 is Messiah the Prince and not a coming prince from a Roman system. This cannot be correct. First, Jesus told his fellow Jews that their enemies were going to destroy them (Luke 19:43), not that He was going to be responsible for it. Second, if verse 27 refers to the Messiah, then the prophecy could not be fulfilled, because as previously shown, Messiah was rejected and only judgment awaited the people and city of Jerusalem.

Verse 27

"And he shall confirm the covenant with many for one week: and in the midst of the week he shall cause the sacrifice and the oblation to cease, and for the overspreading of abominations he shall make it desolate, even until the consummation, and that determined shall be poured upon the desolate."

Verse 27 deals with the seventieth week. The death of the Messiah caused the sacrifices to cease in the lives of those who accepted Him, but in reality the sacrifices continued until A.D. 70 when the city and the Temple were destroyed.

Since Israel rejected Messiah, their true Prince, God is going to let them and the whole world be deceived into accepting a false prince, the coming Antichrist (Revelation 13:3). For this to happen, it was necessary for Israel to become a nation again and for Jerusalem to be restored. On May 14, 1948, after 1,878 years, Israel again became a nation. Today Israel is a viable nation among the nations of the world, capable of making covenants with other people and nations. Israel is not well received by many nations, the United States being its main supporter. And significantly, among the religious community in Israel, there is a desire to see the Temple rebuilt and sacrificial offerings reinstituted. The people continue to abide in unbelief concerning the Lord Jesus Christ. The spiritual blindness is still upon them, and therefore they are open to Satan's deception when his man, the Antichrist, comes on the scene.

When the Antichrist comes, he will make some kind of seven-year (one-week) covenant with Israel. It will possibly have something to do with rebuilding the Temple. The sacrifices will begin for the first time since A.D. 70. After three and a half years, the Antichrist will cause the sacrifices to stop. He or an image of him will be set up in the Temple, and he will command all to worship him. Jesus warned of this: "When ye therefore shall see the abomination of desolation, spoken of by Daniel the prophet, stand in the holy place, (whoso readeth, let him understand:) then let them which be in Judea flee into the mountains" (Matthew 24:15-16).

Another translation may give more insight on this: "He will confirm a covenant with many for one 'seven.' In the middle of the 'seven' he will put an end to sacrifice and offering. And on a wing [of the temple] he will set up an abomination that causes desolation, until the end that is decreed is poured out on him" (Daniel 9:27, NIV).

The apostle Paul added, "Let no man deceive you by any means: for that day shall not come, except there come a falling away first, and that man of sin be revealed, the son of perdition; who opposeth and exalteth himself above all that is called God, or that is worshipped; so that he as God sitteth in the temple of God, shewing himself that he is God" (II Thessalonians 2:3-4).

The Seventieth Week in the Book of Revelation

In the Book of Revelation, the seventieth week is clearly divided into two segments of three and a half years each. For the first three and a half years, the Jews are allowed to offer their sacrifices and offerings. But then they are stopped, and trouble begins for Israel. In Revelation we read: "But the court which is without the temple leave out, and measure it not; for it is given unto the Gentiles: and the holy city shall they tread under foot forty and two months" (Revelation 11:2). Forty-two months is the same as three and a half years, based on a prophetic year in the Bible of 360 days.

The important thing to realize is that the Book of Revelation was written many years after the first coming of Jesus. Yet it uses the same time frame as the seventieth week of Daniel's prophecy. In Revelation, John wrote about things in the future from his day. Thus there is a gap in the prophecy between the sixty-ninth and seventieth week. The seventieth week is yet to be fulfilled. Preterists try to get around this by saying this does not refer to the seventy-week prophecy. But it does because it is a part of the actions of the Antichrist against Israel. And it fits the time frame of one week or seven years as found in the seventy-week prophecy. It is talking about the "prince that shall come" and his dealings with Israel.

"And I will give power unto my two witnesses, and they shall prophesy a thousand two hundred and threescore days, clothed in sackcloth" (Revelation 11:3). The witnesses are in Jerusalem and are slain by the Antichrist. "And when they shall have finished their testimony, the beast that ascendeth out of the bottomless pit shall make war against them, and shall overcome them, and kill them" (Revelation 11:7).

"A thousand two hundred and threescore days" (1,260 days) is the same as three and a half years. So in this one passage of Revelation that is dealing with Israel and the Antichrist are found forty-two months and 1,260 days. These add up to seven years.

One method used by preterists to deny that these numbers refer to the seventieth week is to say the days actually symbolize years. For example they say the 1,260 days are really years and then apply them to historical events such as the length of the so-called Dark Ages. There is no justification for such an interpretation. If the numbers do not have literal meaning in the passage of Scripture where they are given, then how can changing them and applying them to something else have literal meaning?

Daniel had no problem believing in the literal numbers given by Jeremiah concerning the length of the

Babylonian captivity, and it caused him to seek the Lord when he realized the time was near. "In the first year of his reign I Daniel understood by books the number of the years, whereof the word of the LORD came to Jeremiah the prophet, that he would accomplish seventy years in the desolations of Jerusalem" (Daniel 9:2).

The seventy-week prophecy will end when Jesus Christ returns to earth at His second coming. It is then that the Beast (Antichrist, prince to come) will be destroyed. "And I saw the beast, and the kings of the earth, and their armies, gathered together to make war against him that sat on the horse, and against his army. And the beast was taken, and with him the false prophet that wrought miracles before him, with which he deceived them that had received the mark of the beast, and them that worshipped his image. These both were cast alive into a lake of fire burning with brimstone" (Revelation 19:19-20).

The location of the Second Coming will be the land of Israel. In fact the Lord will return to the Mount of Olives from which He departed when He ascended.

> Behold, the day of the LORD cometh, and thy spoil shall be divided in the midst of thee. For I will gather all nations against Jerusalem to battle; and the city shall be taken, and the houses rifled, and the women ravished; and half of the city shall go forth into captivity, and the residue of the people shall not be cut off from the city. Then shall the LORD go forth, and fight against those nations, as when he fought in the day of battle. And his feet shall stand in that day upon the mount of Olives, which is before Jerusalem on the

> east, and the mount of Olives shall cleave in the midst thereof toward the east and toward the west. . . . And the LORD shall be king over all the earth: in that day shall there be one LORD, and his name one (Zechariah 14:1-4, 9).

When this passage is fulfilled, then will the six promises of the seventy-week prophecy be fulfilled for Israel and the city of Jerusalem. God keeps His promises. His Word is forever settled in heaven.

Phillip A. Dugas earned an M.A. in exegetical theology from Western Seminary. He taught eschatology for thirteen years at Christian Life College in Stockton, California, and is at present pastor of Abundant Life Church UPC in Portland, Oregon.

8

Refuting Preterism's View of the Seventy Weeks

John T. Larabell

Until recently, all Apostolics have placed the fulfillment of the seventieth week of Daniel's prophecy in the future, understanding that some of the prophecy in Daniel 9:24-27 was fulfilled at Christ's first advent and that some will be fulfilled at His second advent. Some Oneness Pentecostals, however, have recently promoted the partial preterist view of this prophecy. Therefore, Apostolics must ask, Is the partial preterist view of Daniel 9:24-27 scriptural? Using the previous chapter as a foundation for the proper understanding of the seventy weeks of Daniel, we will, in this chapter, closely examine the partial preterist teaching concerning Daniel 9:24-27 and will demonstrate that it is, in fact, unscriptural and should thus be rejected by Apostolics.

"Seventy weeks are determined for your people and for your holy city, to finish the transgression, to make an end of sins, to make reconciliation for iniquity, to bring in everlasting righteousness, to seal up

vision and prophecy, and to anoint the Most Holy" (Daniel 9: 24, NKJV).

The prophetic portion of the ninth chapter of the Book of Daniel begins with the angel Gabriel speaking to Daniel of what is to befall his people, the Jews. Gabriel tells Daniel that "seventy weeks" are determined for the Jews and Jerusalem. These seventy weeks are for a specific purpose; indeed several purposes are mentioned in verse 24. The phrase "seventy weeks" is a Hebraism unfamiliar to English speakers. The Hebrew phrase translated as "seventy weeks" (*shavuim shivim)* literally means "seventy sevens," or "seventy periods of seven." While the Hebrew word *shavua* in the modern usage means "week,"[1] the biblical usage could mean this or more generally a period of seven of something, be it days, years, etc.[2] Attaching the meaning of years to the periods of seven, making them "weeks of years," is the best interpretation. This is so for several reasons, the first of which is that in context it would be almost meaningless if Gabriel were speaking of seventy literal weeks of seven days. In verse 2 of the same chapter, Daniel "understood by the books the number of the years specified by the word of the LORD through Jeremiah the prophet, that He would accomplish seventy years in the desolations of Jerusalem" (NKJV). So the chapter itself is dealing with long periods of years, not with seventy weeks of days, or 490 days. Apart from a few exceptions, most expositors here speak of "year-weeks." They fully realize that if they were to abandon this idea, then the rich messianic prophecy contained in these verses would be lost.[3]

Edward J. Young, however, represents a common

opposition to the idea that the "sevens" are weeks of years. He notes that, if the text were referring to "weeks," then we would expect the feminine plural *shavuot* since the regular word for "week" is feminine. He then points out that what we actually find in the text is the maculine plural *shavuim*. He concludes that we should therefore interpret this simply as periods of "sevens," with no exact length of time indicated.[4] He continues, "Consequently, since these numbers represent periods of time, the length of which is not stated, and since they are thus symbolical, it is not warrantable to seek to discover the precise length of the sevens. This cannot be done, nor, for that matter, can the length of any of the individual sevens be discovered or determined."[5] Young's use of the phrase "and since they are thus symbolical" betrays a certain presupposition to approaching the biblical text. He makes a good point, but seriously jumps the gun when he assumes that the numbers are symbolical just because there is not a clearly stated length of time. Young goes too far with his assumption. Rarely does biblical prophecy work in symbolic, allegorized periods of "a long time," and Daniel especially offers extremely detailed prophecies about future events. To assume that attaching a length of time to the "sevens" cannot be done is far-fetched.

In fact, this concept of "sevens" is common in the narrative world of the Old Testament, and this manner of expressing time was both known and used by the Jews. Leviticus 25, for example, is one place among others that mentions similar ways of indicating time.[6] Kevin J. Conner states that "the Hebrew mind was saturated with the concept of the 'weeks of the Lord' and the whole context of Scripture shows that God indeed was shadowing forth the redemptive week in the patterns of the sevens in Israel."[7] Whether or not we should go as far as Conner does, the fact remains that interpreting the seventy "sevens" as seventy weeks of years is perfectly in line with the Jewish mindset of the time.

Leon Wood makes an interesting observation regarding the seventy weeks:

> Furthermore the seventy-year period of captivity was based on the idea that seventy of these sabbatical years had not been kept. Knowing this, Daniel would have recognized that the seventy years of the captivity represented seventy sevens of years in which these violations had occurred; he would have understood Gabriel to be saying simply that another period, similar in length to that which had made the captivity necessary, was coming in the future experience of the people.[8]

Wood apparently sees the 490 years as almost a mirror of the time covering the seventy "sabbath-years" that Israel neglected before the captivity, with the captivity of seventy literal years as chastisement for the seventy sabbath-years that Israel ignored. This fits well with the idea that God, during the time of the captivity, recognized Israel as "not My people" (*lo-ammi*), and when speaking to Daniel, Gabriel refers to the Jews as "your people" and to Jerusalem as "your holy city."[9] This prophecy is intended, then, to deal with the future plans that God has for the Jewish people and Jerusalem. The seventy weeks are said to be "determined" for Daniel's people and his holy city. The verb translated "determined" or "decreed" in many translations is *nechtak*, which means "divide" or "determine."[10] This seems to carry the sense that the seventy weeks are divided out and set in place for the future of the Jewish people.

Gabriel proceeds to tell Daniel the purpose of these seventy weeks: Within 490 years six things will be effected upon the Jewish people and Jerusalem. According to Wood, they can be divided into two groups: The first three are negative in force, speaking of undesirable matters to be removed; and the last three are positive, giving desirable factors to be effected.[11]

The first purpose mentioned in verse 25 is "to finish the transgression." Based on the context of the passage, this is most likely referring to Israel's rebellion against God. Again, the prophecy is concerning the Jews and Jerusalem, so the transgression is that of the Jews. The placing of the definite article before the word "transgression"[12] seems to make the sentence refer to a particular transgression committed by the Jews, and not the transgressions of humanity in general. Robert Culver notes that *lekale*, translated "to finish," has no connection with atonement, but rather to restrain or cause to cease.[13] He thinks that an "age of obedience will be ushered in" among the Jews and that this verse is not speaking of the sin problem of humanity.[14] This may not be the best conclusion, however, since this "age of obedience" for the Jews only is not mentioned elsewhere in Scripture.

The second purpose mentioned is "to make an end of sins." Though English translations often read "and to make an end of," the Hebrew text actually reads "and to seal up."[15] While "to finish the transgression" probably refers to the transgression of the Jews, this phrase likely refers to Christ's sacrifice on Calvary to deal with the sin problem of humanity. This would fit in the context of the prophecy since Jesus was the Jewish Messiah who wept and died in Jerusalem.

The third purpose mentioned is "to make reconciliation for iniquity." While partial preterists rightly state that Christ is the one who makes reconciliation for iniquity, some go astray when attempting to refute a futurist interpretation of the seventy weeks.[16] Their view is in error here when it assumes that the futurist interpretation insists that the "reconciliation for iniquity" will take place during the future seventieth week. On the contrary, futurists typically hold that Christ is the one who effects the reconciliation at Calvary. Furthermore, an Apostolic futurist position does not believe that God will reinstitute animal sacrifices to atone for iniquity during the seventieth week. An Apostolic position holds to an "already/not yet" view of eschatology, with some portions of verse 24 as already fulfilled, and portions to be fulfilled in the future.

The fourth purpose mentioned is "to bring in everlasting righteousness." One partial preterist has attempted to exegete this phrase by defining *righteousness* using the 1828 edition of *Webster's Dictionary*.[17] It is odd that he would cite *Webster's Dictionary* as an authoritative source on this matter since *Webster's* obviously cannot give authoritative definitions of words in the Hebrew text. An appeal to *Webster's* only undercuts the legitimacy of his position. The author also states here that only one who is filled with the Holy Spirit could live up to *Webster's* definition of righteousness. Basing the interpretation of a biblical prophecy on a definition in *Webster's* is a hermeneutical disaster waiting to happen.

A futurist interpretation sees "everlasting righteousness" as being partially fulfilled at Calvary, but only completely fulfilled after the second advent of Christ that ushers in the Millennium. The beginning of "everlasting righteousness" occurred when the new covenant was put into effect by Christ's sacrifice on Calvary, but it will not be fully realized until the Millennium when Christ sets up His rule on this earth.

The fifth purpose mentioned is "to seal up vision and prophecy." The interpretation of this purpose is the subject of much debate. According to some partial preterists, this phrase has a dual meaning: one being the fulfillment of messianic prophecies and the other being a "blindness" that was put on Israel in judgment (hence the "sealing up of vision").[18] The first interpretation is acceptable. To say that this concerns Jesus' coming and the fulfillment of the seventy weeks is likely what this phrase refers to. While a preterist would attempt to explain this portion of the prophecy as being totally fulfilled by A.D. 70, a futurist would, again, place part of the fulfillment at Calvary with Jesus' first advent and part at His second advent. This follows the "already/not yet" theme woven throughout the New Testament. The second interpretation, however, is unacceptable. It is unlikely that Israel's blindness and judgment are the subject of any of this prophecy, and the culmination of this prophecy is not a "coming in judgment."

The last purpose mentioned is "to anoint the Most Holy." It, too, is difficult to interpret and subject to much debate. The Hebrew *qodesh qodashim* literally means

"Holy of Holies." There is no definite article, which leads the NRSV to translate the phrase as "a most holy place." This or "a holy of holies" is probably the best translation of the two words since this term is never used of people but always of the Temple. Some partial preterists attack the dispensationalist and futurist view of this phrase, boldly asserting that it cannot refer to the Holy of Holies in a third Jewish Temple.[19]

Dispensationalists and futurists do claim that the Holy of Holies refers to a Third Temple. This Temple is prophesied of in the Book of Ezekiel. However, contrary to what some partial preterists insist is a dispensational belief, most dispensationalists do not believe this future Temple will be a place where the Mosaic law is reinstated as a means of salvation. The Third Temple will be a place from which Christ will reign in Jerusalem. Any sacrifices that will be offered there will most likely be simply a memorial to Christ's work on Calvary. Ezekiel's Temple is different from the Temples built under the Mosaic law, and the ministry of the priests therein was different from their ministry in the law. The allotment of land for the twelve tribes and the wide river flowing to the sea all depict a peaceful state of Israel during the Millennium. (See Ezekiel 47-48.) We must remember that this Temple was never built and that this scene of the city and the condition of the restored Israel has never been seen. Partial preterists often go further in their assertion of the identity of this "Holy of Holies," saying that this phrase refers to Jesus Christ.[20] Here the partial preterists make another interpretive error. They appear to translate the phrase *velimshoach qodesh qodashim* as "and to anoint the most high." This is an erroneous translation of the

Hebrew phrase, which should be translated as "and to anoint a Holy of Holies." This Hebraism, "Holy of Holies," is always used (with a definite article) to refer to the Holy of Holies in the Temple; it is never used to refer to a man. Translating it as "most high" is unacceptable.

Partial preterists often attempt to conclude their discussion of verse 24 by stating that all of the six items listed were to be fulfilled in the seventieth week.[21] Although preterists are correct when they assert that none of the six points of verse 24 was fulfilled during the first sixty-nine weeks and that they must all be fulfilled during the seventieth week, the seventieth week is clearly set apart as a separate week in which the Messiah will fulfill all six points—but He was not cut off in the midst of the week. A preterist interpretation needs to see the Messiah being cut off in the middle of the week in order for that particular view of prophecy to work. If all of these things were accomplished in sixty-nine-and-a-half weeks, then what is the purpose for Gabriel telling Daniel that seventy weeks are determined for the Jews and Jerusalem? This brings into discussion the whole issue of the "gap" between the sixty-ninth and seventieth weeks. Some partial preterists almost begin to delve into conspiracy theory when criticizing dispensationalism, claiming that this position was set in place in order to deceive the church, since it allegedly introduces seven more years of obedience to the Mosaic law.[22]

To say that dispensationalism with a "gap theory" was put in place in an effort to deceive the church and to create seven more years of law keeping has absolutely no ground in fact. There is not a shred of evidence supporting this claim. To make this claim and then label this teaching

"Dispensational Theology" is again out of line. Few, if any, dispensationalists believe that God will reinstitute seven more years of the Mosaic law as efficacious for salvation. As far as can be ascertained, Apostolics who are dispensationalists do not believe this. There will be an attempt by the Jews to return to sacrifices in the restored Temple according to a dispensationalist position, but this is not the same as God restoring the validity of these sacrifices as a means of salvation. Some preterists go even further to make more accusations, saying that the Rapture, the Tribulation, and the Antichrist were created by dispensationalists in order to give their teaching of a return to the Mosaic law credibility.[23] Here again, preterists miss the point and create a straw man named Dispensationalism. While some dispensationalists somewhere may think that God is going to change covenants and re-establish "law keeping," they are in the minority. Dispensationalists will say that the Antichrist will make a covenant with the Jews (this is not the same as God making a new covenant plan with humanity) and that the Jews will begin once again to offer sacrifices since they believe the Mosaic law never ended in the first place. This does not mean that these sacrifices will be "acceptable" to God. The law of Moses was never intended to serve as a means of salvation, and it never will. Preterists are correct when they assert that the New Testament does not mention any return to the law for salvation; futurists wholeheartedly agree.

"Know therefore and understand, that from the going forth of the command to restore and build Jerusalem until Messiah the Prince, there shall be seven weeks and sixty-two weeks; the street shall be

built again, and the wall, even in troublesome times" (Daniel 9:25, NKJV).

Here it is evident that the first sixty-nine weeks were to be completed before Messiah the Prince came on the scene. The weeks would start with a command to rebuild Jerusalem and would culminate at or before the coming of an anointed ruler. The timing of this command and the identity of the anointed prince is of key importance to the interpretation of this verse. A conservative futurist view would contend that the prince is the Messiah, Jesus Christ. However, taking more of a historicist slant, Donald Gowan notes that *nagid* ("prince" or "ruler") is used in reference to Temple officials in I and II Chronicles and Nehemiah, and he thinks it refers to the high priest Joshua, or Jeshua, (Ezra 3; Haggai 1:12; 2:2; Zechariah 3) as the "Anointed Prince" of verse 25.[24] C. L. Seow concurs with this view, holding to what appears to be a historicist view of the seventy weeks.[25] Seow exegetes this verse by using the New Revised Standard Version (NRSV), which contains a reading that appears to support his view. The NRSV reads, "Until the time of an anointed prince, there shall be seven weeks; and for sixty-two weeks it shall be built again with streets and moat, but in a troubled time." This places the coming of "an anointed prince" after only forty-nine years (more or less, since the times are merely symbolic in this view); then after the sixty-two weeks, the city is rebuilt. The placement of the semicolon in the NRSV shows the translators' acceptance of the Masoretic punctuation of the verse. The presence of an *atnach* (similar in function to a comma or semicolon) with "seven weeks" shows that the Masoretes divided the verse here. However, one must remember that punctuation marks were not a part of the original Hebrew text and were placed centuries later only where scribes perceived them to belong.[26] This was likely an attempt by Jewish scribes in the Middle Ages to rid the verse of an incredibly accurate messianic prophecy pointing to Jesus Christ. In their view, this was not "changing the text" per se, as long as the original consonantal text was left intact. The reading followed by many other translations that keeps the seven weeks and sixty-two weeks together is the preferred reading.

The question when the command to restore Jerusalem was given is up for much debate. According to Culver, "An examination of the evidence leads to the conclusion that only one decree reported in the Old Testament fits the specifications as a 'commandment to restore and to build Jerusalem.' This was the one made by the Persian king Artaxerxes Longimanus (465-423 B.C.) in the year 445 (perhaps 444) B.C. and executed by Nehemiah."[27] No indication of how long this rebuilding took is suggested in the prophecy; the emphasis is on the amount of time between the command and Messiah the Prince. Holding to a 445 B.C. date for the command would place the conclusion of the sixty-nine weeks, or 483 years later, at approximately A.D. 38, which was several years after Christ's crucifixion. These calculations are based on a 365-day year. However, if one uses a 360-day year, which fits with the Jewish lunar calendar, then one gets 476 years. This would place the end of the sixty-nine weeks at approximately A.D. 31, or A.D. 30 if one accounts for the fact that 1 B.C.-A.D.1 is only one year. Using a generally accepted A.D. 30 date for the Crucifixion, the coming of Messiah the Prince could be placed at Jesus' triumphal entry into Jerusalem, just a short time before the Crucifixion. This would be fitting since Daniel's prayer and the prophecy concern not just the Jews, but Jerusalem in particular. The triumphal entry was where Jesus was displayed as a humble ruler who came in the name of the Lord, so to see this as the coming of Messiah the Prince is attractive.

The details concerning the rebuilding of Jerusalem are of secondary importance here, but they certainly do coincide with the events surrounding the rebuilding of the wall in the days of Nehemiah. Many partial preterists believe that the command was given by Cyrus, which does not make a substantial difference in the understanding of the prophecy. However, the fallacies of some partial preterists are more evident when they once again use poor hermeneutics to explain the prophecy. They often read their own prophetic views into the text, jumping to conclusions that are not inherent in the Scriptures themselves. Preterists see the coming of Messiah the Prince as the equivalent of the "confirming of the covenant" spoken of in verse 27, which they say takes place before the "cutting off" of the Messiah in verse 26.[28] They place the "confirming of the covenant" in Jesus' ministry and the "cutting off" in the midst of the seventieth week.

"And after the sixty-two weeks Messiah shall be cut off, but not for Himself; and the people of the prince who is to come shall destroy the city and the sanctuary. The end of it shall be with a flood, and till the end

of the war desolations are determined" (Daniel 9:26, NKJV).

A typical partial preterist claim is that "after" instead of "at" the sixty-two weeks means that the Messiah was "cut off" during the seventieth week. This is said to coincide with Jesus dying after three and a half years of ministry.[29] To say that "after" automatically necessitates that the cutting off of the Messiah would take place during the seventieth week is a grammatical fallacy. The word translated "after" is *aharey*. As used in this verse, this word does not necessarily imply that the "cutting off" will take place a certain time period after the close of the sixty-nine weeks. It could just as well mean something like "when the sixty-nine weeks are completed."[30] As Wood points out, "Nothing is said as to how long after."[31]

The phrase translated "and not for Himself" in the NKJV is alternately translated as "and will have nothing" in other versions. Literally translated, the Hebrew means something like "and there will not be to Him/for Him." A very literal rendering would favor some of the newer translations, but the translation in the NKJV and other older translations is an acceptable idiomatic rendering of this phrase. This would then indicate that the Messiah would either be "cut off" (killed) for others or that He would be destitute at His death; either one fits Jesus' crucifixion, but the more idiomatic rendering is arguably a better fit.

A certain partial preterist offers a unique viewpoint on the identity of the "prince who is to come" in verse 26, but relies on an obscure and inappropriate source. He notes that in the 1611 edition of the King James Version, the letter "p" in the word "Prince" is capitalized in verse 26, meaning that it refers to Jesus.[32] This is interesting since preterists will also say that this destruction of Jerusalem and the Temple mentioned in verse 26 was carried out by Roman armies in A.D. 70. Saying the "prince who is to come" is Jesus would confuse their own teaching. In either case, this is another example of hermeneutical error. Hebrew letters do not have upper-case or lower-case forms. The translators understood this prince to refer to Jesus, and so they capitalized the word to make this clear. Just because the translators decided to do this does not guarantee that they interpreted correctly. Though we may agree with the translators, we cannot decide interpretive issues on whether or not the translators capitalized a word. His argument should be dismissed as irrelevant.

"Then he shall confirm a covenant with many for one week; but in the middle of the week he shall bring an end to sacrifice and offering. And on the wing of abominations shall be one who makes desolate, even until the consummation, which is determined, is poured out on the desolate" (Daniel 9:27, NKJV).

A futurist interpretation of this verse would identify the "he" that is confirming the covenant as the future Antichrist. The pronoun "he" would have as its logical antecedent the one described in verse 26 as the "prince who is to come." It is possible, though unlikely, that this could be referring to the Messiah from verse 25 and the beginning of verse 26. However, the context of this verse rules out this possibility. If the Messiah was to confirm a covenant with many for one week, what does this mean? If this was Jesus "confirming" the new covenant with His death on the cross, then in what way was it only for one week? If this was the Messiah bringing in the new covenant that would lead to "everlasting righteousness" as outlined in verse 24, then what does "for one week" mean? And in what way would the Messiah's people, the Jews, destroy Jerusalem and the Temple?

A common preterist answer to these questions is that this verse does not really say the covenant will be a seven-year covenant, only that the confirming will take place during the final week.[33] So in this view, "he shall confirm the covenant with many for one week" does not say the covenant will be seven years long, but it is pertaining to the one remaining week of the seventy weeks. This explanation is really the only way preterists can deal with the opening phrase of verse 27. To say that to confirm a covenant "for one week" does not really mean "for one week" is farfetched, but it is the only way to make this an everlasting covenant fulfilled by Jesus. Contrary to what partial preterists will say, an examination of the Hebrew grammar in this phrase really says nothing to imply anything other than the "making strong" of a one-week covenant. This does mean that the covenant was to be just seven years long. This was a covenant made "with many," presumably with the Jewish people, but possibly recognized by Gentiles as well. The new covenant that Jesus ushered in at Calvary simply does not fit this "one-week" description. This "he" therefore is not a reference to the Messiah spoken of in verse 25.

The identity of the "abomination" in verse 27 is another important issue for partial preterists since in their teaching this event must have taken place in A.D. 70. This has led to some interesting attempts to identify this abomination. A number of partial preterists like to use a reference by Josephus to a certain John Levi of Gischala, an apostate Jew who secretly collaborated with the Romans in order to take control of the Temple, but who was later killed by the Romans because he would not leave the Temple.[34] This, they claim, fits very well with scriptural descriptions of the abomination. This is, again, reading historical events back into the text that likely have nothing to do with the prophecy. Strangely, many partial preterists appeal to the works of Josephus at length as authoritative history while shunning other historical sources as corrupt and untrustworthy.[35] Saying that all of these prophecies (Daniel 9:27; Matthew 24:15; II Thessalonians 2:3-9) were fulfilled in a Jewish collaborator with the Romans is incredible, but it is the only way preterists can make these verses refer to someone other than the future Antichrist. These verses of Scripture are not "easily seen as being fulfilled" by John Levi of Gischala and can be used to refer to the future Antichrist. At least one partial preterist offers another interesting opinion pertaining to the abomination of verse 27, referencing a marginal note in the original 1611 edition of the King James Version.[36] This marginal note reportedly gives "with the abominable armies" as an alternative rendering of "and for the overspreading of abominations." This is said to somehow refer to the A.D. 70 destruction of Jerusalem. Here is another example of using an obscure reference to "prove" a theological point. He holds the translators of the King James Version to be scholars of such high repute that their theological views are authoritative and even their marginal notes can be used to build Bible doctrines. The translators of the King James Version probably understood Latin much better than Hebrew and probably relied heavily on Jerome's Vulgate in their translation of the Old Testament. Furthermore, neither the Hebrew text nor the Septuagint contain any reference whatsoever to "armies." Why the King James translators included this in the marginal notes is up for speculation; regardless, the marginal notes should not be regarded as authoritative proof that Roman armies are what is prophesied of here. Assumptions like this are exactly what make some partial preterists lose credibility.

Another weakness of the preterist view is a failure to deal with the final three and a half weeks of the seventy weeks. For example, if the stopping of the sacrifices was really Jesus' death putting an end to the Mosaic system, then what of the second half of the seventieth week? Rodney Stortz, a preterist, contends that the last three and a half years of the seventieth week were the first three and a half years of the church's existence as it experienced persecution by the Jews. He argues that this corresponds to the prophecy in Revelation 12 of the woman with the man-child being persecuted by the dragon.[37] This reflects another viewpoint within preterism and is even more farfetched and allegorical than the view espoused by most. Stortz says that the woman being harassed by the dragon is the infant church experiencing persecution. If this were correct, then the church gives birth to Christ! To avoid this conclusion, some will state that the woman represents "God's people," which changes from Israel to the church. This way, the woman would have to change identity after Christ is born, and the phrase mentions nothing of a "rejection" of God's plan by the woman and then a changing of her identity (and her persecution of her former self!). Neither scenario works in trying to tie Revelation 12 with the first years of the church and the Great Tribulation. If this view were accepted, then all of the prophecies pertaining to A.D. 70 (according to preterists) would have a double fulfillment or be irrelevant since the seventy weeks were fulfilled three and a half years after the birth of the church.

Verse 27 presents the most variation of interpretations of the seventy-weeks prophecy. A futurist view would assign the "he" in the first sentence to the future Antichrist. However, a preterist view would argue that "he" is referring to Messiah Himself. Wood offers several strong counterpoints to the preterist view that there is no "gap" between the sixty-ninth and seventieth weeks:

> First, the text itself treats the seventieth week separately from the first sixty-nine, suggesting something unique about it, such as that it occurred only after a gap in time. Second, the text further indicates directly that a time-gap of at least forty-three years existed. This number of years elapsed after the close of the sixty-nine weeks, while the crucifixion and destruction of Jerusalem occurred, both of which are mentioned in verse 26 prior to the reference to the seventieth week in verse 27. This fact alone destroys the basic idea of continuity for all seventy weeks. Third, the idea of fitting this seventieth week into the life of Christ is quite impossible, as noted. Neither His life nor His ministry lasted seven years. Sometimes it is noted that His crucifixion came approximately at

> the close of the first half of such a period (three-and-a-half years after the baptism, which is correct) and that the last half could refer to the continuation of His ministry from heaven. But, if so, why stop in that continued ministry after only another three-and-a-half years? Nothing is known to have occurred at that time to support this suggestion. Fourth, the idea of a time-gap should not be thought strange, for it has already been seen in chapters 2, 7, and 8 and will be seen again in chapter 11. The rationale for such a gap is simply that there was a need to speak prophetically of both advents of Christ, and there was no need to describe the history between them, particularly since that history would concern Gentiles primarily, and Gabriel's message concerned Jews (v. 24). Fifth, the message of Gabriel already implied a time-gap, because in verse 24 the six matters specified called for both advents of Christ to fulfill them, as noted. Sixth, in Matthew 24:15 (cf. Mark 13:14), Jesus referred to the "abomination of desolation, spoken of by Daniel the prophet," as something yet future to His time, and, as will be shown presently, Jesus was referring to a feature of this seventieth week which is mentioned here in Daniel 9:27.[38]

Wood's points are convincing and difficult to refute by preterists. The whole issue of the gap is a hot button for preterists, but their arguments really will not stand up since they want to actually divide one of the weeks! At this point the futurist standpoint of placing a division between two of the weeks is more logical that splitting a week up into two pieces.[39]

There are several main facts to consider when interpreting this verse. If the preterist view is to be taken here, there needs to be a bit of "stretching" of the text in order to make this be fulfilled with the Messiah's death. For example, if the covenant referred to here is the new covenant that Christ established, then is the new covenant only a covenant that lasted seven years, or one "week"? Preterists see the "middle of the week" as the Messiah's sacrifice on Calvary, which was the ultimate sacrifice for sins and which puts an end to the validity of animal sacrifices under the Mosaic covenant. While Messiah's death certainly accomplished these things, it is unlikely that verse 26 refers to this.

The "he" that makes the covenant strong in this verse is not referring to the Messiah but to "the prince who is to come." This "prince" will confirm a covenant with "many" people that is to last for seven years, or the seventieth week in Daniel's prophecy. In the middle of this week, or after three and a half years, he will cause the Jewish sacrifices to cease. Saying that the Messiah will "confirm" the covenant at the beginning of His public ministry is highly dubious and appears to be an eisegetical attempt to squeeze the Scriptures into a predetermined mold. A preterist view would have to "back up" the chronology of verses 25 and 26 in order to make the view fit. The Messiah is "cut off," or killed, in verse 26, but then, according to preterists, He confirms a covenant three and a half years before He dies.

Furthermore, preterists say that the destruction of Jerusalem fell within the seventy weeks. However, if the first half of the seventieth week is Jesus' public ministry, which ends with Him being cut off, then how does the rest of that week fit in with the events after the Crucifixion? Where does the latter half of the seventieth week go? Is it thirty-seven years long instead of three and a half? Again, this points out another problem with a preterist interpretation of the seventy weeks. Preterists say that the second half of the seventieth week, or the final three and a half years of the seventy weeks, corresponds to the Great Tribulation of the Book of Revelation. The 1,260 days, or forty-two months, are said to correspond to the three and a half years of the final week in Daniel 9:27. This is referring, in the preterist view, to the war leading up to the destruction of Jerusalem. This actually punches large holes in the preterist argument. For instance, preterists will insist that the seventy weeks are to be taken as a chronological and unbroken chain of 490 years, pointing to what they feel is an absurdity of the futurist view to place a gap between the sixty-ninth and seventieth weeks. However, even a partial-preterist position requires a gap of at least forty years in order to complete the last half of the last week of the prophecy. If the A.D. 70 destruction of Jerusalem is the culmination of the prophecy, then the final three and a half years had to have begun at roughly A.D. 67. This already breaks the "unbroken" 490 years. This inconsistency undermines the preterist interpretation of the seventy weeks. In fact, this is enough to make the entire preterist interpretation of Daniel's seventy weeks fall. Not only is the preterist position inconsistent with Scripture as a whole, it is internally inconsistent. This is certainly troubling considering the tenacity with which some Pentecostal preterists hold to their views.

In conclusion, the partial preterist doctrine is not

hermeneutically sound and should not be regarded as authoritative. There are many attacks in this doctrine on what preterists call "Dispensationalism," but they are readily seen as a straw man erected simply to pit their arguments against. Many of the "proofs" that some preterists use are based on obscure or inappropriate sources, such as the marginal notes of the 1611 edition of the King James Version or the 1828 edition of *Webster's Dictionary.* Partial preterists within the Oneness Pentecostal movement make no scholarly use of the original languages for exegesis; in fact, there is little or no real exegesis of the biblical text. The preterist argument is not scripturally sound regardless of the methods used to present it. The main problem with this viewpoint is that it is inconsistent in its interpretation of Scripture. We have seen that preterism, though arguing against a futurist gap, inserts its own gap in the midst of one of the weeks. Based on the examination of partial preterism set forth here, Oneness Apostolics should reject preterism as unbiblical.

John T. Larabell received a B.A. in Bible & theology with highest honors from Christian Life College, where he studied Hebrew and Greek and taught biblical Hebrew his senior year. He is currently enrolled in the M.Div. program at Urshan Graduate School of Theology.

Notes

[1]Hayim Baltsan, *Webster's New World Hebrew Dictionary: Hebrew/English–English/Hebrew* (New York: Simon & Schuster, 1992), 387.

[2]Francis Brown, R.A. Driver, and Charles A. Briggs, *The New Brown-Driver-Briggs-Gesenius Hebrew-English Lexicon* (Peabody, Mass.: Hendrickson Publishers, 1979), 988.

[3]Harry Bultema, *Commentary on Daniel* (Grand Rapids, MI: Kregel Publications, 1988), 281.

[4]Edward J. Young, *The Messianic Prophecies of Daniel* (Grand Rapids: Eerdmans, 1954), 55-6.

[5]Ibid., 56.

[6]Bultema, *Daniel*, 281. Leviticus 25:1-8 speaks of "sabbaths of years," or periods of seven years. Though this is slightly different than "seventy weeks" of years as found in Daniel, the concept is the same; certainly the ancient Jews were familiar with groupings of years of time, particularly in sevens.

[7]Kevin J. Conner, *The Seventy Weeks of Prophecy* (Blackburn, Victoria, Australia: Acacia Press Pty. Ltd., 1983), 17.

[8]Leon Wood, *Daniel: A Study Guide* (Grand Rapids: Zondervan, 1975), 117.

[9]*ir qodshecha*; literally "the city of your holiness." That this refers to Jerusalem is largely uncontested and seems obvious based on the context. Daniel was praying for the Jews and Jerusalem, and Gabriel's message to Daniel mentions Jerusalem by name (*yerushalayim*) in verse 25. Interestingly the Septuagint (LXX) uses *kai epi ten polin Sion*, "and upon the city Zion," in place of *v'al ir qodshecha*, "and upon your holy city." While the LXX is not a literal rendering of the Hebrew here, this does demonstrate that the translators of the LXX clearly interpreted the text as referring to Jerusalem.

[10]*BDB*, 367.

[11]Leon Wood, *A Commentary on Daniel* (Grand Rapids: Zondervan, 1973), 248.

[12]The word is *hapesha*, "the transgression." This indicates a specific transgression as opposed to using *pesha*, which would mean simply "transgression" in general.

[13]Robert Duncan Culver, *The Histories and Prophecies of Daniel* (Winona Lake, Ind.: BMH Books, 1980), 151.

[14]Ibid.

[15]The difference in translation is based on what Hebrew word actually appears in the text and what word the Masoretic copyists wrote in the margin of the text. So this verse is an example of Kethiv-Qere, with *ulachtom* ("seal

up") being the Kethiv ("what is written") and *ulehatem* ("make an end of") being the Qere ("what is to be read"). This may have been done by the Masoretic copyists for a number of reasons, including grammatical, theological, and esthetic, etc. See Gary D. Pratico and Miles V. Van Pelt, *Basics of Biblical Hebrew: Grammar* (Grand Rapids: Zondervan, 2001), 407-8. This particular Kethiv-Qere may make a difference in the meaning of the text. The Qere pointing indicates that the Masoretes believed the word came from the root *tamam*, meaning "complete, make an end of." According to Wood, numerous Hebrew manuscripts support the Masoretic view, as do the Syriac and Vulgate translations and the Greek translation of Aquila. See Wood's *A Commentary on Daniel*, 249. The word for "sins" is plural in the Kethiv and singular in the Qere, and if the Qere is to be preferred for the verb to which sins is an object, then it makes sense to prefer the Qere here as well. "To make an end of sin" would be following the Qere.

[16]Larry Smith claims that "it is easy to see this point is not referring to a coming 7-year tribulation where the breaking of a covenant by some antichrist causes animal sacrifices to cease, but is instead referring to Jesus Christ's death on Calvary, which satisfied man's payment for sin and offered him a way to walk in close fellowship with God. Jesus' sacrifice stopped animal sacrifices from being acceptable to God, since there is now no scriptural reason for them to ever occur again. His sacrifice also occurred 3½ years into His ministry, which fits perfectly the description of the cutting off in the midst of Daniel's final 70th week (See Daniel 9:27)." Larry Smith, *The 70th Week of Daniel*, (www.rightlydividingtheword.com/articles/70th_week_of_daniel.htm. Web site accessed on 07-19-2005.)

[17]Smith states that "Webster's 1828 dictionary defines righteousness as, 'Purity of heart and rectitude of life; conformity of heart and life to the divine law. Righteousness, as used in Scripture and theology, in which it is chiefly used, is nearly equivalent to holiness, comprehending holy principles and affections of heart, and conformity of life to the divine law. It includes all we call justice, honesty and virtue, with holy affections; in short, it is true religion.' Without being led by the Spirit of Christ, no one would be able to live up to this definition. Webster also described righteousness as, 'The active and passive obedience of Christ, by which the law of God is fulfilled. Daniel 9.' Even Webster connected the work of Christ to Daniel 9, because he also recognized that Jesus was the one who ushered in everlasting righteousness for mankind, and thereby fulfilled this 4th point." Larry Smith, *The 70th Week of Daniel.*

[18]Smith says, "This prophecy seems to carry a two-fold meaning. One interpretation says it fulfills and completes the prophecy concerning Jesus' coming during the time of the 490 years, and was not totally completed until the conclusion of the 70th week. Another interpretation suggests the word

translated 'seal' deals with the blindness that is put on Israel because of their rebellion. This blindness made them unable to see the prophecy fulfillment happening around them. Regardless which of these may be the better interpretation, they both end with judgment coming against Israel coming because of her rejection of the New Covenant." Larry Smith, *The 70th Week of Daniel.*

[19]Smith states, "Dispensationalists claim this refers to a future Jewish Temple. That could not be the case since there is not one scripture that says God will ever again have another physical Temple built, nor is there any that says He will ever again use its sacrificial system. Besides that, God never really wanted a dwelling place built by hands, and will never choose to return to one." Larry Smith, *The 70th Week of Daniel.*

[20]Smith says, "These truths show that this 'anointing of the most high' must be referring to something greater than a building . . . something greater like the most Holy ONE—Jesus. He was the One who was called 'Emmanuel,' which the Bible says is interpreted, 'God with us.' Jesus' coming allowed God's presence to dwell—tabernacle—with man. The anointing of significance that could fulfill this point from Daniel 9:24 happened at Jesus' baptism [. . .] That anointing was the inauguration of Jesus' ministry for it manifested Him as the Messiah of God and ushered in the beginning of Daniel's 70th week. Jesus went from this anointing and began systematically fulfilling all the Messianic signs of Isaiah 61." Larry Smith, *The 70th Week of Daniel.*

[21]Smith writes, "Not one of these six things was fulfilled during the first 69 weeks, so that means they must all be fulfilled during the 70th week. That is why it is set aside as a separate week, because during that the week Messiah would come and fulfill all 6 of these points <u>by being cut off in the midst of the week.</u> This would bring about the Abomination of Desolation which would end in the destruction of the city (Jerusalem) and the sanctuary (Temple). This judgment all took place within the generation after the death of Jesus just as He predicted in Matthew 23 & 24." Larry Smith, *The 70th Week of Daniel.*

[22]Smith has stated that "some in an effort to deceive the Church and create seven more years of law keeping created a 2000-year gap theory and said all these things are yet future and are to be fulfilled when the Lord comes the second time. This teaching is known as Dispensational Theology. This theory began in 1830, and gained popularity in the 1900's by the printing of the Scofield Bible that featured Dispensational footnotes and the writings of Clarence Larkin." Larry Smith, *The 70th Week of Daniel.*

[23]Smith states, "There is never any mention of this so called gap in the Bible, nor to my knowledge, are there any references to it in history before that time. Dispensationalists then placed a rapture in front of this week to give their teaching some type of substance, and then make the seven years a future tribulation period dealing with a covenant of antichrist instead of Jesus Christ. They

make this covenant change when they teach that there will be a future return to law keeping and animal sacrifices for salvation. The scriptures of the New Testament deny that salvation according to the law covenant can ever happen again after Christ came and made one sacrifice for the sins of mankind forever." Larry Smith, *The 70th Week of Daniel.*

[24]Donald E. Gowan, *Daniel* (Nashville: Abingdon Press, 2001), 135.

[25]C.L. Seow, *Daniel* (Louisville, Ky.: Westminster John Knox Press, 2003), 148-49.

[26]Page H. Kelly, *Biblical Hebrew: An Introductory Grammar* (Grand Rapids: Eerdmans, 1992), 16.

[27]Culver, *Histories and Prophecies,* 153.

[28]Smith states, "From the time that Cyrus gave the command to rebuild, until Messiah the Prince was revealed to Israel and began to confirm the New Covenant with them during the final week, would be 483 years. This Messiah the Prince would cause the sacrifice and the oblation (animal sacrifices) to cease in the midst of the week, because his blood, being shed for the sins of Israel, would replace animal sacrifices forever. This would then officially bring in the new covenant, though the actual offering of it did not stop till 70 AD. This Covenant was prophesied in various scriptures in the Old Testament, especially in Jeremiah 31:31-34, and quoted in Hebrews 8:8-13. There the writer of Hebrews described this as being the New Covenant that had replaced the Old Covenant. Clarence Larkin claims in his book Dispensational Truth that this Covenant has nothing to do with the Church, but, he says, it applies only to Israel in the Millennium, the New Heaven, and the New Earth. Larkin's statement is in direct contradiction to those of the Book of Hebrews and to those found in the rest of the New Testament, yet some men still claim that their Dispensational doctrines are biblical truths." Larry Smith, *The 70th Week of Daniel.*

[29]Smith says, "Notice that this does not say "AT" but "AFTER" the 69 weeks that Messiah will be cut off. What is after 69? 70! This shows that this occurrence had to take place during the 70th week. Scriptures and history agree with that for they show that Jesus was crucified after 3½ years of ministry. That would have made Him cut off in the midst of the 70th week." Larry Smith, *The 70th Week of Daniel.*

[30]*Compiler's Note*: Randall Price has pointed out, "The events in verse 26: 'the cutting off of Messiah,' and of 'the people of the prince,' are stated to occur after the sixty-nine weeks. If this was intended to occur in the seventieth week, the text would have read here 'during' or 'in the midst of' (cf. Daniel's use of *hetzi*, 'in the middle of,' verse 27). This language implies that these events precede the seventieth week, but do not immediately follow the sixty-ninth. Therefore, a temporal interval separates the two" (Randall Price,

Prophecy of Daniel 9:27 [San Marcos, Tex.: World of the Bible, n.d.], 22. As quoted in Thomas Ice, *The End Times Controversy*, 334.) That is the reason why the prophecy is divided in seven, then sixty-two, then the final seven. Something of note happens between the sixty-ninth and the seventieth week, but it was not revealed at the time the prophecy was given.

While some people mock the idea that a prophecy's fulfillment could be divided by an unspecified amount of time (a gap), the Lord Himself gave us an example of such a division in Luke 4:16-21: "And he came to Nazareth, where he had been brought up: and, as his custom was, he went into the synagogue on the sabbath day, and stood up for to read. And there was delivered unto him the book of the prophet Esaias. And when he had opened the book, he found the place where it was written, The Spirit of the Lord is upon me, because he hath anointed me to preach the gospel to the poor; he hath sent me to heal the brokenhearted, to preach deliverance to the captives, and recovering of sight to the blind, to set at liberty them that are bruised, to preach the acceptable year of the Lord. And he closed the book, and he gave it again to the minister, and sat down. And the eyes of all them that were in the synagogue were fastened on him. And he began to say unto them, This day is this scripture fulfilled in your ears." Notice that Jesus found a certain place and read. He stopped reading at a specific point and then declared the fulfillment of that passage. What is notable is that He did not finish reading the whole prophecy. In Isaiah we see it goes on: "To proclaim the acceptable year of the LORD, and the day of vengeance of our God" (Isaiah 61:2). The day Jesus read the prophecy only part of it was being fulfilled. There is an unspecified time gap between the "preaching of the gospel to the poor" and "the day of vengeance of our God." That intermission is the period between His first coming and His second coming. (See also Revelation 12 where there is an unspecified interval between verses 5 and 6; also in Zechariah 9:9-10; Hosea 3:4-5; Micah 5:2-3; Amos 9:10-11; Isaiah 54:7.)

[31]Wood, *Daniel*, 255.

[32]"The original 1611 edition of the KJV version of the Bible has capital letter 'P' for the word 'Prince' in verse 26. This would make it a reference to the same Prince as the 'Messiah the Prince' of verse 25, which was a reference to this Prince—the promised Messiah Jesus." Larry Smith, *The 70th Week of Daniel.*

[33]Smith says, "The scriptures do not teach that this covenant is a 7-year covenant. The scriptures say that the prince will confirm the covenant to the Jews for one week, which is showing this will happen during the final week of the 70-week prophecy. The covenant itself could be an everlasting covenant, which is exactly what the scriptures declare it to be. If the scriptures bear this out, then we know the prince in this scripture would be Messiah the

Prince, which was cut off in the midst of the week causing the sacrifice and the oblation (animal sacrifices to no longer be accepted by God) to cease. . . . Notice it says He shall 'CONFIRM THE COVENANT WITH MANY FOR ONE WEEK.' This does not mean that the covenant was just seven years long, but it is dealing with the one week that is left of the 70 weeks in which the Messiah will confirm the covenant with many. This week had to begin with Messiah the prince being anointed at His baptism. This was verse 24's anointing of the most holy. This fulfilled one of the 6 requirements of the 70th week." Larry Smith, *The 70th Week of Daniel.*

[34]Smith writes, "Josephus wrote extensively about an apostate Jew named John Levi of Gischala. John fled to Jerusalem when the city was under Roman siege, and while there he presented himself as a God-sent savior that came to help his people fight against the Roman Armies [. . .] This resistance could have been the resistance that Paul spoke of in 2 Thessalonians 2:3-9. John took over the control of the Temple, set himself up in the Temple as the Jewish savior, looted the vessels of the Temple for their Gold, and caused the daily animal sacrifices to cease. Later Titus asked John to leave the Temple. John flatly refused and his refusal was the very reason why the Temple was razed with the city. Paul's words about a man of sin sitting in the Temple are easily seen as being fulfilled in the above scenarios, and cannot be used to make the prince in Daniel 9:26 & 27 into a future antichrist of our day." Larry Smith, *The 70th Week of Daniel.*

[35]*Compiler's Note:* Their constant appeal to the writings of Josephus turns preterism into a "newspaper eschatology" of sorts. As Thomas Ice has pointed out: "They search first-century 'newspapers' for events that comprise the closest fit to a specific passage and usually cite it as a fulfillment of that passage" (*The End Times Controversy*, 35). This is the more disturbing since preterists are quick to condemn certain futurists who employ those questionable tactics.

[36]"In the margin of Daniel 9:27, the translators of the 1611 edition of the King James Bible added this alternative rendering, 'or with the abominable armies.' This means even the scholars that translated the original 1611 King James Version of the Bible believed Daniel 9:27 referred to an army that would make Jerusalem desolate. Most scholars taught this same doctrine for nearly 1800 years, then the theory of Dispensationalism came along and it became distorted." Larry Smith, *The 70th Week of Daniel.*

[37]Rodney Stortz, *Daniel: The Triumph of God's Kingdom* (Wheaton, Ill.: Crossway Books, 2004), 172-73.

[38]Wood, *Daniel*, 122.

[39]Ibid., 255.

9

The Great Tribulation

William B. Chalfant

"For then shall be great tribulation, such as was not since the beginning of the world to this time, no, nor ever shall be" (Matthew 24:21).

An essential key to understanding the end-time scenario is the correct placement and evaluation of what many call the Great Tribulation. In Daniel 9:24-27, the angel Gabriel revealed to the prophet Daniel that a period of "seventy weeks" had been "determined" upon Daniel's "people" and upon Daniel's "holy city" (Jerusalem). As discussed in the last two chapters, each week actually represents a seven-year period, so the total period the prophecy deals with is 490 years. Moreover, the context of the prophecy proves that it deals exclusively with the Jews, i.e., the nation of Israel.

The seventy weeks are divided up into three segments: seven weeks, sixty-two weeks, and one week. Though preterists claim that the details of the seventieth week (the final seven-year period) were fulfilled in the first century, these details could not have been since the seventieth week immediately precedes the climactic and glorious personal return of the Lord Jesus Christ to reign over the earth. In addition, if Jesus had been crucified in the "midst of the [seventieth] week" as preterists maintain, then this means that the Great Tribulation, along with the abomination of desolation, occurred in approximately A.D. 33-37. This is untenable if one holds that there are no gaps in the seventy weeks as most preterists do. Some preterists attempt to escape this problem by maintaining that the 1,260-day Tribulation period is not even associated with the seventieth week. Other preterists attempt to place the Tribulation in the period of A.D. 66-70, ignoring an approximately thirty-three-year gap between the first half of the seventieth week and the last half of it. The truth is that Jesus was not crucified in the midst of the seventieth week, but rather He suffered at the very close of the sixty-ninth week.

The Abomination of Desolation

Daniel 8-12 conclusively shows that the "abomination of desolation" (*bdelugma tes eremoseos* in the Greek translation of the Old Testament, the Septuagint) initiates the 1,260-day Tribulation. Jesus Himself confirmed this when He referred to the "abomination of desolation, spoken of by Daniel the prophet" in His own description of the Tribulation (Matthew 24:15; Mark 13:14). Matthew and Mark translated Jesus' words into Greek using the same words for "abomination of desolation" that are in the Septuagint version of Daniel. Jesus clearly stated that the Tribulation will begin when the abomination of desolation stands "where it ought not" in the "holy place."

Again, Jesus specifically identified the future Tribulation recorded in Matthew 24 and Mark 13 with the Tribulation spoken about in Daniel 12. Jesus even referred to Daniel 12:1 and 12:11. Daniel 12:1 informs us that the prophesied events of Daniel 12 are indeed contemporary with the prophesied events of Daniel 11:

> But tidings out of the east and out of the north shall trouble him: therefore he shall go forth with great fury to destroy, and utterly to make away many. And he shall plant the tabernacles of his palace between the seas in the glorious holy mountain; yet he shall come to his end, and none shall help him. And at that time shall Michael stand up, the great prince which standeth for the children of thy people: and there shall be a time of trouble, such as never was since there was a nation even to that same time: and at that time thy people shall be delivered, every one that shall be found written in the book (Daniel 11:44-12:1). The phrase "at that time" links Daniel 11 and 12. The "vile person" of Daniel 11:21 is the same evil leader who confirms a "league," or a covenant, in Daniel 11:23. He is the same evil leader who later pollutes the sanctuary with the "abomination that maketh desolate" (Daniel 11:31). He is the same evil leader who is disturbed by "tidings out of the east" and so leaves the "glorious land" (Israel). (Compare with Revelation 9:14-16; 16:12.)

A review of chapters 8-12 of Daniel in the Septuagint will show that Daniel consistently used similar terminology to describe the "abomination" event:

> Yea, [the little horn] magnified himself even to the prince of the host, and by him the daily sacrifice was taken away, and the place of his sanctuary was cast down. And a host was given him against the daily sacrifice by reason of transgression, and it cast down the truth to the ground; and it practised and prospered. Then I heard one saint speaking, and another said unto that certain saint which spake, How long shall be the vision concerning the daily sacrifice, and the transgression of desolation [*hamartia eremoseos*], to give both the sanctuary and the host to be trodden under foot? (Daniel 8:11-13).

Notice in this passage that it is the evil "little horn" who causes the taking away of the "daily sacrifice." The phrase "the transgression of desolation" is very similar to the phrase "the abomination of desolation." It has the same setting. This vision in Daniel 8 is important because this is the vision (Daniel 9:21-23) that the angel Gabriel explains in Daniel 9:24-27. Gabriel says of the "little horn" in the previous vision: "And he shall confirm the covenant with many for one week: and in the midst of the week he shall cause the sacrifice and the oblation to cease, and for the overspreading of abominations he shall make it desolate [*bdelugma ton eremoseon*], even until the consummation, and that determined shall be poured upon the desolate" (Daniel 9:27).

It is clear from the context of chapters 8-12 that the prince or leader of Daniel 9:27 who causes the daily sacrifice to cease is the same prince in the vision of Daniel 8 called "the little horn." Moreover, this is the same prince as the "vile person" of Daniel 11:31: "And arms shall stand on his part, and they shall pollute the sanctuary of strength, and shall take away the daily sacrifice, and they shall place the abomination that maketh desolate [*bdelugma ephanismenon*]." Contextually, this individual cannot possibly be the Christ as some preterists and others maintain.

Daniel 12:11 says that these events take place when the Tribulation begins: "And from the time that the daily sacrifice shall be taken away, and the abomination that maketh desolate [*bdelugma eremoseos*] set up, there shall be a thousand two hundred and ninety days."

The Historical Uniqueness of the Tribulation Assures Us It Has Not Yet Occurred

While it is true that the church has gone through over nineteen hundred years of extensive tribulation, it is not the concentrated event of 1,260 days prophesied in the Bible. Gabriel called the specific 1,260-day Tribulation a "time of trouble" that is without historical parallel "since there was a nation" (Daniel 12:1). The angel also indicated that the entire nation of Israel was involved and that this Tribulation would involve the individual angel that is assigned to protect the nation of Israel.

Jesus also confirmed the historical uniqueness of the Tribulation in Matthew 24:21 ("since the beginning of the world to this time, no, nor ever shall be") and in Mark 13:19 ("from the beginning of the creation which God created unto this time, neither shall be").

This historical uniqueness definitely excludes the possibility that the Tribulation occurred during the Jewish revolt of A.D. 66-70, since the loss of life then was obviously far less than later Jewish persecutions, such as the Spanish Inquisition and the atrocities of the Holocaust. While thousands may have been killed in the Jewish revolt, millions were tortured and slain in the Holocaust. They were herded into gas chambers. Lampshades were made out of their flesh. Jews, including women and children, were hunted down all across Europe and methodically destroyed. There is little doubt that Josephus exaggerated the casualties in the first-century Jewish war with Rome. G. A. Williamson, the renowned translator of *The Jewish War*, stated that Josephus "habitually" exaggerated "figures of every sort."[1]

The Time of Jacob's Trouble

Jeremiah also mentioned the Tribulation and actually identified it as "the time of Jacob's trouble":

> And these are the words that the LORD spake concerning Israel and concerning Judah. For thus saith the LORD; We have heard a voice of trembling, of fear, and not of peace. Ask ye now, and see whether a man doth travail with child? wherefore do I see every man with his hands on his loins, as a woman in travail, and all faces are turned into paleness? Alas! for that day is great, so that none is like it: it is even the time of Jacob's trouble; but he shall be saved out of it (Jeremiah 30:4-7).

Interestingly, not only did Jeremiah prophesy that a unique event was coming upon the nation of Israel, but he stated that "[Jacob] shall be saved out of it."

Both Jeremiah and Daniel used the word "trouble"

(Hebrew *tsor*) in describing the Tribulation. Like Jeremiah 30, Daniel 12:1 also prophesies deliverance for the Jews in the Tribulation: "Thy people shall be delivered, every one that shall be found written in the book."

This cannot fit the idea of an A.D. 66-70 Tribulation. Both the Old Testament and the New Testament passages on the Tribulation show that the actual coming of the Lord to personally reign on earth in the glorious Millennium (Revelation 20:1-6) occurs immediately after the Tribulation ends. These passages show that the end times are connected with the Tribulation and the personal return of Jesus to earth. In order to do away with a future Tribulation and to explain Matthew 24:29 and Mark 13:24, some preterists have substituted an A.D. 70 "coming in judgment" for the actual future coming of the Lord.

There is little scriptural support for the preterist idea that much of the prophecy written in the New Testament was given to reflect the end of the previous Mosaic age, which effectively expired at Calvary. Why would the New Testament writers devote so much time to an age and a covenant that had already ceased to exist?

Both the prophets and the Lord Himself connected the Tribulation directly to the Jews and not to the New Testament church. Here are the reasons why we must conclude that Jesus saw the Tribulation as primarily involving the Jews:

1. The Tribulation begins in the nation of the Jews, and only those who are in Judea are told to flee (Matthew 24:16; Mark 13:14).

2. Jesus' command that those who are on their housetops when it comes time to flee Jerusalem should

not take the time to go back down into their houses before fleeing applies most clearly to Jews (Matthew 24:17; Mark 13:15). It is well known that even today the Jews in Israel continue to make their housetops habitable and still have stairs outside on the sides of their houses.

3. Jesus recommended that people should pray that their flight would not be on the Sabbath (Matthew 24:20). The New Testament church does not keep the seventh-day Sabbath as the Jews do.

Luke 21:20-24 Does Not Mention the 1,260-Day Tribulation

The reader may wonder why Luke 21 has not been mentioned thus far in our discussion of the Tribulation. While there are brief references in Luke 17 to tribulation woes, it is important for a number of reasons to stress that the excursus in Luke 21:20-24 does not even refer to the Tribulation as Matthew 24 and Mark 13 do. Luke 21:20-24 rather tells about "the days of vengeance," which pertain to the Roman armies and the resistance fighters during the Jewish revolt of A.D. 66-70. This is crucial to understand.

What is potentially confusing about Luke 21:20-24 is that the immediate context of Luke 21:25-28 describes the cataclysmic events following the Tribulation as seen in Matthew 24 and in Mark 13, but there is an important difference in Luke. Luke 21:25-28 corresponds with Matthew 24:29-31 and Mark 13:24-27, and both of these passages describe the future second coming of Christ, but Luke 21:20-24 refers to the first-century siege of Jerusalem by the Roman armies under Titus.

Preterists link all three passages and proclaim a first-century Jewish Tribulation based on Luke 21:20-24. For example, one preterist writes:

> Luke made the same statement as Matthew concerning the Abomination of Desolation, except he revealed what the Abomination of Desolation was.
>
> Luke 21:20: "And when ye shall see Jerusalem compassed with armies, then know that the desolation thereof is nigh."
>
> This is the same statement as Matthew, except Luke replaced the phrase, "abomination of desolation" with what it actually was, "Jerusalem compassed with armies." If you accept all Scripture as being divinely inspired, then this Scripture needs no further interpretation since it leaves no room for guesswork. Here in Luke, Jesus is clearly saying that the instrument He would use to bring the desolation was the Roman army who would surround Jerusalem in preparation for her destruction.
>
> The Abomination was actually the abominable sins of Israel, which are revealed in Ezekiel chapters 8 and 16. The judgment, however, would be carried out by a heathen army just as God has always done in the past. This is the judgment that was to be brought against those that refused the seal of God.[2]

First of all, while we accept all Scripture as divinely inspired, this interpretation of Luke 21:20 leaves plenty of room for guesswork. None of the references in Daniel, Matthew, or Mark to the abomination of desolation states that the abomination is "armies surrounding Jerusalem." Certainly, the Book of Daniel demonstrates that armies are involved in the Tribulation, but armies should not be confused with the abomination of desolation itself. There is abundant evidence that armies themselves are not the abomination. This is also true of the armies of Rome in the first century.

Jesus said that the abomination of desolation will "stand in the holy place . . . where it ought not." The Roman army located on the outside of the city of Jerusalem besieging it, as preterism proposes from Luke 21:20-24, does not fit Jesus' description.

Nothing is said in any of these passages about the abomination actually being the "abominable sins of Israel," as some preterists propose. No reference is made in any of these passages to Ezekiel 8 or Ezekiel 16.

The following are some of the significant differences between Luke 21:20-24 and the description of the Tribulation in Matthew 24 and Mark 13:

1. Both Matthew 24 and Mark 13 say that the abomination of desolation described in Daniel initiates the Tribulation; whereas Luke 21 says the "days of vengeance" begin when the armies of Rome surround Jerusalem. The appearance of the Roman armies was the signal to flee to the mountains before the entire city was cut off. But for those who will face the Antichrist, or the Beast, in the future, their signal to flee is the abomination of desolation standing in the holy place where it ought not to be. There is a difference between Roman armies standing outside of the holy city and an abomination that can be "set up" (Daniel 12:11) and which stands in a "holy place" where it ought not to be.

The apostle Paul obviously referred to the Beast of

Daniel in II Thessalonians 2:3-4. Paul did not declare this as a personal vision, and so he must have derived this teaching from the Book of Daniel. No other Old Testament prophecy besides that in Daniel reveals that an evil man claiming to be "God" will appear in Jerusalem. Moreover, II Thessalonians 2:8 reveals that this man Paul referred to will be destroyed in the same manner that the Beast will be "destroyed." (Compare Isaiah 11:4 and Revelation 19:20-21 with Daniel 7:11.)

2. Regarding the Jewish war of A.D. 66-70, Jesus warned the Jews in Luke 21:20-24 to flee to the mountains (this would be the typical place of refuge), but He also added, "And let not them that are in the countries enter thereinto" (Luke 21:21). This advice was good in the Jewish war because it was relatively safe at that time to remain dispersed and out of Judea. In the future Tribulation, however, the existing modern technology of tracking satellites, high-tech identification devices, and the ability to swiftly travel from one place to another will mean that, even though the Tribulation is localized in Judea, it will not be safe anywhere in the world, especially if the Beast controls the nations of the world with such technology. Therefore, it is not surprising that Jesus said nothing in Matthew 24 or in Mark 13 about people "in the countries [entering] thereinto." That advice would not help in a future Tribulation where the Beast had power over the nations and Jews worldwide could be hunted down. It would, however, help in the A.D. 66-70 revolt in Judea.

3. Significantly, Jesus used two different words to describe the circumstances of the two different events (the first-century Jewish war and the future Tribulation).

In Luke 21:20-24, Jesus called the first-century Jewish war a time of "great distress" (*anangke*), while he used *thlipsis* for the future Tribulation (Matthew 24:21; Mark 13:19). While there are similar points of meaning in these two words, there are also differences. Since we believe in verbal plenary inspiration, we believe that the word *anangke* in Luke 21:20-24 is purposely referring to a different type of situation than the *thlipsis* of Matthew 24 and Mark 13.

The Romans in the first century did not come with a demonic intention to religiously persecute and exterminate the Jews. Even the preterists, who quote extensively from Josephus, admit that. In fact, if preterists wish to emphasize Josephus's *Jewish War* to support a first-century Tribulation, then they must admit that Josephus made a hero of Titus and the Roman armies. Scarcely demonic! On the other hand, a close examination of the true Tribulation will reveal that the forces of the Antichrist are indeed demonic.

The Beast is demonically inspired and will desire to completely destroy the Jews. Perhaps this is why the Lord used the term *anangke* concerning the first-century Jewish war and used the term *thlipsis* in Matthew 24 and in Mark 13 to describe the demonic pressure of the Beast.

4. Anyone with a Bible that shows the paragraph divisions in the Greek text can see that a new section in the Greek text begins with Luke 21:25. Thus there is a probable break between verse 24 and verse 25, which describes the events immediately following the future Tribulation. The account in Luke is certainly not in the same order as Matthew 24 and Mark 13. It specifically makes no mention of the abomination of desolation and

does not identify the passage as a "tribulation" but rather as "the days of vengeance."

5. Finally, Luke 21:20-24 has a completely different ending than the descriptions of the Tribulation in Matthew 24 and Mark 13. In Luke 21:20-24 the Jews "fall by the edge of the sword" and are carried away captive into all nations. This describes the worldwide dispersion of the Jews by the Romans. This worldwide dispersion basically remained in effect until modern times when the nation of Israel was miraculously reborn in 1948.

In Matthew 24 and Mark 13, there is no mention of any worldwide dispersion of the Jews. The Beast does not attempt to carry the Jews captive "into all nations" but rather seeks to exterminate them. This is completely different from Luke 21:20-24.

The Times of the Gentiles

The worldwide dispersion of the Jews seen in Luke 21:20-24 was to last until "the times of the Gentiles" were fulfilled. The "times of the Gentiles" are described in Daniel 2. This passage in Luke has no reference to the "fulness of the Gentiles" in Romans 11, which speaks of salvation. Rather, the "times of the Gentiles" speaks of the rule of the Gentiles through imperial systems. The golden image of Nebuchadnezzar's dream reveals this. Daniel 2 portrays the coming of the Lord Jesus Christ as the "stone made without hands" smashing the Gentile system or image on its feet. This certainly did not happen in the first century. Thus Luke 21:20-24 cannot refer to the same events as Matthew 24 and Mark 13.

Some preterists[3] maintain that Revelation 11 also speaks of "the times of the Gentiles" and that the forty-two months of the Tribulation represent the "times of the Gentiles" in Luke 21:20-24. This is not the case at all, since it is obvious, from our knowledge of the centuries of the worldwide dispersion of the Jews initiated by the Romans (and the earlier Babylonian diaspora) and from the regathering of the Jews to the modern, reborn nation of Israel, that forty-two months would never suffice to refer to the dispersion of the Jews. Revelation 11 is not connected to Luke 21:20-24.

In order to maintain only a forty-two-month duration for the "times of the Gentiles," preterists separate verse 24 of Luke 21 into two separate activities: (1) the exiling of Jews into all nations by the Romans (the worldwide dispersion) and (2) the treading down of Jerusalem. By dividing up verse 24 like this, they maintain that the treading down of Jerusalem is the forty-two-month treading down of Jerusalem in Revelation 11:2. However, Jesus linked the treading down of Jerusalem with the Jewish rebellion of A.D 66-70 and with the worldwide dispersion in Luke 21:24.

The context of Revelation 11 does not complement the meaning of the excursus in Luke 21. For one thing, Revelation 11 makes the prophesying of the two prophets (two martyrs) concurrent with the "times of the Gentiles." In Daniel 2 (the premier chapter dealing with the rule of the Gentiles over Israel), the "times of the Gentiles" come to an end only with the personal return of the Lord Jesus Christ.

In Revelation 11, the Beast kills the two prophets (martyrs or witnesses). They are publicly resurrected and ascend into heaven (Revelation 11:11-12). Then the kingdoms of the world become the kingdoms of Christ.

This cannot possibly fit the first century and the period of A.D. 66-70. It does, however, fit the idea of a future Tribulation that ends with the actual physical coming of the Lord Jesus Christ and the wrath of God upon the Gentile system of the Beast.

Attempts to make Luke 21:20-24 correspond with the Lord's description of the future Tribulation and to make it describe a first-century Tribulation must fail because of the major differences between this passage and the description of the future Tribulation in Matthew 24 and in Mark 13, as well as elsewhere.

How great will the Tribulation, "the time of Jacob's trouble," be? It will be the most ferocious, deadly assault upon a nation since the history of the world began. Yet it cannot compare in glory to the martyrdom of the saints of the New Testament church through over nineteen hundred years of history, which culminates in a greater martyrdom yet before the catching up of the Bride.

The Church

God did not appoint the New Testament church to wrath: "For God hath not appointed us to wrath, but to obtain salvation by our Lord Jesus Christ" (I Thessalonians 5:9). This is the hope of the church. Paul used the first person plural pronoun "us" to refer to the church. But it is the lot of unbelieving Jews and the world to undergo wrath. The Jews will especially suffer the wrath of the Beast, while the Gentiles who have rejected the grace of salvation will suffer the unmitigated wrath of God along with the Jews in the Tribulation. Paul referred to these people simply as "them" and "they" (the third person plural): "But of the times and the seasons, brethren, ye have no need that I write unto you. For yourselves know perfectly that the day of the Lord so cometh as a thief in the night. For when they shall say, Peace and safety; then sudden destruction cometh upon them, as travail upon a woman with child; and they shall not escape" (I Thessalonians 5:1-3).

Until the Beast is revealed, the Scriptures show that there will be no 1,260-day Tribulation. Although the church may be able to spot the Antichrist well before he reveals himself, the church is not looking for the Antichrist. The church is looking for the imminent return of our Lord Jesus Christ!

The nation of Israel is blinded in part today. Paul prophesied that this national blindness would continue until the "fulness" or "full number" of Gentiles is saved (Romans 11:25-27). Then God will take His Bride off the face of the earth at the Rapture. There will be no ministry of the church on earth. It is then that the saga of the seventy weeks, which is determined upon the Jews and Jerusalem, will next be completed (Daniel 9:24-27). The terrible time of Jacob's trouble will unfold, and the prophesied end-time events will come about just as they have been foretold.

God does rule history, and He never will completely cast away His people (Romans 11:22-29). Our eyes ought to be on Jesus. We should be looking for Him to come. The true Bride will know the Bridegroom.

William B. Chalfant received a B.S. from the University of Kansas. He earned a Th.D. from International Bible Seminary in Plymouth, Florida. In the last twenty-six years, he has written several books on church history and has submitted research papers to

UPCI symposiums. He has taught on eschatology for over fifteen years. He is pastor of Truth Tabernacle UPCI in Leavenworth, Kansas.

Notes

[1]Flavius Josephus, *The Jewish War* (Penguin Classics, 1976), 14.

[2]Larry T. Smith, *The Coming of the Lord, the Last Days, and the End of the World* (El Campo, Tex.: Rightly Dividing the Word, 2000), 55.

[3]Michael Blume asserts this on his Web site and in private emails with the author.

10

Mistaken Identity: Preterism's View of Israel

Ken Gurley

A Tale of Two Cities

> "The harlot Babylon is a contrasting type of the chaste Jerusalem and, in one sense, the whole course of history is essentially a tale of these two great spiritual cities."[1]
>
> —Henry Morris

The most oft mentioned cities in Scripture are Jerusalem and Babylon. These two cities share space early in biblical history. Both are found in Genesis 14 when Abraham defeated the forces of Babylon (Shinar, Babel) and paid tithes to the obscure king/priest of Jerusalem (Salem), who in turn offered the father of the faithful both bread and wine. Jerusalem is the city of peace, first led by Melchisedec, king and priest of righteousness. The city of Babylon means "confusion," and it was founded by Nimrod, the man of war (Genesis 10). The former was God's city; the latter was man's city. The blessing of one was peace; the curse of the other was confusion.

The revived forms of these two cities are seen once again at the end of the Bible. In Revelation 17-18, man's city meets her doom. In Revelation 21, God's city returns as a bride from heaven. What began in Genesis culminates in Revelation.

Yet, the doctrine of preterism would have one believe that Babylon is really Jerusalem—Nimrod's city is now Melchisedec's city. One preterist holds the view that the Babylon mentioned in Revelation 17-18 is actually the ancient city of Jerusalem and that her destruction in A.D. 70 is found in these chapters.[2] A Pentecostal preterist agrees with these assertions: "Babylon is called 'the great city' in the book of Revelation. . . . The great city that has fallen in this judgment is Jerusalem."[3] Through preterism, what began as two separate cities—sixty-six books, 1,189 chapters, 54,387 verses, and 773,692 words later—became one and the same.

These two cities will be revisited shortly, but it may be in order to consider the means preterists employ to cause the two to become one. It begins with an allegorical hermeneutic that permits the plain sense of Scripture to be reinterpreted or spiritualized. In this schema, the simple text of Scripture reveals deeper or hidden meanings.[4] This mystical view permits the substitution of Jerusalem for Babylon and vice versa. According to such a view, a simple term like *holy city* can alternatively refer to Jerusalem, Babylon, or a future eternal state—all in the same book. (See Revelation 11:2; 21:2; 22:19.) Nor is this substitution limited to Jerusalem; preterism substitutes a Roman army for Christ's coming and the church for Israel. Such substitution is rife with mistaken identities.

Replacement Theology

As seen in these examples, this allegorical hermeneutic opens the door to "replacement theology." Replacement theology (a.k.a. transference or substitution theology) is the postmillennial/preterist practice of placing the church in Israel's stead. One preterist labels this practice "supersession," the view that the church has "superseded for all times national Israel as the institution for the administration of divine blessing to the world."[5] To go one step further, he describes the typical preterist and postmillennial thought as believing that the church has become "the Israel of God" (Galatians 6:16), the "seed of Abraham" (Galatians 3:29), "the circumcision" (Philippians 3:3), the "temple of God" (Ephesians 2:19-22).[6] To put it plainly, the church is the historic continuation of Israel to the total exclusion of the former.

According to this line of thinking, the Jewish people are no longer chosen or special to God. They are no different than any other group of people. Since the Day of Pentecost, the term *Israel* more aptly describes the church than the Jewish people or nation. Israel's promises, covenants, and blessings now belong to the church while the curses remain on the Jews due to their rejection of Christ.[7]

So complete was the insertion of the church into the "blessings-only" portion of Israel's covenants that preterists interpret not only the New Testament but the Old Testament in light of this theology. This preterist points out that "Judah and Jerusalem" (Isaiah 2:1) and "Israel and

Judah" (Jeremiah 31:31) all represent the "whole of the people of God."[8]

The substitution of the church for Israel, however, poses some weighty questions for most people. Queries such as:

- When and how did replacement theology come into being?
- What pssages of Scripture are used to support this belief?
- If the church has replaced Israel, is there a future for the Jewish nation?

A thorough treatment of these questions is beyond the scope of this chapter, but perhaps enough material can be given to satisfy readers or at least to point each in the right direction.

The Development of Replacement Theology

While the formulation of preterism is a relatively modern phenomenon, the idea that somehow the church replaced Israel is old—very old. One scholar has observed: "It is probably not true to say that in New Testament days Christians claimed to be Israel, as they were certainly claiming by Justin's day" (ca. 100-165).[9] Justin argued that the prophets foretold that God would reject His own people and accept the Gentiles in their place. Tertullian's (ca. 155-230) writings make it clear that, by the end of the second century, it was commonly assumed that the church had absorbed all of Israel's blessings.[10]

How the church came to this viewpoint is a profitable study, but it is not necessarily painless. A few sentences of background might be of assistance. In the life and ministry of Christ, He clearly taught that His mission was not to destroy the law or the prophets, but to fulfill them (Matthew 5:17-18). In the apostolic age, Christianity was treated as a sect within Judaism alongside the Pharisees, Sadducees, and others. The status quo would not be maintained for long.

The destruction of Jerusalem, the growing number of Gentile Christians, and the treatment Christ and Christians had received from the Jews chilled the relationship between Gentile and Jew. After the Second Jewish Revolt (133-135) was put down by the emperor Hadrian, the emphasis of the church shifted nearly completely from its birthplace in Jerusalem to centers of Gentile power, such as Antioch, Alexandria, and Rome. Such a shift only served to enhance the not-so-subtle anti-Jewish comments from the early Christian theologians.

That the church's thinking was influenced by neo-platonic and gnostic thought is revealed by the many different doctrines encroaching on the church during this time.[11] As the church and Judaism drifted further apart, Rome's persecution of the church began. The Jewish community, however, had license to worship as it pleased. This further exacerbated the animosities between the two groups, which ultimately revealed itself when the church became the official religion of the Roman Empire.

With that background, one might understand but never completely agree with the comments made by the early Christian theologians. A rising genre of treatises targeting the Jews emerged during the late second and third centuries. The titles themselves indicate the nature of the writings: *Against the Jews* (Tertullian), *Expository*

Treatise Against the Jews (Hippolytus), *Three Books of Testimonies Against the Jews* (Cyprian), *Eight Orations Against the Jews* (John Chrysostom), *Tract Against the Jews* (Augustine), and so forth.

A sampling of comments from such writings is both illustrative and disheartening:

- "Had the Jews been cognizant of our future existence, and that we should use these proofs from the Scriptures, they would themselves never have hesitated to burn their own Scriptures, which declare that all other nations will inherit eternal life, but that they who boast themselves as being the house of Jacob are disinherited from the grace of God."[12]
- "Your scriptures, or rather, not yours but ours, for you, though read them, do not catch the spirit of them."[13]
- "I know that many people hold a high regard for the Jews and consider their way of life worthy of respect at the present time. This is why I am hurrying to pull up this fatal notion by the roots. . . . The Jews have no conception of [spiritual] things at all, but living for the lower nature, all agog for the here and now, no better disposed than pigs or goats, they live by the rule of debauchery and inordinate gluttony. Only one thing they understand: to gorge themselves and to get drunk."[14]

What might have been inflammatory rhetoric entrenched itself into policy when Constantine issued several repressive edicts against Judaism in favor of Christianity. The first ecumenical council in Nicea (325), which focused on the Arian controversy, also witnessed a further effort to curtail Judaism (e.g., restriction of the Jewish Sabbath). Anti-Jewish rhetoric and sentiment became increasingly vitriolic and remained such through the Middle Ages. Perfunctory readings of the ante- and post-Nicene writings reveal two patterns of thought regarding the ill treatment of Jews: first, the Jews were responsible for the crucifixion of Christ and as such deserved such poor treatment; second, Israel had been replaced by the church. This replacement theology has existed in some form from the post-apostolic age to the present time.

Perhaps it is a worthy aside to note that Jesus Himself was a Jew and that He wept over them as He prophesied of their coming trials (Luke 19:41). On the cross, Christ prayed that those responsible for His crucifixion might be forgiven (Luke 23:34). Paul, the apostle to the Gentiles, once wished himself accursed that his people might be saved (Romans 9:3-4). If the Jews are to continue to suffer—and some seem to think that they should—then let it not be at the hands of those who live a crucified life and should be known for their love.

One might argue that replacement theology was partly, but not solely, responsible for this bias against the Jews. While the doctrine is problematic, the greater issue is what lies behind its use. Doctrine is not formed in a vacuum. People can fasten onto a certain thought or concept that feeds some preconceived notion or prejudice. That there are people who embrace replacement theology who are not anti-Semitic is accepted. However, when present proponents of "the church as Israel" doctrine begin to utilize materials that are decidedly anti-Semitic (e.g., *The*

Protocols of the Elders of Zion, misrepresentations about the Noachide laws, vague Zionist and freemasonry conspiracies, etc.) one must wonder what spirit motivates the use of this doctrine.

Replacement theology, as old as it is, did not appear until a century after Christ and the birth of the church.[15] At Pentecost, a crowd of Jews responded to Peter's message with heartfelt repentance and acceptance. May this happen again and again!

Scriptures Used to Support Replacement Theology

One of the chief lines of defense in this doctrine is found in Paul's letter to the Galatians. The first passage normally quoted is Galatians 6:16, "And as many as walk according to this rule, peace be on them, and mercy, and upon the Israel of God." Preterists and other proponents of replacement theology use this as the benchmark of replacement orthodoxy. Paul, in their eyes, is calling the church "the Israel of God."

Before this verse is examined, it is worthy to note that the word "Israel" is used around seventy-five times in the New Testament—some thirty times in the Gospels, twenty-one times in Acts, twenty-one times in the Epistles, and three times in Revelation. Outside of this passage in Galatians 6, it is difficult to find a single example where it refers to anything other than national or ethnic Israel. Furthermore, the apostle Paul used the word "Israel" a dozen times in his description of a future for Israel in Romans 9-11. So, whatever Paul meant in Galatians 6 should be compared with how he used the word elsewhere.

Paul was God's chosen messenger to the Gentiles, although it was his practice to preach the gospel to Jews first (Romans 1:16; 2:9-10). Paul categorized people into three groups: Jews, Gentiles, and the church (I Corinthians 10:32). At this juncture, Paul clearly observed the Jewish reality distinct from that of the church.

The other verse normally cited, Galatians 3:28, is the stronghold for all sorts of aberrant doctrines: "There is neither Jew nor Greek, there is neither bond nor free, there is neither male nor female: for ye are all one in Christ Jesus."[16] The preterist argument normally is that all of the distinctions between Jew and Gentile are abolished, thus Israel is no more. A cursory examination, however, of the two other couplets in this verse (i.e., "bond nor free"; "male nor female") does not reveal the loss of distinctions. Of the former, Paul identified some as masters and others as slaves several times in his epistles (Ephesians 6:5, 9; Colossians 3:22; 4:1; I Timothy 6:1-2; Titus 2:9). Of the latter, it is obvious that the distinction between male and female is preserved (Ephesians 5:22-25; Colossians 3:18-19; I Timothy 3:12). In Galatians 2:15, Paul contrasted those who were Jews by birth with Gentiles. Paul's argument in Galatians 3:28 is not one of distinctions, but one of preferences. The gospel was truly for whosoever will, regardless of ethnicity, economic status, or sex. This text fails to provide a basis for replacement theology.

Preterists will often boast that the church is the seed of Abraham and therefore the rightful Israel of God (Galatians 3:6-9, 29). A comparison of this passage with Ephesians 2:11-3:6 clarifies what Paul meant by this statement. It does not mean that Gentiles at conversion become "spiritual Jews"; rather it means that believing Gentiles partake or share in the spiritual blessings originally promised to the Jews.

The phrase "the seed of Abraham" encompasses four ideas in Scripture. First, it refers to all the physical descendants of Abraham, including the descendants of Esau, Ishmael, and Jacob. Second, it refers to the Messiah, who is uniquely the Seed of Abraham (Hebrews 2:16-17). Third, it refers to the church as the spiritual seed of Abraham (Galatians 3:29). Although this spiritual seed of Abraham is never called Israel, it is permitted to partake of many blessings promised to Israel. Fourth, it refers to the remnant of Israel, or Jewish believers (Isaiah 41:8; Romans 9:6-7; Hebrews 2:16). This portion of the spiritual seed could be called "truly Israel"; they are Jewish believers in Christ who are part of ethnic Israel and thus rightly called the "Israel of God."

Of the seventeen times where Paul uses the word "Israel" in his writings, he refers to the historic or eschatological Israel, but never to the church.[17] On occasion, Paul praised the Jews who obeyed the gospel. He contrasted the Jews who believed, "the Israel of God" (Galatians 6:16, also "true Israel," Romans 9:6), with unbelieving Jews, the "Israel after the flesh" (I Corinthians 10:18). Paul recognized within the whole of Israel that there was a subset of believing Jews, the elect remnant (Romans 9:27; Romans 11:5). This believing subset is obviously the "Israel of God." To place this phrase in the context of Galatians where Judaizers attempted to make the Gentile Christians come under the law, Paul praises both those Gentile Christians and the Jewish Christians who refuse to subject themselves to the law.

To put it plainly, *Israel* means Israel. For Israel to be something other than itself, then preconceived notions and anagogic hermeneutics must be applied. A Pentecostal preterist states erroneously that "to believe the church is the Israel of God is to believe Acts 2:38 is the everlasting Covenant."[18] A belief in Acts 2:38 as the message of salvation does not also require one to believe that the church is Israel.

The Future for Israel

In the earlier chapter on the origins and implications of preterism, the future of Israel was mentioned in the following biblical event: After Jesus rose from the dead, He appeared unto His disciples over a period of forty days in which He taught them of the "things pertaining to the kingdom of God" (Acts 1:3). The last question the disciples asked Jesus prior to His ascension was, "Lord, wilt thou at this time restore again the kingdom to Israel?" (Acts 1:6). If the apostles' thinking was in error, Jesus would have used this occasion to correct it. He had on many other occasions. But Jesus merely said that it was not for them to know the times or seasons. To carry forward the argument, when Jesus ascended, two angels told the apostles that Jesus would return as they had seen Him go (Acts 1:11). It is doubtful that the angels had in mind a Roman dust cloud.

Is there a future for Israel? Preterists teach that there is not. Preterists believe that the events in the Olivet Discourse and Daniel's seventieth week were completely fulfilled in A.D. 70.[19] One preterist does not see a future for Israel in the Book of Revelation either: "Revelation's main focus of attention (though not its only point) is this: God will soon judge the first-century Jews for rejecting and crucifying his Son, their Messiah."[20] Another preterist is not so mild in his view of Revelation: "The book of Revelation is nothing more than biblical imagery that describes God's destruction of Jerusalem, His removal of the Old Covenant system from the earth, His full establishment of His New Covenant Kingdom in the Earth, and the unveiling, sealing, and deliverance of His New Covenant people."[21] To make it plain, he says, "The first 19 chapters of the book of Revelation are fulfilled, and the remaining chapters of Revelation are being fulfilled in the church."[22]

However, when Israel is allowed to be Israel, an honest appraisal of the Book of Revelation, the Olivet Discourse, and Daniel's seventieth week no longer permits such a bleak portrayal.[23] Due to space limitations, the Book of Revelation will suffice to answer the question of the future for Israel.

One Pentecostal preterist interprets Revelation by comparing it to Deuteronomy and Leviticus; in the process he unwittingly undermines his own view that God has cast off Israel and has no future plan for her. First, he notes that "the language of the book of Revelation is easier to understand after reading Dueteronomy,"[24] apparently thinking that interpreting Revelation in light of Deuteronomy supports his view. Somehow he has ignored a prominent theme in Deuteronomy that proves that God still has a future plan for Israel: the repeated promise that the entire land of Canaan will one day belong to Israel. Deuteronomy says at least twenty-five times that the land of Canaan is a gift to the people of Israel from God (e.g., 1:20, 25; 2:29; 3:20; 4:40; 5:16). Another writer observes that "sixty-nine times the writer of Deuteronomy repeated the pledge that Israel would one day 'possess' and 'inherit' the land promised to her."[25] At no time in Jewish history has Israel ever occupied all this land (see Deuteronomy 1:7; 11:24), and so the nation of Israel will receive this promise in the future.

Second, he interprets the judgments found in Revelation from the paradigm of Leviticus 26. He first contends that in Leviticus 26 God says that He will punish Israel with four sevenfold judgments for her sins (Leviticus 26:18, 21, 24, 28). He then maintains that there are also four sevenfold judgments in Revelation (i.e., seals; trumpets; vials; and, curiously, thunders) and that these judgments parallel those in Leviticus 26. He asserts that these "parallel" judgments refer to the destruction of Jerusalem in Matthew 21:44 but also in Daniel 2:34-35.[26] David Norris has demonstrated in "Preterism, the Allegorical Method, and the Old Testament" that neither Leviticus 26 nor Revelation have four sevenfold judgments, and so equating the judgments of Leviticus 26 and Revelation is erroneous. As he points out, preterists overlook Leviticus 26:29-45 where the Lord promises to punish His people for their disobedience, but also promises not to cast them away forever, but that he will restore them. So this preterist's erroneous comparison of Leviticus 26 with Revelation actually highlights that God did not cast off Israel forever.

God has a future plan for Israel. The future will involve a time of "great tribulation" (Matthew 24:21) and "Jacob's trouble" (Jeremiah 30:7). In Revelation 6-18, John saw troubles come to the world that are nearly unimaginable in scope and destruction. The Tribulation stands as the cataclysmic moment when Israel recognizes her missed Messiah and fulfills Christ's promise that she would not see Him again until she called for Him (Luke 13:35). In the midst of that final time of testing for the world, a beautiful picture is painted of 144,000 witnesses converted from the twelve tribes of Israel during the Tribulation (Revelation 7:1-8). This numbered group from Israel stands in marked contrast to the innumerable company from every nation mentioned in the next passage (Revelation 7:9-17).

In Romans 11, Paul asks the question, "Hath God cast off his people?" Paul replies "God forbid" (verse 1). He explains that Israel's rejection of the Messiah was only partial; some Jews including himself had accepted the message (verses 1-10). Paul also saw that Israel's partial rejection of the Messiah broadened an avenue of grace to the Gentiles (verses 11-29.) Finally, Paul saw that salvation would once again come to Israel (verses 25-36).

Some question has been raised among Pentecostal preterists as to the method of salvation during the Tribulation—an event which they believe to be passed. Scripture answers the question of the gospel message quite clearly. Since Calvary, there is only one gospel, and it is everlasting (Jude 3; Revelation 14:6).[27]

Preterists seem enamored with the idea that God divorced Israel to marry the church.[28] The analogy is pressed that Israel was an adulteress, thus permitting God to divorce her and marry another. Paul's analogy in Romans 11 is a more suitable understanding. The apostle compared the Gentiles to a branch from a wild olive tree grafted into a good olive tree. When the fullness of the Gentiles is complete, Israel will be grafted again into the good olive tree (Romans 11:25-26). Paul's vision for Israel's future coincides with earlier prophecies of God turning in love to these people (Hosea 3:1-5; Zechariah 13:9). John's vision of the New Jerusalem also includes the names of the twelve tribes of Israel on the city's gates (Revelation 21:12). Israel is very much a part of God's plan.

Israel seems to be the great "sticking point" in the preterist scheme of things. One Pentecostal preterist enumerates "nine key issues" that must be discussed by the church, six of which involve Jerusalem, Jews, or Israel.[29] The desire to eradicate Israel from the prophetic picture is easily subdued by Israel's continued existence.

The trip back for Israel is nothing short of miraculous. The scattering of the Jews in the first and second centuries A.D. and their ultimate return to the Promised Land is a testimony of God's grace. From the initial trickle of Jews returning to their homeland in the late nineteenth century to the Balfour Declaration in 1917, the resurgence of a Jewish homeland can be seen. After the Jewish Holocaust of World War II, the nation of Israel was reborn. Currently, nearly 40 percent of the Jewish population lives in Israel.[30] Israel's present existence refutes the notion that God has forgotten Israel.

Back to Babylon

As was mentioned previously, the two most often mentioned cities in Scripture, Jerusalem and Babylon, are very ancient. Preterists contend that the Babylon mentioned in Revelation 17-18 is actually Jerusalem. This replacement allows preterists to believe that the A.D. 70 destruction of Jerusalem fulfilled the downfall of Babylon in Revelation 17-18.

Consistent scriptural interpretation prohibits such a replacement. The Book of Revelation not only lists Jerusalem and Babylon, it also includes the names of many actual geographic sites: Patmos (1:9), Ephesus (2:1), Smyrna (2:8), Pergamos (2:12), Thyatira (2:18), Sardis (3:1), Philadelphia (3:7), Laodicea (3:14), the Euphrates River (9:14; 16:12), and Armageddon (16:16), to name several. It is perhaps universally understood that these places refer to the actual locations mentioned. It seems the specificity of cities, rivers, and valleys should extend to John's identification of Babylon.

Earlier in Revelation, John "spiritually" compared Jerusalem, the city "where our Lord was crucified," to the city of Sodom and the country of Egypt (Revelation 11:8). If John would carefully acknowledge this comparison for a single verse, how much more would he do it for two chapters of comparison with Babylon?

The Book of Revelation means "the unveiling." All preterists assert that Revelation was written before A.D. 70; the majority seem to prefer A.D. 68. Assuming for a moment it was written in A.D 68, then it was written in the midst of Jerusalem's siege and destruction. Why was it then necessary for John to offer a veiled reference to Jerusalem? If this book was written to prophesy and delineate Jerusalem's immediate destruction as preterists maintain, it is odd that there is no specific warning of this impending destruction.

Preterists commonly point to Revelation 1:7 as just such a warning to Jerusalem. One preterist admits, "Many assume the Second Advent is in view here. And upon first reading such seems appropriate. Nevertheless, in its contextual setting verse 7 points to the destruction of Jerusalem and her temple in A.D. 70."[31] A cursory reading of this verse shows otherwise. The Lord's return will be personal—it is "He" or "Him" that is coming. That the

Roman army can be His personal return is unreasonable at best. Coupled with this personal return is the fact that He will appear globally, not just locally. His appearing will not be limited to simply those who "pierced him," but before "every eye" with "all kindreds of the earth" wailing when they see Him. A three-year siege of a relatively small city in the ancient world does not justify this interpretation.

Through the years, Babylon has been compared to Rome or other later cities that represent the same pagan religions and commercial system. Many interpret the apocalyptic vision of Babylon as the culmination of human's self-attainment as seen in its early origins. Still others hold to the possibility that, just as Jerusalem is seen in a new and improved form in Revelation, so Babylon will experience a rebirth in the end time. There are four reasons for this last view: first, a comparison can be made between Babylon in Revelation 17-18 and the prophecies of Babylon in Zechariah 5 and Jeremiah 50-51; second, there is incomplete fulfillment of the prophecies regarding Babylon's destruction (Isaiah 13-14; Jeremiah 50-51); third, the city of Babylon still exists, more recently called Hillah; and fourth, rejuvenated interest in this ancient cradle of civilization. Historian Arnold Toynbee was fond of stressing that due to its location at the crossroads of three major continents, the city of Babylon would be the best place to build a world metropolis.[32] This is, of course, conjecture.

Jerusalem and Babylon stand opposite of each other throughout man's history. One represents peace; the other represents war and confusion. There is little need or reason to make them synonymous terms unless one needs to prove a presupposed prophetic point of view.

Summary

Preterism utilizes a replacement theology to establish its viewpoint. In its schema, the church replaces Israel only to the extent of receiving her prerogatives and blessings. Although preterism cannot be found early in church history, replacement theology can be seen a mere century after the apostolic age.

The verses of Scripture employed for replacement theology are inadequate. The many references to Israel in Scripture negate the idea that she had ceased to exist as a distinct nation or ethnicity. The prophecies found in the Old Testament coupled with those in the New Testament indicate that God will one day turn again to Israel to fulfill the promises made to her.

That the church is the primary focus of this present age is without question. Both Jews and Gentiles are being saved and baptized into the bride of Christ. Yet this does not preclude that, as the church began with a revival primarily among the Jews, it could some day close the way it began.

Notes

[1]Henry Morris, *The Revelation Record* (Wheaton, Ill.: Tyndale House, 1983), 323.

[2]Gary DeMar, *End Times Fiction: A Biblical Consideration of the Left Behind Theology* (Nashville, Tenn.: Thomas Nelson Publishers, 2001), 124-9.

[3]Larry Smith, *The Coming of the Lord, the Last Days, and the End of the World as Taught by Jesus and His Apostles* (El Campo, Tex.: Rightly Dividing the Word, 2000), 74.

[4]It is ironic that this method of interpretation could have been learned by the Jews while in Babylon. There, the captive Jews were exposed to the mysticism and esoteric understandings of gematria, numerology, and deeper insights that with later teachings yielded various gnostic or cabalistic writings. The esoteric view of Scripture teaches that there are four levels of understand ing: the first level being its literal meaning and the fourth level being its mystical or anagogic meaning. Application of such principles tends to lead to theosophy more than theology. See *Jewish Encyclopedia*, article on "Cabala"; as cited in Nesta H. Webster, op.cit., 29 also, "Is Theosophy a Religion?" by H. P. Blavatsky, available at www.blavatsky.net.

[5]Kenneth L. Gentry, Jr., "Supersessional Orthodoxy; Zionistic Sadism," *Dispensationalism in Transition*, Vol. VI, No. 2; Feb. 1993, 1.

[6]Kenneth L. Gentry, Jr., "The Iceman Cometh! Moronism Reigneth!," *Dispensationalism in Transition*, Vol. VI, No. 1; Jan. 1993, 1.

[7]David Chilton says that the Bible "does not tell of any future plan for Israel as a special nation" (David Chilton, *Paradise Restored: An Eschatology of Dominion* [Tyler, Tex.: Reconstruction Press, 1985], 225). Gary DeMar and Peter Leithart maintain that "in destroying Israel, Christ transferred the blessings of the kingdom from Israel to a new people, the church" (Gary DeMar and Peter Leithart, *The Reduction of Christianity* [Fort Worth, Tex.: Dominion Press, 1998], 213.

[8]Kenneth L. Gentry, "Postmillennialism," Darrell L. Bock, ed., *Three Views on the Millennium and Beyond* (Grand Rapids: Zondervan, 1998), 36.

[9]Michael Green, *Evangelism in the Early Church* (Grand Rapids: Eerdmans, 2003), 145. Green cited Justin, *Dialogue with Trypho*, 11.

[10]Justin, *Dialogue*, 59-60; Tertullian, *Against the Jews*, complete works.

[11]Michael Green noted, "The church was becoming increasingly Gentile, and increasingly antipathetic to Judaism and its Law and cultus. The Epistle of Barnabas, as we have seen, used the Jewish exegetical method of allegorizing as ruthlessly as Philo. The result was that it transferred the law entirely into the Christian camp, and maintained that the Jews had no right to it because though it was given to them, they were not worthy to receive it on account of their

sins." Green, *Evangelism*, 151.

[12]Irenaeus, *Against Heresies*, 3.21.

[13]Justin, *Dialogue*, 29.

[14]John Chrysostom, *Eight Orations Against the Jews*, 1, 3, 4.

[15]C. Marvin Pate, *Four Views on the Book of Revelation* (Grand Rapids: Zondervan, 1998). "There is no clear-cut example of the church being called 'Israel' in the New Testament or in the church fathers before A.D. 160."

[16]Compare with Colossians 3:5-11.

[17]R. Meyer, "Israel," *New International Dictionary of New Testament Theology*, ed. Colin Brown (Grand Rapids: Zondervan, 1975), 2:315; also G. C. Berkouwer, *The Return of Christ* (Grand Rapids: Eerdmans, 1972), 344; see also Ernest De Witt Burton, *A Critical and Exegetical Commentary on The Epistle to The Galatians* (Edinburgh: T & T Clark, 1920), 358. See also, S. Lewis Johnson, Jr., "Paul and 'The Israel of God': An Exegetical and Eschatological Case-Study," in Stanley D. Toussaint & Charles H. Dyer, *Essays in Honor of J. Dwight Pentecost* (Chicago: Moody Press, 1986), 187-189.

[18]"Prophecy Debate on Preterism Between David Norris and Larry Smith," Houston, Texas, January 31, 2005; Defenders of the Faith Conference on Apostolic Doctrine and Apologetics, sponsored by Los Pentecostales de Royalwood (faithdefenders@hotmail.com).

[19]Smith, *Last Days*, 7.

[20]Gentry, *Three Views*, 46.

[21]Smith, *Last Days*, 20.

[22]Ibid., 7.

[23]Many passages speak of a future for Israel: Leviticus 26:40-45; Deuteronomy 4:27-31; 30:1-6; Isaiah 2:2-3; Jeremiah 23:5-6; Ezekiel 36:10-11, 22-32; 39:25-29; Hosea 3:4-5; Amos 9:11-15; Micah 4:6-7; Zephaniah 3:14-15; Zechariah 8:2-3, 7-8, 13-15; 12:10; Romans 11:15, 25-27.

[24]Smith, *Last Days*, 21.

[25]Walter C. Kaiser, Jr., *Toward an Old Testament Theology* (Grand Rapids: Zondervan, 1978), 124-25.

[26]Smith, *Last Days*, 28-29.

[27]Preterists need only to look at fellow adherents in the postmillennial camp who presently advocate a return to keeping the law. "The theonomic postmillennialist sees the gradual return to biblical norms of civil justice as a consequence of widespread gospel success. . . . The judicial-political outlook of Reconstructionism includes the application of this justice—defining directives contained in the Old Testament legislation" (Gentry, *Three Views*, 19).

[28]Larry Smith, *Last Days*, 75; "John is presenting the dramatic covenant lawsuit against Israel for her adultery" (Gentry, *Three Views*, 73).

[29]Larry Smith, "Response to David Norris" (UGST 2003 Oneness Symposium), 10.

[30]Thomas Ice, *The Truth Behind Left Behind* (Sisters, Ore.: Multnomah, 2004), 69.

[31]Gentry, *Three Views*, 46.

[32]Morris, *The Revelation Record*, 348-49.

11

Dating the Book of Revelation

J. R. Ensey

For preterism to stand up under historical or theological scrutiny, adherents must prove that the Book of Revelation was written before A.D. 70—actually before A.D. 67. Mark Hitchcock explains:

> It is critical to observe that the preterist position requires more than just a pre-70 date. According to [preterist Kenneth L.] Gentry, Revelation anticipates the destruction of Jerusalem (August A.D. 70) the death of Nero (June A.D. 68), and the formal imperial engagement of the Jewish War (spring A.D. 67). Therefore, for preterists, the earliest Revelation could have been written (the *terminus a quo*) is the beginning of the Neronic persecution in November A.D. 64, and the latest possible date (the *terminus ad quem*) is spring A.D. 67. The date Gentry favors is A.D. 65.[1]

With this overwhelming burden of proof, preterists are publishing reams of material in an attempt to assign an early date that would reflect the persecution under the Roman emperor Nero as the primary subject of the Book of Revelation. However, throughout the centuries of Christian history, the vast majority of scholars have set the date of composition in the last years of the first century, ca. A.D. 95-96. Who is right? The answer is critical to the preterism debate: If John wrote Revelation after A.D. 70 when Jerusalem was sacked, burned, and the Jewish Temple was destroyed, then its prophecies obviously do not pertain to those events. Futurists can live with either date, but preterism requires the early date; otherwise the doctrine fails. We should not establish major doctrines on such an uncertain premise. In desperation to affirm an early date, some preterists have even resorted to questioning the authorship of Revelation; however, conservative scholars continue to identify the apostle John as the author.

Since John does not specify a date for his writing, we must depend on other internal and external evidence. Preterists are convinced that the events described in the Book of Revelation are historical—hence, *preterism*, basically meaning "past." Are we to believe the internal and external evidence that support a late date, or are we to join the relatively recent attempt to apply the symbolism of Revelation to events of the first century? To find the answer, let us examine the evidence on which to base our conclusions.

The External Evidence

The external evidence for the late date of Revelation is abundant. The references of the early church theologians and historians to John's exile during the reign of

Domitian, the type of persecution Domitian employed, and the actions of his successor point to a late first-century date for the Apocalypse (the Book of Revelation). R. H. Charles wrote, "The [external evidence] almost unanimously assigns [the writing of Revelation] to the last years of Domitian."[2] That opinion is widespread throughout the theological and historical communities.[3]

There are many direct and indirect references in early church writings that Domitian banished John to Patmos. There are also other direct references that Domitian banished John, but without specifying the location of his banishment. The earliest of these is from Irenaeus (ca. 130-202), bishop of Lyons in Gaul. He was a disciple of Polycarp, who in turn was a disciple of the apostle John. We would thus expect Irenaeus to know when John wrote Revelation. In *Against Heresies* (ca. 180-199), Irenaeus wrote:

> We will not, however, incur the risk of pronouncing positively as to the name of Antichrist; for if it were necessary that his name should be distinctly revealed in this present time, it would have been announced by him who beheld the apocalyptic vision. For that was seen no very long time since, but almost in our day, towards the end of Domitian's reign.

What was seen "no very long time since . . . towards the end of Domitian's reign"? "The apocalyptic vision."

Eusebius of Caesarea, the noted church historian who flourished during the reign of Constantine, certainly had no quarrel with the record of John's authorship or of the date of his writing Revelation. Here is his clear statement of John's persecution under Domitian and banishment to Patmos:

> It is said that in this persecution the apostle and evangelist John, who was still alive, was condemned to dwell on the island of Patmos in consequence of his testimony to the divine word.
>
> Irenaeus, in the fifth book of his work *Against Heresies*, where he discusses the number of the name of Antichrist which is given in the so-called Apocalypse of John, speaks as follows concerning him: "If it were necessary for his name to be proclaimed openly at the present time, it would have been declared by him who saw the revelation. For it was seen not long ago, but almost in our own generation, at the end of the reign of Domitian."
>
> To such a degree, indeed, did the teaching of our faith flourish at that time that even those writers who were far from our religion did not hesitate to mention in their histories the persecution and the martyrdoms which took place during it.
>
> And they, indeed, accurately indicated the time. For they recorded that in the fifteenth year of Domitian Flavia Domitilla, daughter of a sister of Flavius Clement, who at that time was one of the consuls of Rome, was exiled with many others to the island of Pontia in consequence of testimony borne to Christ.[4]

These quotes from Irenaeus and Eusebius are only two of many more testimonies that demonstrate that the early church writers believed in a late date for the Book of Revelation. Regarding the reliability of the testimony of Irenaeus, *Barnes' Notes on the New Testament* comments:

> It will be recollected that he [Irenaeus] was a disciple of Polycarp, bishop of Smyrna, who was himself the disciple of the apostle John. He had, therefore, every opportunity of obtaining correct information, and doubtless expresses the common sentiment of his age on the subject. His character is unexceptionable, and he had no inducement to bear any false or perverted testimony in the case. His testimony is plain and positive that the book was written near the close of the reign of Domitian, and the testimony should be regarded as decisive unless it can be set aside. His language in regard to the book of Revelation is: "It was seen no long time ago, but almost in our age, at the end of the reign of Domitian." (Lardner, ii. 181) Or, as the passage is translated by Professor Stuart: "The Apocalypse was seen not long ago, but almost in our generation, near the end of Domitian's reign." There can be no doubt, therefore, as to the meaning of the passage, or as to the time when Irenaeus believed the book to have been written. Domitian was put to death A.D. 96, and consequently, according to Irenaeus, the Apocalypse must have been written not far from this time.[5]

A nineteenth-century theologian suggested that Irenaeus meant that John himself, rather than the Apocalypse, was seen during the reign of Domitian.[6] Henry Alford, commenting on the expression, which he quotes in the Greek, confirms that the Apocalypse is the subject of "was seen": "For such is the only legitimate understanding of the construction."[7] Preterists, however, disagree with Alford. One says:

> In this passage, it must be noted that the subject of the verb "was seen" is ambiguous in the Greek language and may be either "it" referring to the Apocalypse, or "he" referring to John himself. . . . If one chooses to select "it" meaning the vision, we have the Apocalypse being written at the later date. If "he" is chosen, meaning John, then the Apocalypse is written at the earlier date because he, John, would have been seen "almost in our own generation."[8]

Kenneth Gentry posits that John and not the Apocalypse is the subject of "was seen" and thus understands Irenaeus's topic to be the long length of John's life rather than the time when he saw the apocalyptic vision.[9] It is clear, however, that Irenaeus was referring to the vision of the Apocalypse. Even Philip Schaff, an early-date advocate, understands Irenaeus to refer to the Apocalypse and not to John and calls Irenaeus's record "a clear and weighty testimony."[10]

Hegesippus (ca. 150) was an early chronicler and a source for Eusebius's history of the church. Eusebius cited him at least twice as a source, and many are convinced that he was quoting Hegesippus when he wrote his key statements about the events and timing surrounding John's exile and vision: "At this time [Domitian's persecution], as the story goes, the Apostle and Evangelist John was still alive, and was condemned to live in the island of Patmos for his witness to the divine word."[11]

If validation from early writers and historians of Domitian's practice of exiling Christians is necessary, Eusebius provided it in the forgoing context, pointing out that "in the fifteenth year of Domitian Flavia Domitilla, daughter of a sister of Flavius Clement, who at that time was one of the consuls of Rome, was exiled with many others to the island of Pontia in consequence of testimony borne to Christ."

The reign of terror unleashed by Nero and later by Domitian may have decimated the ranks of Christian leaders, but it by no means left the empire without a witness. Christianity was alive and well after those two tyrants had done their worst. Contemporary historians and writers have given one or the other higher marks for cruelty. Both were vicious. They both used torture and death to evoke denunciation of Christ. But unlike Nero, Domitian was also willing to punish Christians through the confiscation of their property, exile, and making them slaves instead of torture and death.[12]

Victorinus, who served as bishop of Pettau (in modern Austria) ca. 300 and who died in the persecution of 303-304, expressed what was evidently common knowledge at that time:

> When John said these things he was in the island of Patmos, condemned to the labour of the mines by Caesar Domitian. There, therefore, he saw the Apocalypse; and when grown old, he thought that he should at length receive his quittance by suffering, Domitian being killed, all his judgments were discharged. And John being dismissed from the mines, thus subsequently delivered the same Apocalypse which he had

> received from God. . . . The time must be understood in which the written Apocalypse was published, since then reigned Caesar Domitian; but before him had been Titus his brother, and Vespasian, Otho, Vitellius, and Galba. These are the five who have fallen [kings in Revelation 17:9-11]. One remains, under whom the Apocalypse was written—Domitian, to wit.[13]

Tertullian (ca. 150-225), an early Christian apologist and writer, also affirmed that Domitian was somewhat more retrained than Nero had been in persecuting Christians. In chapter 5 of his *Apology*, he wrote, "Domitian, too, a man of Nero's type in cruelty, tried his hand at persecution, but as he had something of the human in him, he soon put an end to what he had begun, even restoring again those whom he had banished."

According to Victorinus, the apostle John was not among those released by Domitian, but by Nerva, his successor.[14] Even if he had been released by Domitian, since Domitian's reign did not begin until A.D. 81, Revelation had to have been written after that date.[15]

Domitian was so hated for his excesses that even his own wife joined the others who were plotting to assassinate him. Upon Domitian's death, Nerva reversed many of his cruel judgments, and John was subsequently released. Domitian's reign ended in A.D. 96, and this has provided the traditional means for dating the Book of Revelation.

Around 236, Hippolytus, in chapter 1 verse 3 of his *On the Twelve Apostles*, wrote:

> John, again, in Asia, was banished by Domitian the king to the isle of Patmos, in which also he wrote

> his Gospel and saw the apocalyptic vision; and in Trajan's time [98-117] he fell asleep at Ephesus, where his remains were sought for, but could not be found.

Jerome (340-420), a learned scholar who became one of the notables of Roman Catholicism after publishing the definitive Latin translation of the Bible, wrote of John in chapter 9 of *Lives of Illustrious Men*:

> In the fourteenth year then after Nero, Domitian, having raised a second persecution, he was banished to the island of Patmos, and wrote the Apocalypse, on which Justin Martyr and Irenaeus afterwards wrote commentaries. But Domitian having been put to death and his acts, on account of his excessive cruelty, having been annulled by the senate, he returned to Ephesus under Pertinax and continuing there until the time of the emperor Trajan, founded and built churches throughout all Asia, and, worn out by old age, died . . . and was buried near the same city.

In *Against Jovinianus*, book 1, Jerome, drawing on the chronicles of Tertullian, also wrote:

> John is both an Apostle and an Evangelist, and a prophet. An Apostle, because he wrote to the Churches as a master; an Evangelist, because he composed a Gospel, a thing which no other of the Apostles, excepting Matthew, did; a prophet, for he saw in the island of Patmos, to which he had been banished by the Emperor Domitian as a martyr for

the Lord, an Apocalypse containing the boundless mysteries of the future.

Sulpicius Severus (360-425) was an ecclesiastical historian. In chapter 31 of book 2 of his *Sacred History*, he states:

> Then, after an interval, Domitian, the son of Vespasian, persecuted the Christians. At this date, he banished John the Apostle and Evangelist to the island of Patmos. There he, secret mysteries having been revealed to him, wrote and published his book of the holy Revelation.

The historian Mosheim (1694-1755) sums up the impact of the emperor Domitian upon the early church:

> In the year 93 or 94 a new assault was made upon the Christians by Domitian, an emperor little inferior to Nero in baseness of character and conduct. . . . The persecution was undoubtedly severe: but it was of short continuance, as the emperor was soon after murdered. In the midst of this persecution, John the apostle was banished to the isle of Patmos. It was there that John received the Revelation (Revelation 1:9).[16]

Domitian, rather than Nero, reached deep into Asia Minor where John lived with his heavy hand of persecution. Historian Henry Chadwick confirmed the differences in the persecution under Nero and that under Domitian, and in the process helps to confirm the late date of John's banishment and vision:

> The Neronian persecution was confined to Rome and its environs and was not due to any sense of deep ideological conflict between church and state; it was simply that the emperor had to blame somebody for the fire [that destroyed much of Rome]. . . . The later persecution under Domitian, on the other hand, directly and oppressively affected the brethren in Asia Minor; in fact, his persecution affected the very ecclesias to whom the Apocalypse was addressed. The Asiarchs (local rulers in Asia Minor) under Domitian enforced Caesar worship and carried out the imperial edict against Christians of this area with some zeal.[17]

Virtually all of the references to the dating of Revelation from the first three centuries support the Domitian period. The Neronic dating theory "has no foundation in the evidence of Christian antiquity and originated in a desire to interpret part of the prophecy [as referring to] the reign and fate of the Emperor Nero."[18]

The *Abingdon Bible Commentary* gives this background information in support of the Domitian date:

> That the book belongs to a date later than the Pauline era is evident from the condition of the churches, the presence of Nicolaitanism and widespread persecution. Ancient tradition was almost unanimous in assigning the book to the later years of Domitian's reign, when the emperor's demand for divine honours, his widespread use of informers, and his special enmity against the Christian church established a reign of terror from which there was

> no relief till his death in A.D. 96. With this most modern scholars agree. It was not till Domitian's edict that Asia became the scene of persecution against Christians.[19]

To these witnesses we could add Paulus Orosius (ca. early fifth century), Primasius of Hadrumentum (ca. 540), Andreas of Cappadocia (ca. 600), and Venerable Bede (ca. 700), the father of English history.[20]

With such testimony given so far and wide and over a number of centuries, a consensus about the date of Revelation is evident among the early Christian leaders and historians. Only a small minority of ancient writers seem to have preferred an earlier date, and often for reasons other than those provided by contemporary preterists. In this case, we are wise to acknowledge and acquiesce to the preponderance of the evidence.[21] However, defenders of the Neronic date put forth several arguments that they believe prove an early date for Revelation:[22]

1. Tertullian (ca. 200) mentions the early date, i.e., the time of Nero's persecution. While Tertullian mentions both Nero and Domitian, he does not date the Apocalypse. However, he does note in his *Apology* that Christians suffered banishment under Domitian.[23]

2. A later Syriac translation of the Bible dates Revelation to the time of Nero. The earliest Syriac version did not include the Apocalypse, because the translators did not regard it as canonical. The title page of the version that does include Revelation is itself dated to the sixth century, 450 years after it was written. It should not carry great weight in this controversy, because of its late date

and because no one knows who made the version or on what authority the translators relied.[24]

3. Clement of Alexandria related that the apostle John "after returning from Patmos, journeyed into the hills to reclaim a wayward disciple."[25] According to preterists, this achievement would have been physically impossible for the aged John if it happened after A.D. 95.

Clement did relate an account of a dedicated apostle who, if the story is correct, still found it possible—on horseback and at an advanced age—to expend himself in the service of his Lord. Clement referred to the apostle in this account as "aged," a term inappropriate at the time of Nero, for John lived some thirty-four years beyond this date. He was truly aged at the time of his release from Patmos in A.D. 96, but had evidently been physically able to work in the mines while confined to Patmos. Clement's testimony agrees with that of Irenaeus, who had written that the apostle John lived for several years in Ephesus after his release from Patmos. Irenaeus wrote, "And all the presbyters of Asia, that had conferred with John, the disciple of our Lord, testify that John had delivered [the Apocalypse] to them; for he continued with them until the times of Trajan [98-117]."[26] Some traditions put the death of John at the very end of the first century, suggesting that he was almost one hundred years old.

The Internal Evidence

In the effort to establish an early date for Revelation, some preterists have resorted to claiming that the apostle John was not the author of the Apocalypse, speculating that it was written much earlier by an unknown person and only attributed to John much later. This claim contradicts the Book of Revelation's own testimony that John was the author: "And he sent and signified it by his angel unto his servant John" (1:1); "John to the seven churches which are in Asia" (1:4); "I John, who also am your brother . . . was in the isle that is called Patmos, for the word of God, and for the testimony of Jesus Christ" (1:9); "I was in the Spirit on the Lord's day . . . and I turned to see. . . . I saw . . ." (1:10, 12).

But was this John the apostle John? Certainly there were other men of his time named John, but this writer was enduring persecution and had been banished to the isle of Patmos. Why should we question the identity of the author when the early writers of history provide a myriad of testimonies that it was John, the beloved apostle of the Lord? Among them were Clement of Alexandria, Origen, Tertullian, Victorinus, Eusebius, Epiphanius, Severus, Jerome, and others. Origen, as representative of this group, stated that "a Roman Emperor banished the apostle John into the isle of Patmos, for the testimony which he bore to the word of truth."[27] Irenaeus, in *Against Heresies*, said repeatedly that the author of the Gospel of John was also the author of the Apocalypse. Hippolytus testified of John's authorship in section 9 of his work *De Antichristo*: "Blessed John, apostle and disciple of the Lord, tell me what thou didst see and hear respecting Babylon." He then quoted Revelation 17 and 18 as John's response. There is therefore little question that the apostle John was persecuted under Domitian, exiled to the isle of Patmos, received from the Lord the revelation, and recorded the same as he was instructed (Revelation 1:19).

Dionysius of Alexandria (ca. 190-270) was skeptical of John's authorship, basing his doubts on the stylistic differences between the Gospel and the Apocalypse. His argument fails when we consider that we should expect stylistic differences since the two books differ dramatically in both subject matter and genre.

Admittedly, certain phrases of the Book of Revelation give some support to the preterists. For example, Revelation 1:1 says, "The revelation of Jesus Christ, which God gave unto him, to show unto his servants things that must shortly come to pass." This seems to indicate that weeks, months, or at the most a few years might be all the time remaining—as man counts time—before the events would unfold. But note that similar statements—"must shortly be done"; "the time is at hand"; "behold, I come quickly; and my reward is with me" (22:6, 10, 12)—also precede resurrections, judgments, a marriage supper, a new heaven and new earth, and other major happenings in the book. None of these occurred before A.D. 70; yet they are described as events that "must shortly come to pass." How are we to understand such phrases, if not in the light of God's prerogative to reckon time in His own way (II Peter 3:8)? We must employ sound hermeneutics in order to understand such statements.

We must seek to understand the phrase "things which must shortly come to pass" in light of other scriptural examples of the same expression. For example, Daniel declared that certain things would occur "in the latter days"; the Apocalypse describes these things as happening "shortly" (Greek *en tachei*). The expression literally means "in haste" (quickly, suddenly), indicating that the events are to be fulfilled rapidly. As the events unfold, John speaks of them as coming to pass quickly (Revelation 11:14). A form of the word occurs in Revelation 22:20: "Surely I come quickly." The events foretold include the decay and fall of empires, conflicts among nations, and the apostasy. Centuries would be required for the fulfillment of these things before the millennial reign of Christ would begin. They did, however, *begin* to happen shortly after they were revealed to John, and they continue in their succession until all are fulfilled in the new heaven and the new earth. The Apocalypse itself indicates an extended period of time before God saves His servants out of their affliction: "They called out in a loud voice, 'How long, Sovereign Lord, holy and true, until you judge the inhabitants of the earth and avenge our blood?' Then each of them was given a white robe, and they were told to wait a little longer, until the number of their fellow servants and brothers who were to be killed as they had been was completed" (Revelation 6:10, 11, NIV).

The phrase *en tachei* occurs in Acts 12:7 (rise up quickly), Acts 22:18 (get out quickly), and Acts 25:4 (depart shortly). In these passages the meaning is clearly "within a short time." In Luke 18, however, the expression is used in a different sense. There is a long-range implication similar to that in the Apocalypse: "And will not God vindicate his elect, who cry unto him day and night? Will he delay long over them? I tell you, he will vindicate them speedily [*en tachei*]. Nevertheless, when the Son of man comes, will he find faith on earth?" (Luke 18:7-8, RSV). Henry Alford, in his commentary on the Revelation, expounds on these expressions. He writes:

> What things must shortly come to pass (i.e., before long)? This expression must not be urged to signify that the events of the apocalyptic prophecy were to be close at hand: for we have a key to its meaning in Luke 18:8. Here long delay is evidently implied, though the term *en tachei* is used, as in Revelation 1:1. . . . So that we are driven to the very same sense of *en tachei* as that of Luke, viz. to God's speedy time, though He seem to delay. . . . It remains to observe that these words cannot with any fairness be used as furnishing a guide to the interpretation of the prophecy. They are far rather to be regarded as a prophetic formula, common to Him to whom a thousand years are as one day, and used in order to teach us how short our time, and the time of this world is.[28]

While Peter preached on the Day of Pentecost, he appealed to the prophecy of Joel 2:28-29, which suggests that Peter believed that the "last days" had then begun (Acts 2:17)—yet we are still here. The prophecy and the terminology are better understood in retrospect. The events of the first three chapters of Revelation dealing with the churches of Asia did indeed begin to occur as we reckon time. But notice that the Lord still says "quickly" in chapter 22 in reference to His coming with rewards for "every man" (22:12). Preterists assume that this quick coming refers to His coming in judgment upon the Jews and Jerusalem in A.D. 70. But "every eye" did not see Him, nor did "they also which pierced him" (1:7) see Him, nor did "all the kindreds of the earth wail because of him" (1:7). None of these things happened in A.D. 70.

A few hold that, since there were only seven churches

mentioned in Asia Minor, only seven might have existed in the mid 60s, thus hinting at an early date. However, were there not churches in Iconium, Lystra, Derbe, Galatia, Colosse, Hierapolis, Pontus, Cappadocia, and in Bithynia (Acts 13:51; 14:6-20; 16:1-2)? Doubtless other towns had congregations of believers also. Perhaps the Lord chose to specifically address these churches to bring certain facts and principles to light. Perhaps God wanted to use the number seven for reasons of His own. Regardless, biblical history affirms that more than seven churches existed in Asia Minor at the time John wrote Revelation.

Furthermore, a pre-70 date would be insufficient time for the churches named in Revelation to mature and decline to the point described by Jesus. Consider that in the early 60s Paul commended the Ephesians with a message of comfort, peace, and grace (Ephesians 6:22-24). But in Revelation they had "left [their] first love" (2:4). The Smyrna congregation had already embraced members of "the synagogue of Satan" (2:9). The church at Pergamos was hosting Nicolaitans, a Gnostic sect.[29] These Nicolaitans (2:14-16) were among those who, near the end of the first century, began a campaign of mutilating the sacred books of the Christians. Perhaps this practice evoked the closing denunciations of the Apocalypse: "For I testify unto every man that heareth the words of the prophecy of this book, If any man shall add unto these things, God shall add unto him the plagues that are written in this book: And if any man shall take away from the words of the book of this prophecy, God shall take away his part out of the book of life, and out of the holy city, and from the things which are written in this book" (Revelation

22:18-19). Other churches addressed by Jesus had similar failings, even harboring and accommodating a woman with the spirit of Jezebel (2:20). A few months or years after the epistle was directed to them would be insufficient time for such decline to take place in seven of the prominent churches of Asia Minor. But if we add thirty years to the number, then we can easily understand how developments could have taken them to where they were when Jesus sent His Word to them via John. And according to Polycarp, bishop of Smyrna (ca. 110), the church in Smyrna did not even exist in the early to mid 60s.[30]

We should also note that the reference to "the first day of the week" as "the Lord's day" (Revelation 1:10) was uncommon terminology until near the close of the first century.[31] Also, it may be significant that John addressed the letters to the seven churches to "the angel of the church," or the presiding elder. Before this time the elders of a church were classed together, but here we see each church having a singular head, or "messenger." This suggests a development in church structure from the early to mid 60s.

Some preterists appeal to Revelation 11:1-2 as evidence that the Temple still stood in Jerusalem. We should not take this verse literally, but symbolically and prophetically. Was John, though in exile, somehow to travel to Jerusalem and measure the Temple? Of course not. Additionally, the angel specifically told John that the court of the Gentiles was to be trodden underfoot for forty-two months. A literal interpretation would have the Romans destroying only part of the Temple and not the Holy or the Most Holy Place. We know, however, that the Romans did indeed destroy the entire Temple complex with hardly a stone left upon another. Thus we cannot understand these verses literally, but symbolically and prophetically.[32] The forty-two months actually represent the first half of the Great Tribulation.

Preterists generally interpret Revelation as though Nero was the beast whose head was wounded but afterward healed. But there is no record of Nero rising from the dead as some of the ancient pagan soothsayers had prophesied. His death preceded the destruction of Jerusalem by two years, so he could not have been active in Revelation 19. Moreover, an enormous army of "two hundred thousand thousand" horsemen (Revelation (9:16) never attacked Jerusalem in the first century—or anywhere else in history!

Many preterists also say that the gematrical value of the name "Neron Kaiser [Caesar]" is 666.[33] How many other potential antichrists have been "anointed" by such numerical values? Trying to make Nero the Antichrist of Revelation 13:16-18 because of the numerical value of the letters of his name demands far too much supposition. Hitchcock explains:

> For the mathematical value to fit Nero Caesar, the Greek form of his name must be transliterated into Hebrew (*nron qsr*). The sum of 666 can be reached only by transliterating the Greek form of this one title for Nero into Hebrew. If the Latin form of the name Nero Caesar is transcribed in Hebrew characters (*nro qsr*), then the total adds up to only 616.85. One wonders why John, writing to a primarily Greek audience in western Asia Minor, would not use a Greek form instead of a Hebrew form? However, even if one

> agrees that this specific title (Nero Caesar) is the correct one and that the correct form is the Greek transliteration into Hebrew (*nron qsr*), there is still another hurdle—should the vowels be included? The calculation for Nero Caesar from Hebrew equals 666 only if the Hebrew letter *yodh* is omitted from the word Caesar (*qsr*). This is a defective spelling.[34]

Robert Mounce summarizes the problems preterists face on this issue: "What is not generally stressed is that this solution asks us to calculate a Hebrew transliteration of the Greek form of a Latin name, and that with a defective spelling."[35] After studying how creatively people throughout history have made practically any name equal 666, G. Salmon formulated three "rules" for doing this (the preterists have followed them in making Nero fit the number of the Beast): "First, if the proper name by itself will not yield it, add a title; secondly, if the sum cannot be found in Greek, try Hebrew, or even Latin; thirdly, do not be too particular about the spelling. . . . We cannot infer much from the fact that a key fits the lock if it is a lock in which almost any key will turn."[36]

There is no clear internal evidence in the Book of Revelation supporting its fulfillment in A.D. 70. The entire theoretical structure of preterism crumbles when we establish that John wrote Revelation in the mid 90s, long after Nero was dead and Jerusalem destroyed. When the early date linchpin is removed, preterism falls apart. Instead of being virtually absorbed with no more than two events—the death of Nero and the fall of Jerusalem—the Book of Revelation reveals the future of the church, its Rapture/resurrection, its judgment at the

Bema, its marriage consummation to the heavenly Bridegroom, the wrath of God on all citizens of the earth who rejected faith in Jesus Christ, the binding of Satan, and the millennial reign of Christ and the church.

Other Considerations Affecting the Dating of Revelation

Here are questions that come to mind when we think about the Second Coming in the context of the preterist viewpoint:

Did Nero recover from a deadly wound by the sword that caused all the world to marvel (Revelation 13:3)? No.

Did Nero, or any Roman antichrist, have a "front man," the false prophet with two horns "like a lamb" (Revelation 13:11-12)? No.

Did Nero have a false prophet that produced a cosmic show: fire coming down "from heaven on the earth in the sight of men" (Revelation 13:13)? No.

Did Nero have a false prophet that made an image of the emperor for the whole world to worship? Was it made to speak in order to deceive the whole world into worshiping Nero (Revelation 13:15)? No.

Did Nero have a false prophet that imposed a mark on the foreheads and hands of the entire populace of the Roman Empire, without which no one could buy or sell (Revelation 13:16)? No.

Did two witnesses turn water to blood and plague all the earth with drought during the three years preceding A.D. 70? Did Nero kill them? Did they lie dead in the streets of Jerusalem with all the world beholding the scene (did they have TV back then)? Did all the world give gifts to one another because of it (Revelation 11:3-10)? No.

Did an innumerable host of all kindreds and people and tongues come out of the Tribulation (Revelation 7:9-17) that preceded the destruction of Jerusalem in A.D. 70? No.

Was the Antichrist—"who opposeth and exalteth himself above all that is called God, or that is worshipped; so that he as God sitteth in the temple of God, showing himself that he is God"—destroyed "by the brightness of his coming" (II Thessalonians 2:4, 8) in A.D. 70? No.

Did the marriage of the Lamb (Revelation 19:7-9) take place without anyone knowing? No.

If we are in the Millennium and if the devil is incarcerated in the pit, why is he called the god of this age (II Corinthians 4:4; Luke 4:5-6)? Was he stopped from deceiving all nations in A.D. 70 (Revelation 20:2-3, 7-8)? No.

Did the saints commence ruling with Christ, sitting on thrones with Christ, reigning as kings and priests (Revelation 20:4-6), ruling with a rod of iron (Revelation 2:25-27) in A.D. 70? No.

The resurrection takes place when Jesus returns. Did a last "trump[et]" (I Thessalonians 4:16-17) sound then? Was there a resurrection in A.D. 70? Did the dead in Christ rise (I Thesssalonians 4:16)? Did the living follow them to meet the Lord in the air? No.

Did a bodily change from natural to spiritual take place then (I Corinthians 15:50-55)? No.

If these "no" answers are correct—and no historian has ever left a record to suggest otherwise—then these events are still future and preterism is wrong.

Conclusion

The internal and external evidence demonstrate that John wrote the Book of Revelation in ca. A.D. 95-96. Thus the events prophesied in it must occur later than the fall of Jerusalem in A.D. 70. When an assumption about the Scriptures flatly contradicts the reliable testimony of multiple scholarly and respected Christian witnesses who lived much closer to the time of the writing of Revelation than we do, we should seriously consider whether the assumption is erroneous. It is inconceivable that the preponderance of early historical witnesses to the late date of Revelation would be off by thirty years. They seemed to be stating facts as they were commonly believed; whereas the preterists seem to be misunderstanding the Scriptures and ignoring history. When these early witnesses wrote, there was no great debate about futurism and preterism. They were not trying to favor one doctrine or another, but were merely stating accepted facts and presenting the extant record.

There are too many references in Revelation to the growing and maturing church, to future events such as the Marriage Supper of the Lamb, and to the entire scope of Christian experience to limit its prophecies to a Jewish tragedy in the first century. While that episode was epochal to that community, the unfolding of history throughout two millennia—especially in the twentieth century—makes it clear that the long-range purposes of God are involved. For these and other reasons Apostolics have embraced the premillennial, futurist perspective of eschatology.

J. R. Ensey holds degrees in theology and education and served as president of Texas Bible College for fourteen years. He currently directs the extension campus program for Texas Bible College, serves as president of Advance Ministries of Willis, Texas, and is associate pastor of Living Way Church in Montgomery (Conroe), Texas.

Notes

[1]Mark Hitchcock, *The Endtimes Controversy*, Tim LaHaye and Thomas Ice, eds. (Eugene, Ore.: Harvest House Publishers, 2003), 125.

[2]R. H. Charles, "The Revelation of St. John," *International Critical Commentary, Vol. 1*, S. R. Driver, A. Plummer, C. A. Briggs, eds. (Edinburgh: T & T Clark, 1920), xci.

[3]For example, M. Kiddle, *The Revelation of St. John* (London, 1940), xxxvi-xliii; L. Morris, *Revelation* (Leicester, 1987), 35-41; J.P.M. Sweet, *Revelation* (Philadelphia, 1979), 21-26; R.H. Mounce, *The Book of Revelation* (Grand Rapids: Baker Book House, 1998), 15-21.

[4]*The Church History of Eusebius*, Book 3, Chapter XVIII.

[5]*Barnes' Notes on the New Testament.*

[6]The suggestion was quoted by the Bishop of Ely in the *Journal of Theological Studies* for April 1907. It originated with a French theologian, M. J. Bevan, Lausanne, 1887. Swete, *Apocalypse of St. John*, cvi.

[7]Henry Alford, *The Greek Testament*, "Revelation: Place and Time of Writing," 230.

[8]www.christeternalchristianchurch.com; Learning Activity #39: "Dating the Book of Revelation."

[9]Kenneth Gentry, *Before Jerusalem Fell* (Atlanta: American Vision, 1998), 45-67.

[10]Philip Schaff, *History of the Christian Church* (Grand Rapids: Eerdmans, 1950), 1:834.

[11]Hugh Lawlor, *Eusebiana: Essays on the Ecclesiastical History of Eusebius Bishop of Caesarea* (Oxford: Clarendon Press, 1912), 52-53.

[12]There is no record of Nero using exile as a means to persecute Christians. (It would have been strange indeed for Nero to kill Paul and perhaps Peter also during his rampage against Christians but only to exile John, the closest disciple to Jesus during His earthly ministry.) Nero insisted on being addressed as *dominus et deus* ("master and god"). Christian believers, of course, refused to do this and thus received the brunt of his viciousness.

[13]Victorinus, *Apocalypse*, 10:11; 17:10.

[14]Eusebius, *Ecclesiastical History*, 3:20.10.

[15]Rusty Entrekin, *When Was the Revelation of Jesus Christ Written?*; www.thingstocome.org/datrev.

[16]Mosheim, *Institutes of Ecclesiastical History*, 1:55-59.

[17]Henry Chadwick, *The Early Church* (New York: Pelican Books, 1967), 26-27.

[18]Henry Alford, *How to Study the New Testament* (Alexander Strahan, publisher, 1867), 225.

[19]*Abingdon Bible Commentary*, 1367-68.

[20]Hitchcock, in *The End Times Controversy*, 136-37.

[21]F. J. A. Hort, although an early date advocate, calls the external evidence for the late date "undoubtedly weighty." He concludes, "On the one hand the tradition as to Domitian is not unanimous; on the other it is the prevalent tradition, and goes back to an author likely to be the recipient of a true tradition on the matter. . . . If external evidence alone could decide, there would be a clear preponderance for Domitian." F. J. A. Hort, quoted by Hitchcock, *The End Times Controversy*, 139.

[22]The following three arguments were put forth by H. A. Whittaker, *Revelation: A Biblical Approach* (Honest Truth Publishers, 1976), 54-55.

[23]Quoted by Eusebius, *Ecclesiastical History*, Book III, Ch. XX

[24]*Barnes Notes on the New Testament*, "Revelation," xlviii.

[25]*Clement of Alexandria*, Translation by G. W. Butterworth, 363.

[26]*Against Heresies*, Book II, Ch. 22.5; Book III, Chs. 3-4.

[27]Quoted by Dr. Enoch Pond, *The Apocalypse; When Written, and By Whom*; www.covenanter.org, 2.

[28]Alford, *The Greek Testament*, "Revelation," 544-47.

[29]Gnosticism, at least in its embryonic stages, existed in the time of Paul, but it probably could not have developed the heresiarchs which were already leading the saints into "the doctrine of Balaam."

[30]R. C. H. Charles, *Revelation*, Vol. 1 (New York: Scribner's Sons, 1920), xciv.

[31]Pond, *Apocalypse*, 6.

[32]Both Daniel and Ezekiel wrote of temples that did not exist at the time of writing (Daniel 8:11-14; 9:27; 11:31; 12:11; Ezekiel 40-48).

[33]Gentry, *Before Jerusalem Fell*, 193-97.

[34]Hitchcock, *The Endtimes Controversy*, 142.

[35]Robert H. Mounce, *The Book of Revelation*, The New International Commentary on the New Testament, gen. ed. F. F. Bruce (Grand Rapids: Eerdmans Publishing Co., 1977), 264. Quoted by Hitchcock in *The End Times Controversy*, 142.

[36]G. Salmon, *An Historical Introduction to the Study of the Books of the New Testament* (London: Murray, 1904), 230-31.

12

The Impending Peril of Full Preterism

Steve Pixler

Introduction

Any discussion of preterism is incomplete without considering indetail the extreme form of preterism that argues that (1) all prophecy concerning the Second Coming was fulfilled in the destruction of Jerusalem in A.D. 70 and that (2) we are now living in the endless age of the new creation. This form of preterism is most often called "full preterism." But perhaps the best and simplest label for this form of preterism is "pantelism" (from *pan*, "all"; *telos*, "end" or "fulfillment")[1] since proponents of this view believe that all biblical prophecy has been fulfilled.

Pantelism is a fringe form of preterism that has increased in popularity in Restorationist (particularly Churches of Christ), Reformed, and Baptist circles in the last few decades. The idea has been around for a while, but it has not gained dominance as an eschatological view. However, its influence is rapidly increasing as an outgrowth of historic preterism, or partial preterism, which has become widely accepted in the last century, especially within Reformed circles.

Most pantelists trace the roots of their ideas back to nineteenth-century writers, such as J. S. Russell, Milton S. Terry, and Ernest Hampden-Cook, though all pantelists would insist that their eschatology is a restoration of New Testament doctrine. Russell's work *The Parousia* is probably the single most influential pantelist volume written to date, with Max King's *The Spirit of Prophecy* a close second.

The most vocal recent proponents of pantelism are Church of Christ author Max King and his son, Timothy King, Ward Fenley, Don Preston, Ed Stevens, Walt Hibbard, Kelly Nelson Birks, John Bray, and John Noe. There are numerous volumes now available defending this view, though most of the debate takes place via Internet publishing.[2] Several scholarly critiques of pantelism are now available from authors of various eschatological perspectives, signifying that pantelism is gaining wider acceptance and provoking closer scrutiny.[3]

Though pantelism is rare among Oneness Pentecostals, it does exist—and it is growing. Pentecostals have traditionally been riveted to a futurist fulfillment of end-time prophecy and have been motivated by the "blessed hope" to zealous evangelism and fervent personal holiness. The expectation of Christ's return has always been a staple of Pentecostal preaching and practice. Pentecostals have differed on the timing of Christ's return, but basically all have agreed that Christ is coming physically to this earth in the future.

However, pantelism is gaining a greater influence among Pentecostals due to the rise of preterism, just as it has among the evangelical community. This is not surprising, because, as many have recognized, pantelism is preterism taken to its logical conclusion. We can, therefore, expect more Pentecostal preterists ultimately to embrace pantelism.

The issues pantelists raise must be addressed and their questions answered. Space constraints limit this chapter to an introductory critique, rather than a thorough refutation of pantelism. But hopefully this introduction may contribute to a fruitful discussion of this urgent topic and help Apostolics understand the perils of this eschatological view.

Defining Pantelism

Pantelists are similar to preterists in many ways, but they take the idea of past fulfillment to an extreme and end up with a distinct eschatology all their own. And as we shall see, their unique eschatology forms the basis for a complete revision of all theology. When pantelism is through formulating its view of prophecy, it ends up with a deviant form of doctrine that no longer resembles any form or expression of Christianity at all, in particular Oneness Pentecostalism. This radical change in their view of the end distorts their perspective on the beginning, the end, and everything in between.

Since pantelism is similar in many ways to preterism, those who are confronted with these views for the first time often confuse them. Though preterism often paves the road that leads to pantelism, the final destinations are miles apart. Preterism anticipates the literal return of Christ in the future, the resurrection of the dead, the rapture of the church,[4] the final judgment, and the re-creation of the physical universe. Pantelism denies all of the above. Pantelism believes that *all* prophecy has been fulfilled and that the present state of things shall continue forever. In this sense, pantelism is strangely unique and uniquely dangerous to the Apostolic faith.

Pantelists have developed their own eschatological hermeneutic that interprets all prophetic passages according to three principles: (1) *radical imminence* (the view that all of the "time texts" that speak of Christ's return as near to first-century believers must be taken in a strictly literal fashion); (2) *radical consistency* (the view that all of the passages that speak of Christ's coming again must refer to one and the same event); and (3) *radical spiritualization* (the view that all of the events surrounding the Second Coming are primarily spiritual and invisible in nature).

The first principle—*radical imminence*—is generally shared with preterists, but the second principle—*radical consistency*—is where the preterist and pantelist's paths diverge. Indeed, pantelists pride themselves on their consistency and deride "timid" preterists as absurdly inconsistent in their exegesis. (Many futurists would agree.) Pantelists insist that they are the only students of prophecy who are willing to face the difficult conclusions that faithful and consistent exegesis requires.

Radical Imminence

How does a sincere student of prophecy become a pantelist? He starts by becoming a preterist. As a preterist, he interprets the time texts in a woodenly literal manner. When the Lord says that His coming is near, the preterist takes it in a strict and unconditional sense. The time texts are also considered alongside the prophecies that link the coming of the Lord to the destruction of Jerusalem, which occurred in A.D. 70. So the preterist, as a true believer who cannot faithfully accept that the predictions of the Bible are in error, seeks an explanation for how the coming of the Lord actually could have occurred in the first century. He finds this explanation in the events surrounding the destruction of Jerusalem in A.D. 70.

The preterist comes to see the coming of the Lord in the first century as an invisible, spiritual "judgment-coming" when Israel is judged for her covenant sins and Jerusalem and the Temple are destroyed. However, the preterist divides the coming of the Lord in judgment upon Israel from the still future visible return of Christ to judge all nations. Thus, the preterist interpretation rests upon the claim that the New Testament church expected a near-coming of the Lord and a distant-coming of the Lord. The *parousia* passages are then divided into "near" and "distant" passages based on context. Basically, some *parousia* passages are fulfilled and others will be fulfilled in the future.[5]

Preterists are generally amillennial or postmillennial and hold that Revelation 20-22 describes past, present, and future events. They believe that the Millennium is being fulfilled presently in the church age, which began with the binding of Satan in A.D. 30-70 and shall end with the loosing of Satan for a final conflict, the return of Christ, and the final judgment. Then, the new creation shall be realized in the total renovation of the physical universe.

Radical Consistency

This is where the pantelist switches trains. The pantelist picks up on a problem that all critics of preterism (including futurists) notice at some point. The division of the *parousia* passages into near and distant categories is seemingly arbitrary and inconsistent. The pantelist notices that the early church seems to speak of the coming of the Lord as a single, near event. The single/near perspective on the coming of the Lord changes everything. The pantelist agrees with the preterist that the time texts are literal, and the conclusion that the coming of the Lord must have occurred in some sense in A.D. 70 is inescapable to him.

But an incipient pantelism begins developing within preterism as the sincere student of eschatology begins to be troubled about the seeming inconsistencies inherent within the preterist near/distant scheme. If he is unable to satisfy his mind on the consistency of preterism and the viability of the near/distant, multiple-comings scheme, then he will either recoil toward a more futurist eschatology, or he will begin drifting toward pantelism. If he refuses to surrender either radical imminence or radical consistency, then pantelism is unavoidable.

The budding pantelist carefully reviews all the *parousia* passages with an eye for consistency. He concludes that the New Testament church spoke of only one expected coming of the Lord and that the coming of the Lord in Matthew 24 and Revelation is the same coming of the Lord Paul spoke of in I Thessalonians 4 and I Corinthians 15. There can only be *one* Second Coming, and it is either past or future. He cannot accept futurism, for his preterist conclusions on the time texts and the faithfulness of Scripture will not allow it. So he is forced by his hermeneutical principles to conclude that the coming of the Lord *must* have occurred in A.D. 70. Admittedly, there are difficulties, but those can be resolved later. For now, the principles of radical imminence and radical consistency are controlling the exegesis.

One place in Scripture where preterist inconsistency is most apparent to the increasingly persuaded pantelist is Paul's letters to the church at Thessalonica. Throughout his first letter, Paul speaks of the wrath that is coming upon the Jews, which, to a preterist, is an obvious reference to A.D. 70. In chapter 4, Paul speaks of the coming of the Lord. And in chapter 5, he speaks again of the wrath of God, seemingly connecting the two together. To the pantelist striving for rigid consistency, chapters 4 and 5 cannot be separated.

This idea is further reinforced because Paul wrote his second letter to respond to misunderstandings that had arisen out of the first. Again, Paul speaks of the coming of the Lord, and there seems to be no distinction in Paul's thought between the wrath that is coming upon the Jews and the coming of the Lord to catch away His church. The man of sin, who sits in the Temple (interpreted by most preterists to refer either to Nero[6] or the apostate Jewish priesthood), is destroyed by the coming of the Lord, the very coming that Paul spoke about in I Thessalonians 4. Paul does not seem to make a distinction. The burgeoning impression is confirmed to the pantelist that the church expected one final return of Christ in the near future. His conversion to pantelism is almost complete.

He reads again through Matthew 24 and Revelation and spends a good deal of time in Hebrews where the coming of the Lord is spoken of as Christ appearing a "second time without sin unto salvation" (Hebrews 9:28) and as "he that shall come will come, and will not tarry" (Hebrews 10:37). Here, the idea of a single/near coming is obvious to the pantelist. All of the comings of the Lord are merged into one single event, and that event is near to the first-century church. Indeed, Matthew 24 plainly states that the coming of the Lord shall occur immediately after the Tribulation, which, to a preterist, now a pantelist, is plainly the destruction of Jerusalem. The distinction between the multiple comings that allowed the preterist to argue that the events of the Great Tribulation are past while the events of the Second Coming are future collapses around the pantelist's head. The unthinkable has become thinkable: The coming of the Lord and everything that it entails is already over, and this present age is the endless age of the new creation.

But how can these things be? The Second Coming *must* have occurred in A.D. 70, the pantelist concludes. But this does not seem right. The Second Coming has always been understood as a visible, universal event at the end of history. Jesus would be seen by the entire world coming on the clouds of heaven. The church would be resurrected and caught up together to meet the Lord in the air. The nations would behold in shock as the saved are taken up into heaven before their eyes. Fiery judgment would be poured out upon Satan and the armies of the earth who join him in his final revolt against Christ and the church. But this traditional sort of Second Coming does not fit very well with a "judgment-coming" of the Lord in A.D. 70. So the Second Coming must be reconsidered and redefined.

To the pantelist, the idea that the Second Coming occurred in A.D. 70 is a matter of consistent exegesis and simple faith in the promises of God. According to the pantelist, the Lord said He would return only once in a time near to the early church immediately after the fall of Jerusalem—so He did! The pantelist points to the obvious historical fact that Jerusalem was destroyed as adequate proof to confirm the point to the faithful who are willing to shake off traditional notions and see what is right before their eyes. Indeed, to the pantelist, the destruction of Jerusalem in A.D. 70 is the single greatest historical proof of the veracity of Christianity. Unlike the resurrection of Jesus, the destruction of Jerusalem is verified by independent sources. Jesus is a true prophet! To question these plain facts is to question the faithfulness of God and Scripture.

What prevents a partial preterist from going all the way and becoming a pantelist is the fact that it seems obvious that the events predicted to occur only at the Second Coming have not occurred. The preterist agrees that there was *a* coming of the Lord in A.D. 70, but it could not have been *the* coming of the Lord. To a preterist, the events of the Second Coming clearly include the visible return of Christ, the physical resurrection of the dead, the corporate rapture of the church, the final judgment, and the re-creation of the physical universe. These events simply have not occurred. If they had, the entire world would have known about it, and history would have recorded it.

But the pantelist brushes this objection aside as inconsistent exegesis and a lack of faith in the explicit promise of God. The Lord said He would come—so He did! Discussion over, question settled. We must accept the fact of Christ's return by faith even if it means that we must overhaul our traditional notions concerning end-time events. We must be willing (so reasons the pantelist) to accept the Word of God even if it means reconsidering and redefining the nature of the Second Coming and associated events. To the pantelist, now feverish with a passion for consistency, we must either sacrifice the faithfulness of God and Scripture by denying that the prophecies came to pass when promised, or we must faithfully and humbly rethink our conclusions to allow for a complete and consistent A.D. 70 fulfillment.

Another thing that prevents many preterists from becoming pantelists is the broad consensus of church history. The Christian faith has always included a future expectation of the coming of the Lord after the events of A.D. 70. Many preterists appeal to the creeds of "historic Christianity" as proof that the Christian faith has always included the blessed hope of Christ's return. But pantelists insist that our faith must be *sola scriptura* and argue that the only acceptable basis for belief must be the Word of God. The preterist responds that we must recognize the importance of doctrinal consensus, that church history and the teaching of our forbears should at least be a factor in our consideration of new ideas. But the principles of radical imminence and radical consistency crowd out all other considerations in the pantelist's mind. He is now persuaded that the pantelist option is the only viable, biblical option.

Radical Spiritualization

The next step for the pantelist is to develop the third principle of his eschatological hermeneutic—*radical spiritualization.* This principle is necessary in order to explain how the events of the Second Coming occurred in A.D. 70 and escaped the notice of history. The seeds of radical spiritualization are sown in preterism. The preterist develops the idea that "a *spiritual* coming of the Lord" occurred in A.D. 70. Preterism conditions the student of prophecy to accept that certain events are spiritual and invisible in nature, that much of the language of prophecy is symbolic and typological.

The pantelist, in his perfervid quest for radical consistency, simply takes this idea to an extreme conclusion: *All* of the events of the Second Coming are spiritual and invisible in nature. Thus, radical imminence and radical consistency lead the pantelist into radical spiritualization, and the foundation of the pantelist hermeneutic is finished. Now the structure must be raised.

Redefining the Second Coming

The pantelist has accepted that the Bible plainly teaches that the Second Coming occurred in A.D. 70. Now he must figure out how to resolve the difficulties that this conclusion raises. The traditional view of the Second Coming has always included the return of Christ, the resurrection of the dead, the rapture of the church, the final judgment, and the re-creation of the physical universe. The pantelist must explain how each of these events was fulfilled in an invisible and spiritual way in A.D. 70. And the pantelist is not afraid of difficulties. He has boldly embraced a view that is contrary to everything he has learned and everyone who has taught him. He is *pantelist contra mundum*, and he does not shrink back from the task. Indeed, his sense of being opposed by the entire world further strengthens his conviction that he is right and increases his unwillingness to listen to those who seek to dissuade him from his error. He *will* explain how the Second Coming is spiritual no matter what it takes to do so, no matter how creative and original he must become. In his mind, the demand of truth makes it so.

It is traditionally held that the return of Christ will be visible to the entire population of the world, that literally "every eye shall see him" (Revelation 1:7). The pantelist, following the lead of preterist interpretation, argues that the language is symbolic (apocalyptic hyperbole) and that "every eye shall see him" means that His return shall be manifest to all in the fall of Jerusalem. The entire world "saw" Christ come again in the news of Jerusalem's destruction, even if they did not recognize what they saw. The coming of the Lord is visible only to the eyes of faith. Therefore, Christ actually did return in a spiritual, invisible coming that was manifest in the destruction of Jerusalem. Pantelists readily acknowledge that a worldwide visible appearance of Christ would be unlikely to escape the historian's notice. But the pantelist argues that the traditional interpretation relies too heavily on a literal interpretation that fails to handle the biblical, prophetic language correctly. Pantelists use the same explanations preterists use to explain how the coming of the Lord could be spiritual; they just take the explanations further.

The Return of Christ

The pantelist reads passages such as I Thessalonians 4 through a radical imminence/consistency/spiritualization lens. When Paul speaks of the hope of the church and God bringing the dead in Christ back with Him, the pantelist reads it as God's descent in judgment upon Jerusalem with the armies of the saints with Him in A.D. 70. When the Lord came upon Jerusalem, He came with a shout, a trumpet, and the voice of the archangel. The pantelist explains that these sounds were spiritual, inaudible noises heard only in the heavens. Just as the voice of God is often confused with thunder, so the sounds accompanying the return of Christ may have sounded like natural phenomena to unbelievers on earth. Indeed, Paul does not insist that unbelievers will actually hear and recognize the sound of Christ's return. Futurists have always assumed it.

Some pantelists, following the lead of many preterists, use examples from Josephus where trumpets were allegedly heard and angels were purportedly seen in the clouds during the Roman siege of Jerusalem as possible proof that the sights and sounds of the Second Coming were actually seen and heard. In any case, the pantelist argues that this actually happened in A.D. 70, just because "the Bible tells me so." The fact that Paul told the early church that "we" shall experience this and that they should "comfort one another" with this hope is proof positive to the pantelist that this experience would happen to the first-century church. Otherwise, the hope would be so distant as to provide no comfort at all to the believers to whom Paul was writing. The pantelist argues that "audience relevance" must be a factor in interpreting each *parousia* passage.

The Resurrection

Next, the pantelist must explain the resurrection of the dead. He must show how the resurrection could have occurred in A.D. 70. So he argues that the resurrection, just like the return of Christ, must have been an invisible spiritual event witnessed only in the heavens. Following the radical spiritualization scheme that he is developing, the pantelist redefines the resurrection into a sort of "translation" where the physical/visible/earthly is transformed into the spiritual/invisible/heavenly.

There are many directions that the pantelist can go from here with his explanations on the spiritual body, for opinions vary widely. But the bottom line is that the pantelist ends up with a "spiritual" explanation of how the dead in Christ could be raised in A.D. 70 when Jesus returned. The resurrection no longer involves opening tombs or ripping the ground open and bringing out physical, revivified bodies as the traditional view demands. The pantelist argues that those things only occurred as signs in specific settings at specific times. But the resurrection of A.D. 70 was simply a matter of believers being translated instantly into the presence of God in the heavens.

Now, this is where the preterist spends most of his time arguing with the pantelist. The nature of the resurrection is one of the major differences between preterism and pantelism. It is also one of the few places where preterists and futurists find common ground.

The preterist asserts that the resurrection is still future and is the transformation and glorification of a physical body. Indeed, the preterist holds the traditional view that the glorified body is a spiritual body, in the sense that it lives by the spirit rather than being dependent upon natural sources, such as food and water, for life. Most preterists also hold that the glorified body is "flesh and bone" but not "flesh and blood."

The pantelist forsakes the traditional view altogether and argues that the glorified body is a form much like the "body" of angels. It is "corporeal" in the sense that it is spatial and dimensional, but it is not a person's fleshly body raised to life again. It is corporeal (bodily) but not carnal (fleshly). The traditional resurrection would necessitate a much more tangible, visible event with graves burst open and tombs emptied of their dead. This sort of physical resurrection must be disproved in order to explain how the resurrection could have occurred in A.D. 70 without anyone noticing. This explanation is also needed to explain how we, who live in the final age (according to the pantelist), shall partake in the resurrection when we die.

One of the passages that the pantelist must spend a good deal of time and creative energy considering and explaining is I Corinthians 15. In this famously difficult passage, Paul addresses at length the subject of the resurrection. He deals with the question of the spiritual body and the form that it takes. The pantelist senses that he may be on firmer ground here, and he eagerly presses his radical spiritualization principle even further.

Somewhere along the way, the pantelist will usually become sensitive to the preterist's charge that his radical spiritualization of *parousia* passages has strayed into a neo-gnostic, neo-platonic, manichean sort of dualism. Such a view separates the spiritual from the physical in an extreme dichotomy that defies the biblical picture of creation. The preterist will generally charge that the pantelist wrongly seeks to make the spiritual form of existence superior to the physical. The preterist argues that God made the physical world to be the medium and manifestation of the spiritual world. To divide creation into disparate and contrary realms is arbitrary and unbiblical. Of course, most futurists would agree.

However, the pantelist insists that he is simply following Paul by asserting that the spiritual body is substantially different from the material body. This "spiritual" view of the resurrection is what makes all of pantelism possible. The astute preterist recognizes this and focuses most of his argument against pantelism here.

One of the greatest problems that the pantelist encounters in I Corinthians 15 is the idea that Paul presents that the resurrection of the dead will bring the ultimate and final defeat of death. This traditionally has been understood as being the absolute end of all physical dying, that death itself will be banished from the new heaven and new earth. Death traditionally has been understood as separation from God and the resultant corruption of sin. This means that the traditional view expects that the general resurrection at the end of history shall remove the curse of sin and the sting of death once and for all. Certainly, if the resurrection entails this kind of physical, visible victory, then the resurrection did not occur in A.D. 70. But once again, the spiritualistic interpretation pulls the pantelist out of a bind. The pantelist, remember, is fully persuaded by now that the Bible plainly teaches that everything happened in A.D. 70, and he must simply seek to understand how the difficult passages square up. Indeed, he must shim them up and make them fit if necessary. The pantelist's structure must be built to measure on the foundation he has laid.

So the pantelist considers the problem for a while

until all the pieces of the puzzle fall into place. The pantelist concludes that the defeat of death is spiritual, not physical. Sin and death were defeated in the resurrection of A.D. 70, and we are no longer under their power. He explains that God never promised to remove the *presence* of sin and death, but rather the *power* of sin and death. The Christian who now lives after the resurrection may still experience the presence of sin in his life, but the power of sin has been broken, and the victory is available to all who believe. The reality and fullness of Christ's victory has come, and we must simply accept it by faith as a *fait accompli* and change the world around us in the power of that realization.

The Rapture

This explanation of the resurrection leads smoothly into the pantelist explanation of the Rapture. The resurrection is the spiritual man breaking free of the chains of physicality into the transformation of glory, and the Rapture is the relocation of the spiritual man from this realm to the one above. They are both parts of the same process, and it is all spiritual and invisible. When the Rapture occurred in A.D. 70, the believers who had already died were resurrected and raptured first, followed immediately by the living saints. All were immediately transformed (resurrected) and translated (raptured). So the Rapture, just like the return and resurrection, was a purely spiritual event unseen to human eyes—except to the eyes of retrospective faith.

The pantelist acknowledges that all Christians are partakers of a resurrection and rapture, even those of us who live after the corporate resurrection and rapture of

A.D. 70. Though the general, or corporate, resurrection and rapture already occurred and death and hades were emptied at Christ's return, present-day Christians shall still have a personal resurrection and rapture at the time of their death. All believers from the time of the end of the age and the dawning on the new creation (A.D. 70) experience the return of Christ (personal revelation), the resurrection of the dead (personal transformation), and the rapture (personal translation) on an individual level.

Indeed, this "spiritual" approach to prophecy demands a radically individualized eschatology. This sort of eschatology has a tremendous effect on the rest of theology, including soteriology and ecclesiology. Since the idea of a corporate resurrection and rapture has no place after A.D. 70, the entire idea of corporate and covenantal categories in redemption is affected. Radically individualized eschatology stirs an unfamiliar, and possibly even unwelcome, question in the pantelist mind concerning the post-A.D. 70 relevance of corporate ecclesial structures (local church congregations), but that must be settled later. For now, he is focused on explaining how the Second Coming, the resurrection, and the Rapture happened in A.D. 70.

The Final Judgment

After explaining how the return of Christ, the resurrection of the dead, and the Rapture occurred in A.D. 70, the pantelist is confronted with the question of the final judgment, when all nations are called before the Judge of all the earth and separated as sheep and goats (Matthew 25). But the framework for his explanation is already in place: The judgment was—not surprisingly—a *spiritual* judgment that occurred at the destruction of Jerusalem. When Jesus returned in A.D. 70, the graves were emptied of all the dead. The righteous and the wicked were judged. They were then sent to their respective eternal dwelling place. The righteous were carried into heaven to be with Christ forever. The wicked were cast "outside" the presence of God into everlasting torment. Now, we face the judgment individually when we die. We go to heaven if we are saved. We are cast "outside" if we are lost. The general judgment is over. The only judgment left is an individual one when we die. The judgment then and now is an invisible spiritual event.

The New Creation

So the return of Christ, the resurrection of the dead, the rapture of the church, and the final judgment all happened in the events that surrounded the destruction of Jerusalem in A.D. 70. This leaves one final explanation. The Second Coming has always been held to be the catalyst for the destruction of the old heavens and earth and the inauguration of the new as described in II Peter 3 (and other similar passages).

Most traditionalists read II Peter 3 as a literal prophecy of the physical destruction and re-creation of the material universe. However, the pantelist is required by his hermeneutic to interpret this passage along with all the others as a reference to the destruction of Jerusalem. So once again, the pantelist pulls out his trusty crowbar and forces Peter's lumber into the pantelist framework. He follows the preterist, who has taught him well how to refer back to Old Testament apocalyptic language to explain the cosmic phenomena as symbolic.

The preterist generally understands the destruction of the old heaven and earth and the formation of the new heaven and earth as symbolic of the transition between the old and new covenants. The pantelist accepts this as manifestly true. But most preterists also insist that this spiritual event is indicative of a future actual renovation of the physical universe. The preterist generally holds to a dual spiritual/typological fulfillment scheme: There is a very real spiritual fulfillment in the transition between the old and new covenants, but there will also be a very real physical fulfillment in the re-creation of the universe.

The pantelist cannot accept this dual fulfillment scheme because of his consistent exegesis. All must have been fulfilled in A.D. 70. It is obvious that such a physical cosmic event did not happen in the first century. So he must clarify what Peter meant. Therefore, the pantelist takes the preterist explanation further and simply denies that Peter ever intended for us to expect a literal physical fulfillment. Peter's prophecy is entirely spiritual. The only biblical expectation of a new heaven and new earth is the spiritual transition between the old and new covenants. The old heavens and old earth symbolize Judaism; the new heavens and new earth symbolize the church. The spiritual explanation comes through again!

The radical imminence/consistency/spiritualization hermeneutic explains every *parousia* passage to the pantelist's satisfaction. He is certain now that he has solved the persistent riddle of eschatology. The answer has been overlooked by everyone for centuries, but he has figured it out. The only problem he now faces is how to explain that the way things are is the way things ought to be. He must convince the skeptical preterist (and highly skeptical futurist) that the world we see around us is in fact the endless age of the new creation. The pantelist must argue that the new creation foretold by the prophets is simply the church in heaven and upon earth surrounded forever by the "outside" world of sin and death.

His critics protest that pantelism abandons the creation to an eternally unredeemed state. The pantelist acknowledges the criticism but insists that there is a biblical explanation awaiting those who look for it. It has to be there somewhere, for the pantelist is certain that all he has concluded so far is inescapable to those who take the Word of God at face value and refuse to be slaves to hidebound tradition. The pantelist has explained "the end of the age" to his satisfaction. Now he sets out to defend the pantelist view that the present age is actually "the age to come."

The Age to Come

The pantelist recognizes that the hardest part of the many hard parts of pantelism to accept is the argument that this present world around us is the promised eternal age of glory presented by the prophets as the hope of Israel. Preterists rightly recognize that the recurring theme of the prophets is full redemption, restitution, and reconciliation. The church and all of creation shall be fully delivered from the curse of sin and death; God's plan of salvation shall then be complete. This present age obviously does not match this biblical expectation. However, the pantelist is persuaded that the end of the age occurred in A.D. 70. So the present age must be the age to come. Simple as that. True, the present state of things does not match the traditional expectation of how the age to come would be. Well, then, the traditional expectation simply must be wrong. Consistent and faithful exegesis demands it. So the pantelist begins the arduous task of redefining the traditional view of redemption, restitution, and reconciliation until it fits his previous conclusions. When he is done, he has, in effect, redefined the gospel itself.

There are several things that the pantelist must explain to defend his view. He must explain the continuing cycle of life, the presence of sin and death, the unbroken curse upon creation, the imperfection and immaturity of the body of Christ, the vast majority of the nations continuing in defiance and unbelief, etc. All of these things indicate the absence of full redemption. Redemption traditionally is expected to be *total* (encompassing all of creation, spiritual and physical) and *final* (bringing a culmination and completion to redemptive history). The pantelist view of redemption is *partial* (encompassing only the spiritual realm) and *continual* (history is infinite, never finished). The pantelist argues that this partial/continual version of redemption is actually more true to the biblical witness than the traditional view.

The pantelist looks over every passage that he can find that speaks of total/final redemption and uses the same instrument of interpretation that he did with the Second Coming. He simply spiritualizes every passage. He insists that the hope of Israel was never intended to be physical. God was always speaking to us about spiritual realities using physical types and shadows. The pantelist uses the teaching of Paul on the distinction between the physical and the spiritual to prove that the spiritual realm is superior to the physical. He argues that those who look for a literal fulfillment of the Old Testament prophets are just simplistic and carnal. It should be obvious, he thinks, that the heavenly state of being is our objective, and he multiplies references to make his point.

Everything must be redefined. The pantelist looks around him and acknowledges that the present state of things does not look much like a new creation. But he insists that we must not look at the world around us, for salvation is *spiritual.* Critics fail to see the truth in pantelism, he reasons, because they refuse to see with the eyes of faith the reality of Christ's presence in the church right now. The church may seem imperfect, but that is because we are seeing only the visible church. But the pantelist argues that the visible church is not the church at all. The church is the invisible body of believers around the world who are truly faithful and pure. *That* church is "perfect and entire, wanting nothing" (James 1:4). The church has reached the fullness and maturity that Paul spoke of in Ephesians 4. We simply must recognize that the perfection of the church is invisible and hidden to the eyes of unbelief.

The pantelist is convinced that the church will always be surrounded by the wicked. To him, it is foolish to teach that there will ever be a time when the wicked do not camp outside the gates of the city. (See Revelation 21:27; 22:14, 15.) However, the church will increase its influence as salt and light in the earth throughout the ceaseless ages of eternity, and the wicked shall be greatly decreased in number. The nations of the earth shall eventually come to acknowledge the Lord as King over all the earth. The pantelist borrows a bit of postmillennial eschatology here and assures us that this present state of woe will not last forever. Of course, he sacrifices a little bit of consistency here, but we must pretend not to notice for now.

The pantelist reads passages where the Word of God seems to indicate that the present earth shall last forever. He lays aside his spiritualizing tool for a moment and borrows the futurist's literal hermeneutic. Obviously, these passages indicate a "world without end" (Ephesians 3:21). The generations of the earth shall continue forever, the families of the earth will continue to marry, give birth, live, and die forever. In the resurrection and rapture, as individual Christians are transformed and translated into heaven when they die, this cycle of life will no longer continue. But in the present age upon earth, the cycle of life has no end.

The new heavens and new earth symbolize the invisible church. We should expect nothing more. God created this world as a place of peace and beauty, and He is not going to destroy it and start over. He will simply transform it by the ever-increasing influence of the church as it realizes the reality of His indwelling Spirit in finished perfection here and now. But the pantelist has no assurance from the Word of the Lord that sin and death will ever be totally and finally abolished. He concluded earlier that the defeat of sin and death was spiritual, that we are free from the power of sin but not the presence of sin. The Christian may live victorious over sin by faith in the finished spiritual work of Calvary. But creation will never be totally and finally free from the presence of sin. The curse is lifted in a spiritual sense—that should come as no surprise.

Another Gospel

Later on, as critics multiply, the pantelist will be required to go into greater detail in defending his views. This is where he will begin tinkering with the doctrines of sin and salvation and develop a completely new gospel. In his attempt to redefine the nature of death and to explain how death can remain in God's new creation, he must deny the legal imputation of Adam's sin and that death has come upon all humanity as a result. He must deny that death is an unnatural process that violates God's initial created order. He must deny that redemption is universal and cosmic. He must deny that there is an end—and objective—to history. He must deny the need for corporate ecclesial structures (churches), for salvation is purely individual and personal. He must deny the corporate and covenantal nature of God's elect people.

Everything is radically individualistic. The transmutation of doctrines is endless, but it has become necessary to defend the basic conclusions of his radical immінence/consistency/spiritualization hermeneutic. The pantelist has taken a long, tortuous journey, and he has finally arrived at his destination all by himself, out in the barren wilderness of hopeless and endless existence.

Practical Implications of Pantelism

The pantelist must now confront a few practical issues concerning church practice and polity. The expectation of Christ's soon return pervades the New Testament. Everything the church says and does is cast in this mold. It is almost impossible to read a passage at random that is not colored in some sense by the "blessed hope." But there are several specific passages that go to the very heart of the mission and ministry of the church that are directly connected to the Second Coming. And the confirmed pantelist, who is now firmly entrenched in his doctrinal isolation, is ready to reevaluate them all in light of his new revelation.

Evangelism

One of the first passages to consider is the "great commission" passage in Matthew 28 where Jesus tells His disciples that He has all power in heaven and earth. He commands them to evangelize the world and make disciples of every nation. Jesus promises that He will be with the church in the pursuit of this goal "until the end of the age" (Matthew 28:20). But, according to the pantelist, the end of the age happened in A.D. 70. If the pantelist follows his own formula for radical consistency, this means that the evangelistic task of which Christ spoke was finished in A.D. 70. The great commission was completed in A.D. 70. That is unsettling, but the pantelist must accept that it is so.

Baptism

But even more unsettling is the corollary of this conclusion: If the great commission is fulfilled, then our mandate to baptize has expired. This means that the pantelist must reconsider the command to baptize and make disciples "until the end of the age." This is even more unsettling for the Pentecostal who embraces Acts 2:38 as "the plan of salvation," for evangelism (which necessarily includes baptism and discipleship) is the *raison d'être* of Pentecostal mission and ministry.

Baptism in Jesus' name is a Oneness Pentecostal distinctive, but if baptism no longer matters, then we are fools to quibble over the formula of baptism. Further, if baptism is no longer commanded in this post-commission age, then Acts 2:38 is no longer "the plan of salvation," and the promise of the Holy Ghost (Acts 2:39) is no longer extended. Since the baptism of the Spirit is "the earnest of our inheritance" (Ephesians 1:14), and since, according to the pantelist, the fullness of the inheritance came in A.D. 70, then we no longer need to seek for a Pentecostal experience. The entire edifice of Pentecostal doctrine collapses when built on a pantelist foundation. And this is just one of the ways that pantelism affects soteriology.

The Lord's Supper

The pantelist must consider the continuing relevance and necessity of the Lord's Supper. Paul says, "For as often as ye eat this bread, and drink this cup, ye do shew the Lord's death till he come" (I Corinthians 11:26). The Lord's Supper proclaims the Lord's death *until He comes.* Now the pantelist has a choice: He can interpret Paul's words quite literally and insist that the observance of the Lord's Supper ended in A.D. 70 or he can argue that Paul did not say that the celebration of the Lord's Supper should *end* at the Second Coming, but rather that the Lord's Supper simply points to the return of Christ, pointing forward for the early church and backward for us. The pantelist may continue to accept the Lord's Supper as a fitting memorial of past redemption, just as Passover commemorates a past deliverance for Israel. But in doing so, the Supper loses its future orientation and eschatological nature.

The pantelist may argue further that Jesus promised to celebrate the Lord's Supper with us in the Father's kingdom, which is the endless age of the new creation. He may multiply references that show the Father's kingdom refers to the everlasting age and argue that we are in the time when Christ promised to share the meal with us. To the pantelist, this supports his contention that the Lord's Supper should continue in the new creation.

However, the pantelist may have some difficulty proving to his critics that the Lord's Supper is destined to continue eternally after Christ returns. First of all, many critics have a real problem accepting the pantelist's claim that Paul saw the Lord's Supper continuing beyond the Second Coming. The language and context of I Corinthians 11:26 seem to indicate that Paul had both the first and second advents of Christ in view as the dual focus of the observance of the Lord's Supper, as the bookends of its practice. Preterists and futurists insist that Paul considers the Lord's Supper an interim, temporary Lord's Day celebration that announces the *past* death, burial, and resurrection of Christ; the *present* communion of Christ with believers and believers with one another; and the *future* return of Christ. If this is indeed the case, then the significance of the Lord's Supper would cease at the Second Coming.

The pantelist must also demonstrate that Christ's promise to "drink [the fruit of the vine] new with you in my Father's kingdom" refers only to the Lord's Supper and not to an actual kingdom feast. The traditional view has held that Christ was referring both to the Lord's Supper, celebrated in the church until the Second Coming, and the Marriage Supper of the Lamb, which would be celebrated literally in the everlasting kingdom of the Father.

The pantelist has his work cut out for him if he wishes to keep the observance of the Lord's Supper in the new creation. Many pantelists simply acknowledge the difficulty and "consistently" get rid of it altogether. Others who wish to evade the more undesirable and less theoretical consequences of their newfound position find a creative way to drag the Lord's Supper past the Second Coming.

Spiritual Gifts

The pantelist must also address the use of spiritual gifts in the new creation. This is particularly important for the Pentecostal pantelist. Paul states in I Corinthians 13 that "we know in part, and we prophesy in part. But when that which is perfect is come, then that which is in part shall be done away" (I Corinthians 13:9, 10). Paul is clearly speaking of a day when spiritual gifts shall cease. The pantelist must conclude that "the perfect" came in A.D. 70. Most pantelists are cessationists and have no problem at all with spiritual gifts ending in A.D. 70. But a Pentecostal pantelist has serious problems here. He must either abandon his Pentecostal experience as a casualty of his radical pantelist hermeneutic, or he must edge carefully away from his rigid insistence on consistency. Either the pantelism or the Pentecostalism has to give. The Pentecostal pantelist may try to explain this as referring to the individual perfection that comes at our death, but that sounds a little thin. In other words (he argues), "the perfect" has come *spiritually* for the entire church, and we shall all experience "the perfect" *personally* when we die. It still sounds thin. It is impossible that Paul had a person's transformation at death in mind when he wrote these words to the Corinthians. Thus, the true pantelist also becomes a cessationist and must, therefore, further redefine biblical theology.

Fivefold Ministry

The pantelist must also confront Paul's teaching in Ephesians on the perfection and maturity of the church. He must consider and redefine the entire book, but particularly chapter 4 where Paul describes the "ascension gifts" that Jesus gave to the church: the gift of apostles, prophets, evangelists, pastors and teachers. Jesus gave the ministry to the church "for the perfecting of the saints" (Ephesians 4:12). But if the church has reached the age of perfection in the new creation, then the ministry is no longer needed. Now the lay-pantelist may readily embrace this idea, but the preacher-pantelist will struggle here. If he remains consistent, he has just "fulfilled" himself out of a job! The pantelist cannot have it both ways: Either he will be consistent and state that the ministry is no longer needed in this perfect age or he will edge around the issue a bit and say that those who have already been resurrected and raptured (obviously) no longer need the ministry but that those who remain here still do. Either way, his argument runs out of steam with a close consideration of Ephesians 4.[7]

The Perfection of the Church

It is hard to argue credibly that the church has "come in the unity of the faith, and of the knowledge of the Son of God, unto a perfect man, unto the measure of the stature of the fulness of Christ" (Ephesians 4:13). And yet, Paul's train of thought in Ephesians is clearly eschatological and teleological. He speaks of the Father "gather[ing] together . . . all things in Christ [in] the dispensation of the fulness of times" (1:10) and how this fullness is the "redemption of the purchased possession" that we now anticipate in the "earnest of our inheritance" (1:14). He speaks of how the church as a "building fitly framed together groweth unto a holy temple in the Lord: in whom ye also are builded together for a habitation of God through the Spirit" (2:21-22).

The pantelist must argue that this perfection was achieved in A.D. 70 at the end of the age when the church received the fullness of the kingdom and the promised inheritance. We must admit that it strains the non-pantelist imagination to look around and equate the present church with this glorious church predicted. No doubt the pantelist would suggest that maybe we just need a more spiritual outlook.

Moreover, while the pantelist is arguing that ecclesial perfection was achieved in A.D. 70, he must simultaneously argue that the temple will remain under construction forever, that it will never be finally and totally complete: We are the lively stones that make up the spiritual habitation of God (2:22), and according to the pantelist, the number of the saved and dying will never be finished. Thus, the temple is never finished. This hardly fits with Paul's thought.

Church Attendance

The pantelist confronts a pervasive eschatological and teleological motif bleeding through every page of Scripture. He must keep his red pencil sharpened and his eraser ready at all times to edit commonly held doctrines.

He cleverly cuts and pastes every *parousia* passage into an A.D. 70 template.

The pantelist can never be accused of lacking explanations. He grabs hold of Hebrews and squeezes the eschatological priesthood of Christ into a brief forty-year tenure, for Christ makes intercession for us until He comes again (Hebrews 10:12-13). The pantelist must grapple with the eschatological purpose of the Christian assembly and offer original answers to the questions raised by fellow pantelists about whether corporate worship is really all that necessary in the new creation (Hebrews 10:25). The church gathers on the Lord's Day in anticipation of the Day of the Lord, but the pantelist insists that the Day of the Lord is past and the judgment is over. So the eschatological impulse of corporate worship is lost completely. Why should we gather together as a sign of our gathering together unto Him when the gathering is already over? The only gathering left for a Christian is an individual "gathering" to Christ when he dies. Pantelism fractures the body and divides worshipers into isolated individuals awaiting their own personal resurrection and rapture.

Conclusion

There are many other practical implications of pantelism, but this gives enough of the flavor to make it distasteful to the serious Bible student. Out of an unreasonable commitment to a radical hermeneutic, the pantelist slowly redefines his doctrine until it is no longer in accord with biblical faith. When he is done, all hope is gone. The world may get better, but it will never get well. The overall health of creation may improve, but it will always have a slight fever. And there are no guarantees against a total relapse. The cancer of sin and death will always be present, though we can bravely hope for gradual remission.

The pantelist, because of his radical imminence/consistency/spiritualization hermeneutic, ends up with another gospel that reduces salvation to a purely personal and spiritual experience and leaves sin and death present upon the earth forever. This is unacceptable. Salvation is corporate and cosmic. God foreordained the church as a covenant community to dwell within the created universe to display His glory for eternity. The church is the spiritual temple of God that is destined to occupy the physical temple of God, the created universe. And the temple will be finished and indwelled by the Almighty. Salvation is covenantal and teleological. It has an end, and it all ends together.

Creation was formed in the beginning to give glory to God. That is its original purpose, and it remains a fallen world until that purpose is recovered. God did not create the physical realm only to abandon it to sin and death. This present world does not glorify God. Sin and death bring no glory to God except as they are defeated by the Cross. But in the pantelist scheme of things, the Cross won only a partial victory. There is no point in time when the victory of the Cross is total and final. The created world shall always be less than it was when God stood back and surveyed His handiwork and proudly declared, "It is good! It is very good!" (Genesis 1). Pantelism reduces redemption, reconciliation, and restitution to a never-completed work. This stands in marked contrast to everything the prophets foretold. The promise of God is to "make all things new" (Revelation 21:5). We are not expected to settle for anything less.

In order to believe in pantelism, we must accept that this present world is the promised "age to come" of the new creation. If that can be disproved, then pantelism is refuted *ipso facto.* All of the other questions raised by pantelists can be debated endlessly, but this is where their doctrine stands or falls. This present world of never-ending sin and death is not God's new creation. They cannot separate the physical world from the spiritual. The material universe was created to be the temple of the Most High. Indeed, the Temple at Jerusalem that was destroyed in A.D. 70 was but a model of the universe God created to be His habitation. The heaven is His throne, and the earth is His footstool. The physical universe will be consecrated by fire just like the physical Temple. The *cosmos* will be made new. The veil of the firmament shall be rent, the heaven of heavens shall become transparent to the earth, the throne of God shall be established among human beings, and God will dwell with the redeemed of every nation. The temple of God cannot be defiled forever. It must be purged entirely, and the burnt offering of the heaven and earth must be cast outside the camp into everlasting fire. The only corner of God's creation that shall remain alienated from Him shall be what burns forever as an everlasting reminder of the holiness of God. But the temple shall be cleansed.

The idea of full redemption and complete salvation is so pervasive that it is somewhat difficult to know where to start when setting out to refute pantelism. It is like arguing with "green-sky" proponents. How do you begin proving that the sky is blue? It seems almost silly to try.

And yet, we must try. Pantelism must be answered. A thorough refutation of pantelism requires a book-length treatment. It is hoped that this chapter has sufficiently introduced Oneness Pentecostals to an idea that is growing among us and that it will get us moving toward better understanding the error in our midst so we may be prepared to refute it.

Steve Pixler is pastor of the Apostolic Church of Fort Worth in Fort Worth, Texas. Before becoming a pastor, he evangelized for ten years. He has submitted several papers to conferences and forums and has recently authored a book, The Beginning of Judgment. *He and his wife, Jeana, reside with their two daughters in Arlington, Texas.*

Notes

[1]In addition to "full preterism," this form of preterism is called by various other names, including "consistent preterism," "Transmillennialism®" (registered by Timothy King to provide exclusive identity to his particular brand of full preterism), "fulfilled eschatology," and "hyper-preterism" (primarily by critics). I have chosen to use "pantelism" as a matter of personal preference and have chosen to use "preterism" primarily to refer to what has been called "partial preterism" in the other chapters of this book.

[2]There are numerous Web sites dedicated to pantelism. Among the most prominent are www.preterist.org, www.preteristplanet.com, and www.preteristarchive.com.

[3]See Keith Mathison (editor), *When Shall These Things Be? A Reformed Response to Hyper-preterism* (Phillipsburg, N.J.: Presbyterian and Reformed, 2004); C. Jonathin Seraiah, *The End of All Things: A Defense of the Future* (Moscow, Idaho: Canon Press, 1999); John MacArthur, *The Second Coming: Signs of Christ's Return and the End of the Age* (Wheaton, Ill.: Crossway Books, 1999); Tim LaHaye and Thomas Ice, *The End-Times Controversy: The Second Coming Under Attack* (Eugene, Ore.: Harvest House Publishers,

2003); Kenneth L. Gentry, "A Brief Theological Analysis of Hyper-Preterism" (www.reformed.org/eschaton/gentry_preterism.html); Jim West, "The Allurement of Hymenaen Preterism: The Rise of 'Dispensable Eschatology'" (http://reformed.org/eschaton/index.html).

[4]There are some preterists who are dogmatic about the fact they do not believe in a Rapture and would rather be "left behind," for according to them, only the righteous remain while unbelievers are "taken away" by God's judgment.

[5]Generally, preterists would divide the passages as follows: *past passages* include Matthew 24 and parallel passages; I Thessalonians 5; II Thessalonians 1-2; II Peter 3 (preterists vary here); most of Revelation. *Future passages* include Acts 1:11; Acts 3:19-21; Romans 8; I Corinthians 15; I Thessalonians 4; and Hebrews 9:28.

[6]It is strange that any preterist would identify Nero as this "man of sin." Paul says that Jesus will destroy the man of sin at His coming, and as James Groce points out, Nero could not have been defeated at Jesus' alleged return in A.D. 70: "Was Nero defeated by the return of Jesus Christ? No, he was not. It is a matter of history that Nero committed suicide on June 9, A.D. 68 . . . [which] puts Nero's death two years before the fall of Jerusalem and the destruction of the Temple. That's . . . two years before preterists claim Jesus returned" (James L. Groce, "How the Apostles Understood the Prophetic Teachings of Jesus," unpublished paper, 2005, 13).

[7]See I Peter 5:1-4. The shepherds of the church are exhorted to lead the flock in anticipation of the return of the Chief Shepherd. Peter's exhortation to the elders is another example of the eschatological character of Christian ministry.